W9-DEJ-760

THE WAY I REMEMBER IT

Ruth Volle

The Way I Remember It

THE MEMOIRS OF MARGARET WEST TAYLOR

With love —

Margaret

TAYLOR PRESS
WHEATON, ILLINOIS

ISBN 0-8423-5321-6

CONTENTS

To My Children and Grandchildren

THESE MEMORIES have been written down to answer the questions you never asked about my growing-up years.

If you don't want to read about my Uncle Fred or Uncle Merle, then skip the first two chapters. But you will miss the interesting fact that my Grandma Trappe was a widow for 52 years after being married for 13 years, and that she raised six children by herself before such a thing as welfare.

The 1920s are described as the "Roaring Twenties," but the only roaring the West family knew about came from the steam trains Papa frequently rode to Washington and California to oversee his growing cheese business. We were *in* the world but not *of* the world. We did not listen to the popular music of the day or the dramatic radio serials.

You will learn, if you didn't already know, that Kenneth Taylor and I met in 1930, when we were freshmen in high school. And after that he figures in nearly every chapter of my life!

In case anyone from outside our family reads over your shoulder, I have included a few chapters of Taylor family lore from your generation. Just a sampling. Not everything that I remember or that you remember. You can write your own books, beginning where I have left off.

1

The Trappe Side

MAMA WAS a Trappe (pronounced "Trappy"). Her parents, Carl Trappe and Emma Schulze, were born in Germany in 1865 and came to America when they were young. I do not know how or when they met. Grandma's confirmation certificate shows that she was confirmed in Waterloo, Iowa, in 1881. They were married October 27, 1888, in East Portland, Oregon. Mama was born in Portland on November 4, 1889. She was christened Louise in the Missouri Synod Lutheran Church.

Martin, William, Marie, Theodore, and Fred joined the family in the next several years. They spoke German at home, and schoolwork was done in German at the parochial school. But German was left behind as they left home and went to work, and I never heard my relatives speak German.

Grandpa Carl was a carpenter, and during the Alaska gold rush, he joined the stampede going north, assuming he could find work with his carpentry skills. His luck must have matched that of most of the miners, for the family has a letter he wrote to Grandma in which he enclosed one dollar. He said he was sorry he could not send more.

Carl died in July 1901 as the result of a fall while working. Mama was not yet 12, and baby Fred was only four months old. Grandma was left with the compact three-bedroom house Carl had built in Sellwood (southeast Portland), a cow, and just enough cash to pay for the funeral. We have a copy of the itemized bill from the funeral home for a total of $48.75. The grave site cost an additional $5.00, and digging the grave was another $5.00.

How did Grandma manage with six children? Mama went to live with and work for her Grandpa Schulze, who was a tailor. That meant one less mouth to feed at 601 Tolman Avenue. Mama attended school only through sixth grade.

Grandma had chickens and a cow and sold milk to neighbors. As far as we know, that was her only cash income for buying staples such as sugar, flour, beans, and rice. But a cow has to be bred to keep producing milk, and eventually it goes dry anyway. Then for a while there is no milk to sell or to feed a hungry brood of children.

Grandma had a large garden and a few fruit trees. She canned fruits and vegetables to see the family through winter months.

Uncle Mart and Uncle Will served in World War I, but I know that only because we have pictures of them in uniform in the family album. None of our relatives were killed or even injured in the war. The only reference I remember hearing when I was young was when the womenfolk recalled having to "make do" because of the food rationing. As far as I was concerned, their "making do" could have been as far back as the Civil War—not while I was a baby.

Uncle Mart got a job in Spokane after the war and lived there all his life. He and Aunt Esther and their two children came to Grandma's for a visit only once every couple of years, so we hardly knew them.

Both Uncle Will and Uncle Ted worked for Papa—their brother-in-law—at the Red Rock Dairy. Uncle Will became business manager.

Uncle Ted took a short course at Oregon Agricultural College (later Oregon State University in Corvallis) to learn the rudiments of chemistry. He tested milk samples for butterfat, impurities, etc. He worked by himself in a little room, surrounded by test tubes, a few steps up from the main floor where the big cheese vats were. When a batch of cheese went off-flavor, they had to trace which farmer's milk was responsible. Maybe the cows had pastured in a field with a strong-flavored weed that had tainted their milk, and the farmer would have to move his cows.

Uncle Ted married a woman named Marie. They both belonged to the Trails Club, a Portland-based hiking and wilderness club. The first time I climbed Larch Mountain was with them and a group from the Trails Club. We stayed overnight in the cabin the club had built near the top.

Aunt Mae (we never called her by her real name, Marie) worked in the office of Jantzen Knitting Mills until she retired. Most of that time she was in the order department. She kept us supplied with foreign stamps for our stamp collections and with Jantzen swimsuits. As soon as she could afford it, she bought a roadster. Of course Grandma Trappe and Grandma West never learned to drive. Aunt Mae lived with Grandma Trappe and was her basic support until Grandma died in 1953 at age 88. Papa helped, too, at least in early years. I remember seeing him slip Grandma a check on Sunday evenings after we had been at her house for Sunday dinner. After Grandma's death Aunt Mae lived alone until her death in 1980, just short of her 85th birthday.

Uncle Fred apparently struck out on his own and headed for California as soon as he was old enough to leave home. I think that he and Aunt Mae were the only ones to finish high school. He always lived in California. My siblings remember that once he showed up when we were vacationing in Neskowin, but that would have been the only time we ever saw him. He died in 1994 at the age of 93.

Since Papa and Mama were both the oldest in their families, and they married earlier than their brothers and sisters, our first cousins were all younger than my older sisters, Harriet and Lois, and me. But some of Mama's first cousins, Bernette and Helen Schulze, were our age. They fondly remember coming out from Portland to our little farm and playing games with us and picking all the berries they could eat.

2

The Atwater/ West Side

GRANDMA WEST was an Atwater. Most of the Atwaters in the States are descendants of David Atwater, who, with his brother, Joshua, and sister, Ann, emigrated from England in 1637 after the deaths of their parents. They were Puritans and were among the very first settlers of New Haven, Connecticut. The Atwater genealogy we have was published in 1900, so my grandparents' and my father's names are in it, but not Uncle Elwin's.

Grandma (Helen Maria Atwater) was born January 16, 1860, the sixth child of Thomas Judson Atwater and Julia Van Schaick, in Prescott, Wisconsin. Her father was a farmer and was also town treasurer and chairman of the county board.

I know almost nothing about Grandpa West. His family may have come from Kentucky, but we have never tried to trace his roots. The story is that he proposed to Grandma with a shotgun in hand (that Kentucky blood?). Would he really have shot himself if she hadn't said yes? But she did say yes, and she married Charles Wilson West July 26, 1881. Prior to that she had taught school.

Papa (Harry Atwater West) was born June 18, 1885, in Prescott.

He was the second of five sons. (Baby Andrew had died two years before Papa was born.) Uncle Merle was born in 1890, followed in 1897 by Leon, who lived only a few months. Elwin was born in 1900.

Grandpa and Grandma moved to Milwaukie, Oregon, near Portland, when Papa was five. They would have traveled from Wisconsin by train. Grandpa drove a horsecar and later a streetcar when horsecars were phased out.

It must have been in 1909 that Grandpa, Grandma, Papa, and Elwin moved to a small farm near Tigard, Oregon. Merle had already left home.

When I was young, Merle and his wife, Elsie, lived in Milwaukee, Wisconsin. Later they moved to Los Angeles, California. Merle was the black sheep of the family. He didn't espouse the Christian faith, and his whole life seemed clouded. We never knew what he did for a living. He claimed to be an inventor, but the only product we ever saw was aluminum clothespins. But they left metallic marks on clothes, so Mama threw them out. Periodically Uncle Merle would write Grandma and Grandpa or Papa for money. No doubt he called them loans, but I'm sure they were never paid back.

While phones were common in the 1920s, personal long-distance calls were still largely a thing of the future. But once Uncle Merle arranged to call us and Grandpa and Grandma *long distance!* The exact time was set days ahead so he could write and tell us when to expect the call. Eventually the call came through all the way from Wisconsin to the office of the Red Rock Dairy, where we were all assembled, ten miles west of Portland! That was Uncle Merle. When he had money, he didn't necessarily spend it wisely.

The first time I saw Uncle Merle was at Christmas, maybe 1928, when his whole family came on the train. At the time Merle and Elsie had three children—Lyle (who took his own life as a young adult), Gordon, and Florence. Claudia was born later. I remember they gave us more presents than we gave them.

The second time I saw Uncle Merle and Aunt Elsie was in June

1937, when I was on my way to Houston by train for the summer. I stopped in Los Angeles and looked them up. Uncle Merle drove me around Beverly Hills, pointing out the homes of movie celebrities. Aunt Elsie gave me a long cotton housecoat that was a favorite for years. It was a pleasant visit. On my way home from Houston, around Labor Day, I stopped in Los Angeles again to see them, but when I got to their house, they had moved, and none of the neighbors knew where they had gone. I got the impression they had to move for failure to pay the rent.

Uncle Elwin was 15 years younger than Papa. When he was young, he worked for Papa at the dairy. After they had a falling out one day, Elwin walked off the job, saying he was quitting. The next day he showed up for work again, assuming the problem had disappeared overnight. But Papa said no, he had quit—and that was that.

Elwin married Muriel Rae, whose father was a traveling evangelist with the Plymouth Brethren. They had three children, Donald, Rae, and Helen. We hardly ever saw Uncle Elwin's family. Their social times were with the Rae side of the family, as ours were with the Trappes and with Grandpa and Grandma West. I don't remember ever being in their home for a meal.

My cousin Don became a Portland fireman. He and his wife, Naydine, had seven children. It was following my mother's funeral in 1950 that Don decided to enter the ministry. Missouri Synod Lutheran no less! Quite a switch from his Plymouth Brethren background.

Don enrolled in the seminary at Springfield, Illinois, which was for men who had not had college preparation. Naydine worked to put him through school. Once their family joined us in our old house in Wheaton for a Thanksgiving dinner. Following graduation and ordination, Don had a pastorate near Rochester, Minnesota, and Ken and I visited them twice during those years. Later he had churches in California and Arizona, but after retiring, he and Naydine moved back to the Rochester area, where most of their children had settled.

A cross that Don had to bear was that his father never wanted to hear him preach. Even though Elwin and Muriel had left the Plymouth Brethren for Central Bible Church, there was still that old prejudice that the formalism and liturgical order of the Lutheran service meant that something less than the pure gospel was being preached.

Aunt Muriel has died, but Uncle Elwin is still living in Portland (as of the end of 2000) and is being lovingly cared for by their daughter Helen and her husband John, who moved from Tulsa to Portland to assume responsibility for her aging parents.

Grandpa West had one sister, Mary, who married William Irle. Uncle Will was a schoolteacher, probably in a one-room schoolhouse. Once I went with my grandparents to visit them in Buxton, Oregon. Later they lived in Portland, and occasionally Uncle Will and Aunt Mary were included in our family celebrations. They had only one son, Kenneth, who was a banker in Shanghai, China. He married Lillian, who worked in the YWCA, and they had no children. They only came home once during my childhood, bringing Chinese souvenirs for all the family.

3

Mama and Papa Marry

WHEN MAMA was old enough for a real job, she worked in the Stettler Box Factory on the West side of Portland. I'm sure she gave most of her paycheck to Grandma. Harry West also worked at Stettler's, and he rode the same streetcar Mama rode.

Mama was an attractive young woman, and according to Mr. Stettler, she was the hardest working employee in his factory. That fact was not lost on Papa, who himself was never one to shirk. They were attracted to each other, and Mama resolved that if Harry West didn't ask for her hand in marriage, she would never marry anyone! As far as I can tell, Papa didn't work at Stettler's after the Wests moved to the farm in 1909. But he didn't forget Louise. He continued to see her, and eventually he proposed to her.

Papa and Mama were married at Grandma Trappe's home October 2, 1911, with her Lutheran pastor performing the ceremony. I am sure she would have preferred being married in the church, but she was the one to compromise. With his Plymouth Brethren background, Papa did not want to be married in a Lutheran church.

When we children were born, however, we attended the Lutheran church with Mama. Papa was never present for the baptism of any of his children or for the confirmation of Harriet, Lois, or myself. So we West children grew up like no other family that we knew—with parents attending two different Protestant churches for the 40 years of their marriage.

The newlyweds moved to a tiny house on the property next to Grandpa's farm.

Grandpa had several cows. At first Grandma and Grandpa sold the cream to a creamery in Portland. The Oregon Electric Railway trains ran right by the farm, and a cooperative brakeman slowed down enough between the Bonita and Trece stations for Papa to swing the cream can aboard, and a creamery employee would pick it up in Portland.

By the time my parents were married, however, Grandma was making cottage cheese from their milk and cream. Papa would take the cheese to town by train and peddle it door to door. It was highly perishable, and in those pre-refrigeration days, the purchasers would have consumed it the same day they bought it.

Most people did not know how to make cottage cheese. Grandma's product had always been popular with friends and neighbors when she shared it, so it was logical to begin making money from a product that essentially sold itself.

Mama's hard work continued in the rural setting. Quoting from a letter she wrote many years later to daughter-in-law Florence, "I set six or more hens the first season, though I had no previous experience. Also it was taken for granted that I should prune the two acres of grapes on Grandpa's farm, and I had to set out a half acre of strawberries on our rented place, including digging the plants. We also planted a large garden. And I picked crates of strawberries for sale by Grandpa only a few weeks before Harriet was born. You see I had to learn quickly."

Harriet Helen was born in that little house on July 23, 1912. Early the next year my parents rented a place across the road—a house, barn, and pasture—from Harry Ball for $10 a month. And a few months later they bought the eight acres with house and barn for $3,500. Only one acre was cleared.

In 1913 they had a telephone put in. Transportation to and from Portland was still by train. But the next year Papa borrowed $200 to buy his first car, probably a Model T Ford.

Lois Miriam was born in their still-unfinished frame house on August 24, 1913.

Papa was working such long hours at Grandpa and Grandma's as the fledgling dairy business grew that he hardly ever saw Harriet and Lois when they were awake. Since German had been spoken in her childhood home, it was natural for Mama to revert to German in talking to her little ones. And so Harriet and Lois learned German before English. Unfortunately, they later forgot it. I never heard Mama speak German. But I did hear it when we occasionally attended German services at the Lutheran church, especially at the outdoor services on Mission Fest Sunday.

Richard Gail was born on October 6, 1915. He was a "blue baby" and lived only a few months. He had a congenital heart problem, something that no doubt could now be corrected with surgery. Mama and Papa never talked about their little one in heaven. Perhaps they did their grieving beforehand, knowing that he could not live long. I remember going only once to the cemetery and looking for his grave without a headstone. It is in the Pioneer Cemetery in Milwaukie next to the grave of his Grandpa Carl.

I was born at home on March 23, 1917. My parents must have had trouble naming me as my birth certificate says "unnamed female." (After I was married and applied for my first passport, my parents had to sign an affidavit that I was indeed that "unnamed female.") Apparently I was a happy child, for sometimes they called me Merry Sunshine.

Charles Lee was born 18 months after me, on October 17, 1918.

Since I was much closer in age to Charlie than Lois, it was natural that we two played together until I went to school.

Harry and Louise's family continued to grow with the births of Ruth Atwater on April 10, 1921, William Judson on April 18, 1924, and Eunice Marie on January 5, 1929.

4

PAPA

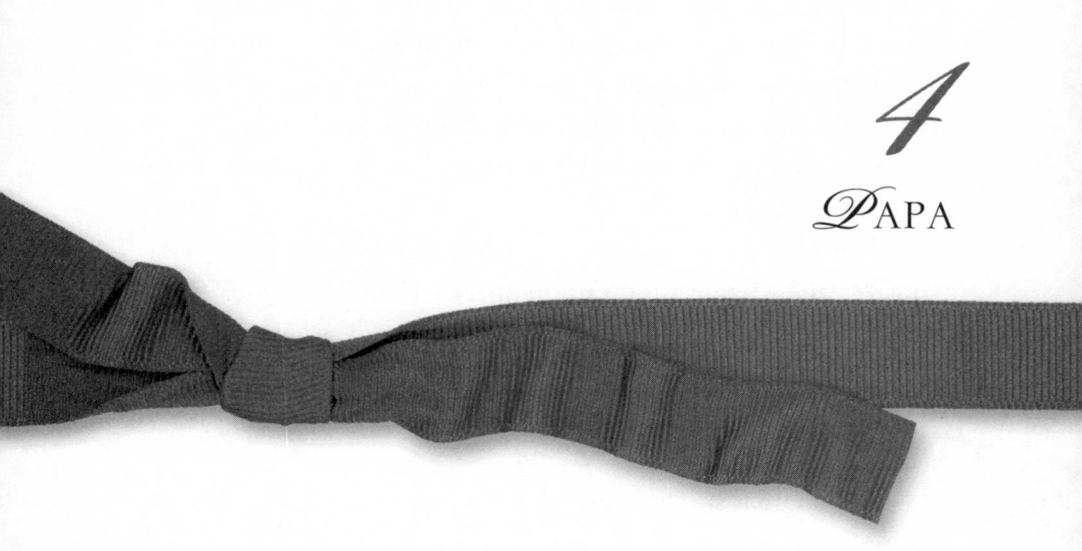

PAPA DESCRIBED himself as a bad boy when young, though he never gave us any details. He was saved when he was 16, and his life changed. He had a second experience of grace in his early twenties, from which he received the assurance of his salvation. According to his report cards (which we still have), his school attendance was erratic. Perhaps that was part of his being a bad boy. He finished eighth grade at age 16, then went to work.

A verse that helped him and became his life verse was Hebrews 11:6, "He that cometh to God must believe that he is, and that he is a rewarder of them that diligently seek him" (KJV). I would say he diligently sought the Lord all his life. Even in his last years, when he was senile and unable to relate to family members, he could still quote Scripture verses and pray.

Papa integrated his faith and his business life. All his conversation was punctuated with Bible quotations, and he did all the talking at supper time. So along with facts and figures about cheese production, sales, and quotas, there were always stories about whom he had witnessed to or the answers to prayer he had heard from a friend at lunch.

The world had no attraction for Papa, and he saw to it that we had as little exposure to the world as possible. We didn't go to movies (then called "picture shows") or dances, or even talk about why we were not going. Hollywood was said to be such a corrupt place that nothing—absolutely *nothing*—good could come out of it. This was in the 1920s!

When I was in seventh grade, I invited Eleanor Plank, a classmate, to go with our family to the International Livestock Exposition in Portland. She saw a billboard on the way announcing the latest movie starring Clara Bow. "I can't wait to see it, can you?" she asked. I just about died. What did Mama and Papa think? But thankfully they didn't say anything.

Need I say that smoking and drinking were strict taboos with Papa? Mama's brothers smoked. Uncle Ted smoked a pipe, and Uncle Will liked a cigar after Sunday dinner, but Papa didn't run them down. But once when a woman was hired to help Mama, she smoked in her room, normally our guest room. The lady had to go. She obviously wasn't a lady, despite her references! John Baden and Win Schroeder, who became my brothers-in-law, almost had to sign on the dotted line that they would give up smoking before they could marry Harriet and Lois.

Papa was a very active Christian layman until he was almost 80. It began when he inherited the tract ministry of Harry Cooper, a friend who died of tuberculosis in 1917 or 1918. This was expanded in 1920 through the opening of the Book Room in one room of an office building in downtown Portland. Other ministries in which he played a key role were listed in the program for his memorial service, as follows:

1921 Became Chairman of the Council of the newly formed Portland Union Bible Classes under the ministry of Dr. B. B. Sutcliffe.

1925	Joined the enlarged Gideon Camp in Portland.
1926	Became President of the Gideon Camp in Portland.
1927	Headed a committee for establishing the Union Gospel Mission, of which he served as Chairman of the Board for 24 years.
1931	Welcomed Dr. John G. Mitchell to the ministry of the Union Bible Classes, which relocated to the Behnke-Walker Auditorium and was renamed Central Bible Church.
1936	Became a charter member of the Board of Trustees of Multnomah School of the Bible.
1936–1938	Served as Vice President of The Gideons International.
1940–1943	Served as Zone Trustee of The Gideons International.
1943–1946	Served as Chaplain of The Gideons International.
1950	Donated the much enlarged Book Room (now under the name of the Christian Supply Center) to Multnomah School of the Bible.
1951–1955	Operated the Christian Supply Center in Boise, Idaho, and continued his activities in Gideons and church work.
1956–1964	In the Los Angeles area: remained active in Gideons and church work, and served on the board of Gospel Recordings, Inc., from 1959 through 1964.

The following tribute to Papa was written by his grandson David C. Schroeder on March 19, 1973, the day of his burial.

On Grandpa West

A giant of a man has fallen.
An old-fashioned saint:
Whose piety caused him to lash out
with personal zeal against the forces of Evil
(including the Sunday comics brusquely seized
from a stunned grandson and tossed into the flames).
Who saw in the young Billy Graham,
in the Gideons, in The Living Bible,
a vision of the gospel
proclaimed in all its old power in fresh new ways.
Who rejoiced to see that Day.
Whose heartfelt prayers will never be forgotten.
Who like Peter never lost his impulsiveness
or his childlike wonder
at God's world and God's ways.
Who walked with his Lord.
And if his Lord gave His all,
why should he hesitate to share
with someone who had less than he?
Grandpa West has gone to be with his Lord.
A hero of the faith.
(I'm glad now I told him so.)
For I feel a strong bond to this saint now sainted.
What he accomplished does not matter,
for I know what he was, and what he meant to me.
I cannot measure his influence;
I simply know that it is there.
He was my grandfather.
And I remember him with pride and love.

5

The Red Rock Dairy

FOR ABOUT THREE years Grandma West made cottage cheese on her wood stove, and that was the main cash crop of their 20-acre farm. The cheese was called Red Rock Cheese. Demand outgrew the limitations of Grandma's kitchen, and during the summer of 1912, a separate dairy house was constructed. Hidden by woods from the country road, it was the site of the growing business for six or seven years.

On the other side of the woods, our family was growing, too, as Harriet, Lois, Gail, myself, and Charlie were all born during those years. Our unfinished house was worked on as time and money permitted, though it still had no indoor plumbing or electricity.

In August 1913, Red Rock Cheese was first advertised in the Portland *Oregonian.* A few weeks later, samples of Red Rock Cheese were given out at a milk show at Meier & Frank department store.

Cottage cheese was a very perishable product, and it became a commercial product only with the advent of refrigeration. It was first sold in meat markets. The cheese was ladled from a white enamel tray in a refrigerated glass case. It was packaged to order by the butcher in half-pound or one-pound cartons with a wire handle. Red Rock Cheese was large curd and very creamy. Modern nutritionists would be horrified at the high level of butterfat!

In 1918 the business was moved from the farm to a modern factory on the highway, a mile from our house. A separate building contained several offices. Some farmers brought their milk directly to the dairy, but the dairy also had a flatbed truck that went throughout Washington County, picking up ten-gallon cans of milk at various farms. At each stop the driver left the same number of empty (and now sterilized) cans he had picked up the previous day. At first Grandpa drove the truck, but after he "retired," Mr. Boyer drove it. Mr. Boyer was an ex-prizefighter who was converted in our neighborhood Sunday school.

The cans had to be marked for each farm, and as soon as they were unloaded, they were weighed to record the amount of milk. The amount was then noted in an account book. Papa had a little sign above the scales: "A false balance is abomination to the Lord: but a just weight is his delight" (Proverbs 11:1, KJV).

Making the cheese itself was not labor intensive, but more and more men were hired to drive vans to deliver the cheese to more and more stores within driving distance of Portland. The vans were cooled with 100-pound blocks of ice, which were made in the dairy's ice-making machine. Soon another factory was opened in Kent, Washington, to serve the greater Seattle area. And not too much later another was opened in Petaluma, California, in the San Francisco Bay area.

Papa traveled frequently to Washington and California as the business expanded. I don't think he had much time to study the set of slim leather-bound books on business management he had purchased. He belonged to the Portland Chamber of Commerce, and he was listed in *Who's Who in America.* He bought a copy, and we children could look up our own names in that fat book.

Speaking of fat books, we had a copy of *Webster's Unabridged Dictionary,* which was displayed on a metal stand with wooden leaves that clamped shut when you weren't using the dictionary. Papa went far with only an eighth-grade education.

Red Rock Dairy had a booth at county fairs and at the Pacific International Livestock Exposition in Portland every year. Samples of cottage cheese on saltine crackers would be passed out, along with recipes and serving suggestions. Here are a couple of entries from Papa's 1926 diary:

> January 22: "Our product was used this week in the Oakland Tribune Cooking School, and we hope this will benefit our business. School had large attendance, and we gave away hundreds of samples."
>
> October 6: "All day at the Machinery Exhibit. Met Prof. Chappell of Oregon Agricultural College. He said they are now working on what constitutes control of body in cottage cheese."

In 1928 my parents went to the International Dairy Congress in London. The following year, the dairy was sold to the Kraft-Phenix corporation. Apparently it was a case of merging or being squeezed out of the market by the larger company from the East. A real bonus for the Kraft company was acquiring the know-how for making Philadelphia cream cheese, which had become a popular Red Rock product in addition to cottage cheese. Red Rock's Kent plant had also been freezing local strawberries in season, which was an early entry in the frozen-food industry. As it turned out, the transaction was strictly a sale—not a merger, as my dad claimed it to be. The following paragraphs are from the Portland *Oregonian* of September 23, 1929:

> Consolidation of the Red Rock Cheese companies of the Pacific coast, largest producers of cottage cheese in the world, and

Kraft-Phenix, Inc. of Chicago, was announced yesterday by Earl Bunting, marketing director of the Red Rock Corporation.

Holders of Red Rock stock, according to Mr. Bunting, will receive more than $1,000,000 in shares of the new company. No change in the policy, products, or personnel of either company will result from the merger.

The history of the Red Rock company, as given yesterday by Mr. Bunting, reads like one of the Horatio Alger books. Twenty years ago, almost to a day, Mr. West, then a mere youth, left his home with the first batch of the now famous Red Rock cottage cheese. It had been made by his mother in the family home near Tigard.

Each day Mr. West trudged from store to store, selling small portions of his cheese to merchants. As a market was established, Mr. West opened his first dairy. Since then the organization has grown with astounding rapidity. The Red Rock Dairy was incorporated in 1920, and in 1922 the Red Rock Creamery company of Washington was formed, followed two years later by the establishment of two dairies in California.

Red Rock products are now handled by about 5,000 retail dealers, according to Mr. West.

It was stock and not money that changed hands. The stock market crash of 1929 occurred within weeks, and I presume the stock that my dad was holding lost a great deal in value.

Despite promises and expectations to the contrary, within a few months the Red Rock officials were out of the management. In a diary entry from 1930, Papa wrote:

June 1: "Having been in the cheese business 21 years, it is only natural that a strange feeling should come over me, realizing that all the old ties and associations are ended. Naturally Mother and Father regret seeing me leave the business."

After leaving the dairy business, Papa started a new business, turning from cheese to investments. The day after writing of his feelings on leaving the "cheese business" after 21 years, Papa wrote:

> June 2: "Moving desk and some furniture into Portland—204 Porter Building. Louis LeTourneau is to be in the office and keep books."

The new company, if it was a company, was called L & H Investment Co. Apparently the Kraft stock was sold in order to make other investments, but what they were, none of us knew. As far as I know, the L & H Investment Co. never handled other people's money.

Decades later, when we West children got together for periodic reunions, the question would always come up: "Where did the money go?" A million dollars was a *lot* of money in 1929. Not that any of us seven were really hankering after that lost treasure. None of our sweat was in it. We were all too young to have played a part in that fast-growing business before it was sold. It was more the mystery of it—where did the money go?

Of course some of it went toward the purchase of a big brick house in Raleigh, a few miles from our former home near Tigard. (Raleigh is the name of a bit of semi-rural suburbia around the private Portland Golf Club.) We moved into that house in January, 1930, and furnished it in part with new furniture. My parents also built a new three-car garage and spruced up the landscaping of the large property. We all greatly enjoyed that house for a number of years.

Eighteen months after opening the office in the Porter Building, Papa wrote in his diary on December 5, 1931, "Business looks not only blue but black and blue! On the other hand, things Christian never looked more promising." He was referring to the Portland Union Bible Classes (later Central Bible Church), the Gideons, the Union Gospel Mission, and the Christian bookstore, in all of which he played a leading role.

After the short-lived L & H Investment Co. folded, Papa got into the growing electrical appliance retail business. His store was on Tenth Street on Portland's West side, just four blocks from his main competitor, Meier & Frank. At first they sold only refrigerators, with Frigidaire as their main line. Later, electric ranges were added. Papa's office was on the mezzanine above the sales floor, where he was available to every Tom, Dick, and Harry he knew in business, the church, the mission, the Gideons, and committeemen from the current interchurch evangelistic effort. Now he had lots to share at supper time, whether we were interested or not.

Early Childhood Memories

OUR HOUSE was on Bonita Road, about a mile from the Red Rock Dairy. Bonita was only a stop on the Oregon Electric line. A yellow wooden shelter, open toward the tracks, served as a station. You had to pull a rope that raised an arm signal so the brakeman would know you wanted to get on. The Southern Pacific Railroad paralleled the Oregon Electric Railway, but the Southern Pacific had no station at Bonita.

Mama was a thorough housekeeper and a stickler for routine. She probably didn't think of it in those terms, though. She would have assumed that every household had a similar pattern: wash on Monday; iron and bake bread on Tuesday; iron again on Wednesday if the family was large; mend on Thursday and wash again if there was a baby in diapers; change the sheets and clean the upstairs on Friday; clean the downstairs and bake bread on Saturday; go to church on Sunday and not do any work other than meal preparation.

That was her routine. Never a thought like "I'll do it if and when I feel like it." Holidays could be a problem: If the Fourth of July fell on Friday, when would the upstairs get cleaned? Some things were done seasonally. For instance, with Oregon's clean air, windows did not need to be washed or curtains laundered very often. And Mama was not one to do a thorough spring cleaning as some homemakers did. Every week's cleaning was thorough! Mama was so methodical that as a child I wondered how she knew when to wash the sugar bowl, but I never asked her. After I was married, I struggled with guilt for years (perhaps my sisters did, too) because I was not as systematic and thorough as Mama.

Mama got all that daily work done in the morning before lunch. After lunch she went upstairs and took a nap. All her life Mama had insomnia, but she resisted taking the sleeping powders that were available, so the naps were important. After her nap she would work in the vegetable and flower gardens, doing what was appropriate for the season. She worked as hard as any man. At five o'clock she came in, started or stoked the fire in the woodstove, changed into a clean housedress, and peeled the potatoes. We almost always had potatoes, no matter what else was on the menu. A dessert like rice pudding, bread pudding, or tapioca pudding would have been prepared in the morning before the fire went out in the woodstove.

During the winter, or on other rainy days, Mama sewed and mended in the afternoon. A large closet off the dining room was her sewing room. She made cotton housedresses for herself and clothes for us girls—dresses, slips, and nightgowns. She pieced a few quilts from the cotton scraps. To keep her hands busy when visiting, she crocheted borders for pillowcases and dresser scarves, as did both of our grandmothers. She also crocheted the wool tams that we wore to school in winter. Our Sunday hats were purchased.

We girls were really bundled up in winter. We wore long underwear, long cotton stockings, a waist that held the garters, bloomers, and a flannel slip—and over that a broadcloth slip—and then a wool jumper or skirt and blouse. We would drape the underwear over a radiator to take off the chill before putting it on. Pulling cotton stockings on over long underwear took some expertise to keep it from looking lumpy.

If one of us had a really bad cold in those days before Kleenex, Mama would tear a worn sheet into squares that were disposed of in the stove after use. Papa was careful to put a clean handkerchief in his pocket every day.

Occasionally Mama would go shopping in Portland. If she wasn't home by five, we girls knew to start the fire and put potatoes on to boil.

Mama telephoned the Schubring & Biederman store in Tigard for groceries, which were delivered. She bought sugar in 100-pound sacks and flour in 50-pound sacks. The flour sacks made good dish towels.

There were three bins under the counter in the pantry, which was like a second kitchen: one for flour, one for sugar, and one for wrapping paper and string that could be reused.

Papa always told us girls that the best thing he had done for us as a father was giving us Mama as mother. We agreed, but of course we couldn't imagine any alternative.

Papa saw to it that we washed our hands before sitting down to supper. Also the boys had to make a stab at slicking their hair down with a brush and water. Stacomb was the product Dad applied to their heads on Sunday before going to church.

When I was very young, we always had Sunday dinner at Grandma Trappe's. Stark Street Gospel Hall and Grace Lutheran Church (Missouri Synod) were not all that far apart on Portland's East side, so transportation to and from church was coordinated between Papa and Mama and their respective churches. Then we drove to Sellwood, where Grandma and Aunt Mae lived. Mama took her nap after the dinner dishes were done. We children liked to walk to the Sellwood park and use the swings, slides, and rings. There was a ferry crossing the Willamette River in Sellwood, and we had to be sure to catch the last ferry when going home from Grandma's. It would have meant quite a few extra miles if we had had to go back to Portland to cross the river on one of the bridges.

Portland was famous for all its bridges as the Willamette River cut the city in two, dividing West side and East side. All of the banks, large department stores, office buildings, hotels, apartment houses, and the big denominational "first" churches were on the West side when I was young. The East side contained single-family homes, with retail stores and services along the main arteries like Burnside, Sandy Boulevard, and Union Avenue. The river itself was lined with docks, as Portland was an important port despite being 100 miles inland.

Papa's self-appointed share in housework was to wash the Sunday dinner dishes when we stopped going to Grandma Trappe's for Sunday dinner. We girls dried. He was fast, used very hot water, and was thorough. The pantry was really clean when we hung up the last dish towel.

"Shoulders back" was a frequent reminder from Papa. Always erect himself, he was intolerant of sloppy posture. He was well groomed, too. He had his hair cut every Friday and saw to it that his suits were well pressed.

From the south side of our house, especially the big porch where we played on rainy days, we could look across two hay fields to see the Oregon Electric passenger trains and the Southern Pacific freight trains. There were only cross-arm warning signs where roads crossed tracks. The signs cautioned motorists and pedestrians to "Stop, Look, and Listen."

Even before we had indoor plumbing or electricity, Mama had a washing machine. It sat in the screened back porch and was operated by a belt from a gasoline engine. She boiled all the white clothes in a copper boiler on the woodstove before transferring them to the washing machine, then through the wringer to the rinse tubs set up on a wooden bench. The first rinse was warm, the second cold, and liquid bluing was added to that to ensure that the white fabrics stayed white and did not turn yellow over time.

There were long clotheslines in the backyard and more on a large porch where the clothes were hung on rainy days. We did not have a basement. Mama ironed everything, including sheets and bath towels. We girls learned to iron by starting with dish towels and Papa's handkerchiefs. Before we had electricity, the heavy irons were heated on the woodstove in the kitchen. Mama had five irons, so there was always a hot one to replace the one that had cooled.

One of the round washtubs was put on the kitchen floor for baths. We didn't have a bath every night. During barefoot days, when we didn't take a bath, we sat on the porch step with a bucket of water to wash our feet before going to bed.

It wasn't as if our town didn't have electricity, but there weren't lines on Bonita Road. I think the homeowners had to put up some money before that was done. Some of our neighbors were pretty poor. The Stevens family lived in a corner of their barn.

Our neighbors may have been poor, but they had pride. Once Mama sent me to the Bows, half a mile away, with a shopping bag of outgrown clothes for their girls. Mrs. Bow said I must have misunderstood my mother and that I was to take them to the Turnbulls, who lived across the road from the Bows. I dragged the bag home, disconsolate, as if it were my fault the good deed had been spurned.

There were wall brackets with glass reflectors for the kerosene lamps in the kitchen and dining room. Elsewhere the lamps were put on tables or bureaus. On winter nights Mama put a lamp at the bottom of the stairs until we were safely in our beds. The lamp chimneys were washed every morning because they would get cloudy from smoke. The wicks were trimmed before the chimneys were put back on the lamps. We girls learned that the hot glass broke if water splashed on a lamp when we were doing dishes. Such carelessness, or playfulness, was not overlooked!

When we did get indoor plumbing, the bathroom was large and accessible only from a door on our screened back porch. If Mama was busy with a baby or just plain too tired, Papa would bathe Charlie, Ruth, and me on Tuesday and Saturday nights. He would put us all in the tub at the same time, and he scrubbed harder than Mama! Also it was he who taught us to clean the ring around the tub. The bathroom was so large that once, when our cow got out of the pasture, she walked in and deposited a cow pie! We children thought that was pretty funny. It was on a Sunday morning while we were at church. Papa changed his clothes and did barn chores in our bathroom!

The back porch also figures in another childhood memory. It was the Fourth of July, and the annual picnic for our extended family was at our place. While we children were setting off firecrackers, someone left a lighted punk (a substance used to ignite the fuses of firecrackers) on the porch table. It ignited the paper wrapping on the Roman candles and skyrockets that were being saved until after dark. Bang, bang, bang! They shot through the open door into the kitchen, where our aunts and great aunts were washing up the picnic dishes. Did they jump fast!

As a young child I occasionally played in the ditch beside the road in front of our house. If I heard a car coming down Bonita Road, I would get up and swing on the gate so the passerby could identify me as "one of Harry West's girls." I was not just somebody who lived in the neighborhood. I was proud of my family identity. And of course, in my mind, everyone driving by knew the Harry West place. And they probably did.

Mama learned to drive "the machine" (the family's first Ford car) before I was born. But after she had an accident one time, she quit and did not drive again for years. While our groceries were delivered and we had our own milk, anything to be purchased from a department store meant a trip to Portland. As the family grew, there were more things to be purchased. Mama had to catch the stage (the bus) near the dairy for the ride into the city, then walk several blocks to Meier & Frank, then walk back to the depot lugging two big shopping bags (especially if she had stopped at the farmer's market on Yamhill Street, near the depot, to pick up fresh lettuce, cabbage, celery, and hominy). When she got off the stage, she would ride home with Papa from the dairy.

But Papa wasn't always home, so it was harder to shop or get to church, and eventually Mama started driving again. By then cars were easier to drive, too. She didn't have to take us to school or to music lessons, as we always walked, no matter what the weather.

I took piano lessons, but music theory was really hard for me to learn—all about sharps, flats, major and minor keys—and practicing the scales was boring. I dreaded music lessons, and Miss Gilbert didn't make them any fun and games either. It was a happy day when Mama said I could quit piano. I was in fifth grade.

Lois kept on with piano lessons through high school and into college. As a consequence, she has been able to use her musical ability in churches wherever Win has served. Now in her mid-eighties, she still plays old songs and hymns in a couple of nursing homes for the enjoyment of residents.

Occasionally Gypsies camped on a piece of vacant property between our place and Grandpa's. They didn't have horses and colorful wagons like I've seen in Europe, but they drove big cars with California license plates. What were they doing in our neck of the woods? Rumors about Gypsies are no doubt the same the world over. They'd steal things in stores, we heard from our friends, and would even kidnap little children. We wondered how much Mr. Schubring lost when several women came in his store at the same time with the very full skirts with deep pockets. Not that we ever saw the women that close up, but it was common knowledge about those *deep* pockets. We wouldn't walk the mile to Grandpa and Grandma's until the Gypsies moved on.

Sometimes we walked up the road when it was time for Papa to come home from the office. He would pick us up, and we would stand on the running board. When one is loved and cared for, such simple pleasures as getting a ride on the running board add up to a happy childhood.

We always had a horse, Old Red, for doing the farmwork. Not all of our small farm was cultivated, for there was a stand of fir trees between our house and the Balls' and a section around the barn that was too rocky. But there was one field for raising hay to feed the horse and cow, so the hired man and Red plowed and harrowed that field and Mama's large vegetable garden each spring.

About 1928 Papa thought we should have a riding horse, too. I don't think any of us children would have thought of asking for one, for we didn't know anyone who rode. After he bought a riding horse and an English saddle, we had to have lessons to learn to ride correctly. None of us children were asking for that, either! We took lessons on Saturdays at the Portland Hunt Club in Garden Home—not all that far from where we lived, but in a different world! The other children taking lessons came out from Portland, and we never even got to know their names. They were properly dressed in vests, jodhpurs, and boots, something Papa hadn't thought of. I wore a Saturday cotton dress, long cotton stockings, and oxfords!

I learned to saddle a horse, mount and dismount, and ride in a ring. Unfortunately, I didn't learn to enjoy doing it. It was a "must," like the piano lessons that had preceded it. And since we only had one riding horse, there was no one to ride with at home. Taking turns going up and down the road wasn't that much fun. Give me a good book!

The horse (I don't remember her name) moved with us in 1930 and was boarded in Nichol's Riding Academy on the other side of the Portland Golf Club. Well, boarding an unridden horse during the Depression was an expense that could be given up. Nobody cried when she was sold.

7

Grandpa West

WHEN THE MODERN dairy plant was built on the highway (not in Tigard itself but at the juncture of Bonita Road and the highway), Papa had a new frame bungalow built for Grandpa and Grandma West on part of the dairy property. He even had steam heat piped from the dairy for their radiators. Since the logo for the dairy was a red rock, Grandpa had a huge boulder placed in the front yard where it would be seen by everyone passing by on the highway—and he painted it fire-engine red.

His energy found outlet in stunts, and he always called a Portland newspaper so a reporter could come and get the story—mostly just a picture! More often than not we first learned about his latest stunt at school when a classmate would say, "I saw your Grandpa's picture in the paper." We hadn't seen it because it would be in an afternoon paper, and we took the more staid morning paper, *The Oregonian*. Mama always said he retired too soon.

When he was driving an Austin car (smaller than a VW beetle), he had an open-air seat made to fit on top, and he called it his Toonerville Trolley, after the cartoon strip. Then he had a trailer made and would appear at grade schools to give children a ride on top and behind. One year for the Rose Festival Parade, he added still another trailer behind the first and had the whole contraption decorated with flowers and full of children. Grandpa's Austin was small enough to navigate the trail up the Lower Multnomah Falls, and he had his picture taken on the bridge to record the event.

One time he had a motorboat tow him on a wide surfboard for 50 miles on the Willamette River from Portland to Salem.

So much for a sampling of his stunts. Grandma would be home reading her Bible, praying for children, grandchildren, and missionaries, or visiting neighbors.

Once Grandpa walked in the annual Fourth of July race between Portland and Hillsboro (18 miles) to garner publicity. He was the oldest contestant by far. The summer I was 13, he decided that Charlie and I should enter the race. It wasn't our idea of fun, but he must have been persuasive. Then he saw to it that there was a prize for the youngest winner. Maybe only that year! There was some conditioning ahead of time, and he had a photographer make a movie strip of us walking as fast as we could.

When the big day arrived, Charlie was nursing a boil on his leg and couldn't join me in the race. It was a warm day, and when I lagged, Grandpa would get out of his Austin and pace me. I came in third in the women's race for a $10 prize! Somewhere in my memorabilia I have the newspaper picture that records it. Grandpa had seen to it that a reporter was on hand.

The walk ended at the Washington County Fairgrounds, where an amusement company had set up concession stands. After showering and resting up, I wanted to ride the Ferris wheel in the worst way, but I wasn't forward enough to ask Grandpa for a dime. The whole $10 went into my savings account.

Of all the grandchildren, I was singled out to accompany Grandpa to home games of Portland's professional baseball team. I'm sure Papa never went to a game in his life, and the few games I saw didn't make me much of a fan.

Once Grandpa took Charlie, Ruth, and me on the steamer *Georgiana* for an all-day excursion on the Columbia River to Astoria and back. We very much enjoyed that experience. Another time I drove to Astoria with Grandpa for an overnight visit with an old buddy from his streetcar days. I must have been 13, for I remember surreptitiously trying out my first little 10¢ tube of Tangee lipstick.

Harriet came home from Houston with her one-year-old daughter Margaret for a much-anticipated visit during the summer of 1939. And who should get off the train with them but Grandpa West! How could that be? Turns out he had boarded the train in Oregon City, the last stop before Portland, in order to be the first to welcome them, but also to share the limelight at the Portland depot.

Grandma West sent me a Christmas card early in December 1942, "because I may not live long," and to let me know she was praying all would go well with the birth of our first child. She died January 11, 1943, five days before her 83rd birthday. She and Grandpa had been married 61 years.

At that time Grandpa was also failing and could not live alone. My parents took him into their home, and he lived with them more than a year. When care for him became too burdensome for Mother, he was put in a nursing home in Hillsboro. He was there only a few weeks before he died on May 28, 1944, at age 86. He was buried next to Grandma in Crescent Grove Cemetery, near the plot where my sister Eunice was laid to rest and where my parents were later buried.

8

Summer Fun

ON SUMMER MORNINGS we would have chores such as digging weeds from the yard, hoeing in the garden, picking strawberries, peas, or beans, or chopping wood. But summer afternoons were free. Mama always took a nap after lunch, so we were careful not to be too noisy or disturb her with requests. Better to have decided ahead of time if we were going to go crawfishing in Fanno Creek or swimming at Oswego Lake.

Both activities were with the Ball children. We had to have permission to leave our place, but the Ball children seemed to be free agents. As long as they came back for supper, they could do whatever they wanted. All the games and play equipment were at our house, so we seldom went to their house. Besides, we couldn't play in their much larger barn, for the stacks of hay were not to be trampled. The Balls milked a number of cows, and sale of the milk supported the family. Mr. Ball was taciturn, and we avoided him if at all possible.

Howard Ball was my age. Once when we were standing around after his big brother Fred came back from hunting, Fred's shotgun accidentally fired and hit Howard's ankle at close range. Boy, did I run for home in a hurry. I had been standing right next to Howard. It took a long time for his shattered foot to heal, and Howard walked with a limp the rest of his life.

For crawfishing we each needed string, a piece of slab bacon, and a nail for weight. One pail was enough to bring home our catch. The challenge was to pull the crawdad out of the water and grab both claws from behind so as not to get pinched. If they were too small, we threw them back. After all, they were to be eaten. But we usually gave our catch to the Balls. Mama didn't much care for our boiling crawfish on the kitchen range. Once Gracia Rundel came up from behind and put a crawfish down the back of my dress. The crawfish did what came naturally and pinched my back. I also did what came naturally—I yelled!

We wore out two platform yard swings while we lived on the Bonita place. They had two seats facing each other and were propelled by pushing your feet on the floor slats. One person could swing alone, or four could be seated, with two more standing. Then we pushed the swing to its limits. No wonder they wore out!

In the summer a hammock made of blue-striped ticking hung across one corner of the deep side porch. A wisteria vine gave shade from the sun. That same porch had the "indoor" clotheslines for drying laundry on rainy days.

Papa hung a swing from the highest ridge pole in the open part of the barn. There were buckles on the sturdy straps, so the swing seat could be replaced with a trapeze bar or two rings. We could swing very high. There was a tree swing in the yard, too.

Another piece of playground equipment, as good as any in the city parks, was a string of four rings. There was a platform for reaching the first ring and a base for shoving off to catch the second ring while releasing the first—and then on to the third and fourth. With enough momentum one could come back to the platform, and another kid had a turn. I'm guessing that Uncle Ted had a hand in building the framework to support the rings, but it would have been Papa's idea.

We could ride a coaster wagon or scooter on the sidewalk from the back door, around the side of the house, and through the front yard to the gate. Beginning with Ruth, a tricycle was added to the parade.

Behind the house was the biggest sandbox you ever saw. Several children could be in it at the same time, making roads for miniature cars, mountains for them to climb, or even tunnels *through* the "mountains"! Hours of fun. If we made mud pies on washday, we might get a few lumps of Argo starch out of the wooden box and make a paste by adding water. Then, with a few drops of bluing, we had blue frosting for our brown cookies drying in the sun.

We always had a hired man to do the farmwork, but jobs such as painting the house, wallpapering, or reglazing a broken window meant hiring the right artisan. Then there were the well drillers, hired when we needed a new deeper well, and sawyers who came around when a load of cordwood had been delivered. We burned wood in the fireplace and the kitchen stove. In the furnace we burned both wood and coal briquettes.

All of us, girls as well as boys, learned to chop wood for the kitchen stove (and *pile it neatly*) and chop kindling to start the fire. Charlie had to keep the woodbin beside the kitchen stove full.

After fir trees had been felled to make way for an orchard and before the stumps had been blasted out, we children were allowed—after asking permission—to play with fire. We gathered up sticks and cones and piled them against the stumps to keep the fire going. When we tried roasting potatoes, we never left them in long enough. The Ball children ate potatoes raw, sprinkled with salt. I never acquired a taste for that.

We had a big yard and could play softball games like "work-up," as we didn't have enough kids for two teams. We also played tag, hide-and-seek, kick the can, stealing steps, and run sheep run. Also a game like Red Rover that included this exchange:

"Here we come."

"Where from?"

"New Orleans."

"What's your trade?"

"Lemonade."

"Give us some if you're not afraid."

Then players from one side would try to tag players from the other side.

A favorite game involved two teams throwing a hard rubber ball over the garage roof, shouting "Ante Ante Over" when throwing the ball. If someone caught the ball before it touched the ground, that team ran around to the other side and tried to tag players on the opposing side, while they ran as soon as they saw the others coming. We could only run around one side of the garage because of the chain-link fence between our yard and the road.

We had most of the indoor games that were current in the '20s. They were kept in cupboards under window seats in our front hall. The games I remember are Parcheesi, Peggity, Pit, Authors, Flinch, Lotto, an Erector set, Tiddlywinks, Rook, Bible-character question games, Anagrams, jacks, Jack Straws, building blocks, Tinker Toys, checkers, a Carrom board, a Nellie Bly board game, and beanbags that we tossed through holes cut into a board.

Authors was a favorite game that was also educational. We learned to recognize the faces and works of Walt Whitman, Nathaniel Hawthorne, Victor Hugo, William Shakespeare, and others long before we read any of their books or plays. Titles included

The Scarlet Letter
The House of the Seven Gables
Les Miserables
The Count of Monte Cristo
Hamlet
Macbeth
A Midsummer Night's Dream

There was a large blackboard in the kitchen where we played tic-tac-toe, dot-to-dot, and word games.

My parents subscribed to a number of magazines. The ones I remember are

National Geographic
The Literary Digest
Sunday-School Times
Our Hope
Woman's Home Companion
A business magazine, like *Nation's Business* or *Forbes*
Saturday Evening Post
The Lutheran Witness
A Lutheran missions periodical in German

Among us children, the *Youth's Companion* was eagerly awaited each week. Of course, Harriet, being oldest, got it first.

Papa did very little general reading because he read the Christian magazines before the others, even if he thought he would read them later. He had a large library of devotional books and Bible expositions by such writers as C. H. M. and A. W. Pink. But you always knew if Papa had read something because he marked passages he liked—mostly check marks in the margin, but he underlined, too. Just as he couldn't converse without quoting Scripture, he couldn't read without marking. I didn't like it that he marked in ink a couple of his favorite hymns in the new Lutheran hymnal I received for confirmation.

Papa didn't read any fiction, as he thought it was a waste of time. I think he had read *Ben Hur* when he was young, or else had seen the play. One exception was *Pilgrim's Progress,* which he rated next to the Bible.

We all had measles when I was two, before my memory, and whooping cough the summer I was four. I remember that because

Ruth was only four months old, and she nearly died. A couple of years later we had chicken pox and smallpox not too far apart. Chicken pox first, so when Harriet became ill and had unmistakable pocks, we knew it must be smallpox. Everybody else in the family was immediately vaccinated, which may have accounted for the fact that we had light cases. The big scabs on our arms where we were vaccinated were the worst part. Smallpox was a serious disease, so we were quarantined, with a sign posted on our front door. When traveling overseas as an adult, I have had to be vaccinated several times because I could never prove that I had smallpox as a child. The few pockmarks that would have been telltale signs have long since disappeared.

Except for those contagious diseases, we were a healthy lot, and the six of us survived rough-and-tumble play indoors and out without a broken arm or leg. We applied a paste of soda and water to numerous bee stings.

When little Ruth lost her grip swinging on the pipe trellis behind Mama's perennial border and hit her head on the sharp edge of the concrete footings, I ran to pick her up, and already the back of her dress was soaked with blood. What a scare! The gash required several stitches. Fortunately, the doctor was only a couple of miles away in Tigard.

I had my back all taped up after an accident the summer our parents were in England. We were having a family picnic at a park on the Pudding River where chutes had been built for water fun. You carried a board up steps to a platform, sat on the board (or belly flopped), and someone would give you a good push. There were rollers on the chute, and the momentum carried board and rider out into the river before slowly sinking. For an added thrill I sat on Grandpa's shoulders while he sat on the board. There was a jerk when the sled started, and I fell off, landing first on the top board of a fence and then on the ground. Poor me and poor Grandpa. But there were no lasting ill effects.

A few years earlier, while directing a play in our hayloft, I stepped backward off the edge, landing on my back on the plank barn floor. I was subdued but not injured, and after I caught my breath, we decided none of us would tell Mama.

We went barefoot all summer, and I hated to leave childhood when it meant wearing shoes all year. Even when we walked two miles or more to swim in Oswego Lake, we went barefoot on gravel roads.

I recently read that the packaged caramel corn, Cracker Jack, is 100 years old. I always associate that with the little candy store in the park at Oswego Lake. Occasionally we West kids would have a nickel to spend, and Cracker Jack gave us the most for our money—plus a prize in the bottom of the box.

There was a tenant house on the far corner of our property, past the barn and chicken house. In my earliest memory, the Hewitt family lived there, and Mr. Hewitt milked the cow and did other farm chores. Other tenants were the Clintons, an older couple, followed by the Personetts, and the Pollards in 1926. From Papa's journal: "Mr. and Mrs. Pollard started to work on our place for $60 per month plus rent, water, garden, and milk. Also extra pay for housework."

The big girls did not always appreciate my tagging along when it came to summer fun. Once they did something about it in an unforgettable way. Under some pretext they got me in the little walled-off feed room inside the barn, then locked the door on the outside and ran off. All kinds of "what ifs" ran through my mind in that dark, stuffy space. What if the hired man didn't show up to milk the cow in late afternoon? Would I ever be found?

What seemed like hours was probably only 15 minutes before softhearted Lois came back and released her little sister. Still, feelings of claustrophobia have stayed with me all my life as a result of that childish prank.

9

Bonita Sunday School

THE BONITA SUNDAY school probably began in a home, but in my earliest memory it met on the second floor of a small grocery and general store near the Bonita train station. It was reached by an outside stairway. Papa was strong on Sunday school. Teachers came out from the Stark St. Gospel Hall in Portland to teach at three o'clock in the afternoon. I don't remember who played the pump organ before Lois was accomplished enough to take over.

When the store with the meeting room burned to the ground, the Sunday school, never large, met at Koopmans' house and later at Boyers'. These two families and others, including some of the Ball children, became rooted in their faith through this neighborhood Sunday school. The children grew up and established Christian homes wherever they moved.

Eventually a hall was built in Bonita just to house the Sunday school. I suppose Papa put up the money, but maybe he got some money from friends at Stark St. Gospel Hall, too. There was no official tie with the Plymouth Brethren, but occasionally we had special evening services, and the speakers would be leading elders from the Plymouth Brethren.

I was too young to understand or appreciate the large charts they brought with them outlining prophecy and the end times. For me the only result was to turn me off to all such charts. That building still stands, but I do not know if services are held there.

Fanno Creek ran by the property. Once while I was standing on the bridge that crossed the creek, my Bible slipped off the railing and got "baptized." Mr. Boyer was really baptized in the creek. Perhaps others, but they were not public services. I just heard Papa tell about it.

"Ole" Olson was the spirited song leader for years. He was very tall, and his wife, Tillie, was very short. We sang gospel songs and the choruses of the day. And the leaders were strong on Bible memorization. Sometimes everybody had to learn a verse starting with the letter *A,* then stand and recite it. Then the leader would choose the "best" verse, such as "All we like sheep have gone astray; we have turned every one to his own way; and the Lord hath laid on him the iniquity of us all" (Isa. 53:6, KJV). Then we were all supposed to memorize that verse for the following week, as well as come prepared to recite a verse beginning with the letter *B*.

If we needed help, Papa or Mama would help us find a verse with special meaning, such as "Be ye doers of the word, and not hearers only" (James 1:22, KJV).

Months later, when we got to *X* and *Z,* we just had to find verses that contained those letters because there weren't any verses that started with them. A favorite for *X* was "Except ye be converted, and become as little children, ye shall not enter into the kingdom of heaven" (Matt. 18:3, KJV).

Mama never came to the Bonita Sunday school or the special meetings. For us children it was our second Sunday school because in the morning we had attended at Grace Lutheran Church. There our memory work was more likely to be the Ten Commandments, even though Lutherans are very strong on grace as opposed to the law. But if you don't know the demands of the law and the awful punishment for disobeying even the smallest commandment, how can you fully appreciate the bounties of God's grace? "For by grace are ye saved through faith; and that not of yourselves: it is the gift of God: Not of works, lest any man should boast" (Eph. 2:8-9, KJV).

The Brethren (that is, the P.B. kind of Brethren) were funny about Christmas, and I don't know why. There was always a program, but it was *after* Christmas, not before. The recitations were not about the birth of Jesus, the angels coming to the shepherds, or even Old Testament prophecies about the coming of the Messiah. Rather, little children might hold up cards that spelled SALVATION, and the first child would say, "*S* stands for sin," and the next one, "*A* stands for all, for all of us have sinned." *L* would stand for love ("We love him because he first loved us"), *V* for verily ("Verily, verily I say unto you"), and so on.

I could memorize easily, and I was given a long poem that must have come out of some British religious periodical. Sort of a tearjerker, but nothing about Christmas. At the end of the program, we would be given an orange and a little box of hard candies. An orange was no special treat for us West children. Mama bought oranges all winter, and we had one in our school lunch every day. But maybe they were too expensive for other families.

Our family's attendance at Bonita Sunday school came to an end when we moved to Raleigh in 1930, but "the wonderful words of life" have reverberated through all of our lives.

10

Grade School

I STARTED SCHOOL at age six and was put in second grade, as I could read well and do simple arithmetic. Third grade would not have been a challenge, but I was too young for that grade.

Tigard Public School was in a new six-room building. Harriet and Lois remember the old school, which was demolished when the new one was built. Two grades (third and sixth) were split up to accommodate eight grades in six rooms. Half of the third grade was with the second grade, and half with the fourth grade. Tigard still didn't have its own high school, so students were bussed to Beaverton High School.

Halfway through sixth grade, about a third of our class was promoted to seventh grade. Consequently, that small hybrid class graduated two years later in January 1930. I was still 12.

The two miles we walked to school took us through woods, road, woods, road, woods, and highway, in that order. The paths through woods were well beaten. Coming out of the last woods, we crossed the railroad tracks and walked on the sidewalk along the highway through Tigard, past Schubring & Biederman grocery store, the bank, the barbershop, Mrs. Lewis's little store of sundries, the pool hall ("Don't you dare look inside!"), then Mr. Nedry's house. On the other side of the highway were Tigard Grocery and Feed store, a butcher shop, and the blacksmith shop. After crossing Fanno Creek, there was a Sealy Mattress factory in an unattractive building and the Johnson Lumber Company.

Then came St. Anthony's Catholic church and school. All very mysterious. Occasionally we could see nuns in their long black habits and tight-fitting wimples as they lined up the children to go into the church. It was so foreign to us, they might as well have been from another planet. There were also two Protestant churches in Tigard.

Past the public school a little ways was Tigardville, with another grocery store, the Grange Hall, and a little bitty shoe-repair shop. I was kind of afraid of bearded Mr. Lenz when I had to take shoes in for him to fix.

When the school bell rang at nine o'clock, we lined up in the central hall by room and *marched* to our respective rooms to the martial beat of a record on the Victrola. Mr. Nedry accented the beat by drumming a stick on the table leg.

We played basketball and indoor softball in the gym. But weather permitting we were always outdoors during recess and the noon hour after eating lunch. From fourth grade on we were expected to divide into teams and play softball or baseball on three different diamonds.

To see educational movies, a grade at a time sat on the stage of the gym, with the curtains drawn to make it dark. The janitor was the projectionist. Occasionally Hollywood movies were shown at the school on a weekend night. A sandwich board by the highway announced the movie to the community. Of course our family never went to any of those.

I saw my first real Hollywood movie sort of by deception. I was in Girl Scouts for a year or two when I was 11 or 12. A short feature about scouting was being shown at a Portland theater, and our leader took a carful of us girls to see it. Mama gave me permission. Maybe Papa wasn't home; in any event, he wasn't involved.

I felt tainted just walking past the posters about coming movies and through the door into semidarkness. There was a Girl Scout short all right, but it seemed *very* short after we saw a full-length movie first! I really was not prepared for that. It was about survivors living on boats marooned in the Sargasso Sea. The boats were all jammed together, with mutiny, provisions running out, etc. I don't remember the plot except it was spooky and probably violent for that day. For sure I couldn't tell my parents about it, but how could I expand the Girl Scout feature into an entire evening's performance? The guilt I felt kept me from wanting to see any more movies—at least for a few years.

There were weekly assemblies at school. Sometimes there were speakers, but what I remember most is singing from the yellow *Community Songs* book—patriotic songs, spirituals, war songs, ballads, and religious songs. We sang them all. This is a sampling:

America the Beautiful
Columbia, the Gem of the Ocean
My Bonnie Lies over the Ocean
Ol' Black Joe
Carry Me Back to Old Virginny
My Old Kentucky Home
The Old Oaken Bucket
Onward, Christian Soldiers
Auld Lang Syne
Coming through the Rye
Gin a body meet a body coming thro' the rye;
Gin a body kiss a body, need a body cry?
Old Folks at Home
Tenting in the Old Campground
When Irish Eyes Are Smiling

Swing Low, Sweet Chariot
The Church in the Wildwood
Annie Laurie
When the Saints Go Marching In
Genevieve, Sweet Genevieve

If one of the older kids suggested that we walk home from school on the tracks instead of the way we usually walked, I would look up at the sign that said, as clear as could be, NO TRESPASSING, Violators Will Be Prosecuted. As a six-year-old, I didn't really know what *prosecute* meant, but it sounded pretty much like *persecute*. I knew that word, sort of, from the Bible. Weren't the Philistines always persecuting the Israelites? It was bad news all around. What if some railroad official came along and started persecuting us? How would we get home? And then would Papa whip us with the leather razor strop?

But the big kids—Harriet, Lois, Ruby, Ivy, Gracia, and Garnet—were so much bigger than I, and they didn't pay any attention to the sign. Neither did the tramps who walked along the tracks. Did railroad people ever persecute—I mean prosecute—them? I think it was because of the tramps that Mama didn't like us to walk home on the tracks, not because of what the sign said.

Our grade school principal and eighth grade teacher, Mr. Nedry, liked the Yukon ballads of Robert Service. We became very familiar with "The Shooting of Dan McGrew," "The Cremation of Sam McGee," and "The Face on the Barroom Floor."

We were encouraged to memorize poetry. Poems I recited before the class in seventh and eighth grade included

I Wandered Lonely As a Cloud
O Captain, My Captain
Abou Ben Adhem
Crossing the Bar

Part of Mr. Nedry's philosophy of education was "no homework." Consequently, we never carried books those two miles to and from school. Harriet, Lois, and I carried lunch baskets covered with a cotton napkin. We ate at our desks in our classrooms.

But starting in fourth grade, we had tests each Friday that we had to take home so parents could observe our progress. One side of the paper had curriculum-appropriate questions in social studies, except that "social studies" as such was still in the future of academia. What we called social studies was American history, Oregon history (sixth grade), geography (every grade), or civics (eighth grade). The back side of the paper had arithmetic problems. Basically these tests were weekly report cards.

Mamie Hardy was the first girl I knew to get a permanent. Her hair had been as straight as mine. One Monday when we were in seventh grade, she came to school with her hair sticking out every which way. Before that, to improve on nature one was limited to making waves with a curling iron, and that was called a marcel. And before electric curling irons, you had to put the iron inside the shade of a kerosene lamp to get it hot. We didn't have any "foolishness" like curling irons at our house.

Since we lived at the edge of the school district, none of my girl classmates lived anywhere near us, so there was almost no visiting back and forth between our homes.

Our family moved from the small farm and its large white frame house to the brick house in Raleigh Hills a few miles away early in January 1930. The move took us to a new school district, but I didn't move with the rest of the family, as I had only a few more days of school before graduation. I stayed with Grandma and Grandpa West.

Then came the Big Snowstorm, like none we had ever experienced. In fact, that part of western Oregon doesn't even get snow every year—just rain, and maybe ice storms. Roads were blocked with snow drifts, and everything came to a halt out in the country. The graduation exercises were postponed for a week. I got so cold walking home to Grandpa's after school that I stopped at Alma Blue's house to get warm. For someone as shy as I was, that was not an easy thing to do.

Women's fashions were making one of their periodic radical changes. Hemlines came down and were uneven. Mama wasn't buying into it, and my pink graduation dress was a typical—up to that point—little girl dress. So was Catherine Crabtree's. The other girls had dresses of the latest style, especially Alma. Mama said it made them look too old. My dress was my Sunday dress the next summer.

Because of our move I lost touch with these girls. Maybe some went right into Tigard High School midyear, but Papa and Mama thought I was too young at 12, so I was kept home until September when I began high school at Beaverton High.

By special arrangement, Harriet and Lois continued to attend Tigard High School instead of transferring to Beaverton. Papa bought them a used car so they could drive to school. They would have been the *only* students who drove to school. I suppose there was some arrangement for tuition, as we now lived in the Beaverton High School district, but maybe not.

Until we moved out of the district, Papa was chairman of the school board. In that position he carried weight in hiring teachers, and he saw to it that a young, redheaded Christian friend, Edna Sandblom, was among those hired. Both Harriet and Lois had her for Latin and/or English. Twenty-one years later she became our stepmother. The rest of us children had become acquainted with Edna the summer of 1928 when she stayed with the six of us for 11 weeks while Papa and Mama took their memorable trip to England and Switzerland.

Reading and Being Read To

THAT READING would be an important part of our childhood is indicated by a diary entry in Mama's handwriting from May 7, 1916: "Harriet is learning to read a little, and I am pleased that she shows an aptitude for learning." She was still several months shy of her fourth birthday!

I was probably four when I learned to read from primers and other easy-to-read books we had at home. Also I memorized easily, and I remember reciting the 23rd Psalm to Mama while she was ironing before I started school.

I looked forward to my birthday and Christmas because it always meant getting books as gifts, not only from Mama but also from both of my grandmothers. Grandma West's choices always came from The Book Room, and that meant they came from Pickering & Inglis in England, publishers for the Plymouth Brethren. The books of fiction may not have been good writing, but they were good moral stories. She also chose books about missionaries, such as *Mary Slessor of Calabar*.

Mama read to us every night after supper when Harriet and Lois had finished the dishes and the baby was put to bed. First the baby was Ruth, then Billy, then Eunice. All of us listened until we were in high school, sprawled on the carpet in front of the big fireplace. We heard many of the books at least twice. There might be a chapter from one of the Uncle Remus books (Joel Chandler Harris) in addition to the adventures of Tom Sawyer, Huck Finn, or Penrod and Sam.

The true stories about cousins who spent their summers at their grandparents' farm in Maine were favorites. They came out in book form after being published in the *Youth's Companion*. I think the author was C. A. Stephens. While my brothers and sisters and I have some of our childhood books, the Stephens books have been lost. Some of the other books Mama read to us were

Little Men
Little Women
Jo's Boys
Eight Cousins
Under the Lilacs
The Prince and the Pauper
Alice in Wonderland
Through the Looking Glass
Robinson Crusoe
Treasure Island
Hans Brinker, or The Silver Skates
Heidi (and other books by Johanna Spyri)
Water Babies
Rebecca of Sunnybrook Farm
Dr. Doolittle
Five Little Peppers
The Secret Garden

We missed out on books by C. S. Lewis and Laura Ingalls Wilder, which had not yet been written.

On Sunday night Mama read from *Egermeier's Bible Story Book.* I think it contained more stories from the Old Testament than are included in most modern Bible story books. Reading from the Bible itself (King James Version, of course, as we had no other translation) came in the morning, right after breakfast before we left for school, or on Saturday before we began our prescribed chores. I don't recall that we discussed what was read, or that we children ever asked questions. Then we knelt by our chairs, and Papa prayed. If Papa was away, then Mama said the Lord's Prayer. I never heard her pray extemporaneously.

When we children were young, we stood by Mama's knee and recited "Now I Lay Me Down to Sleep," which was followed by a goodnight kiss before going upstairs to bed.

When I was young, it eluded me that characters like Abraham, Joseph, Jonah, and Nicodemus were real, historical people who lived on this earth once upon a time. Mama didn't read us stories from Greek or Norse mythology (we got some in school, and I didn't know how to categorize them with other things I was learning), but when I was very young, the Bible characters might as well have been folklore.

All of us Wests agree with Strickland Gillilan, who wrote:

> You may have tangible wealth untold;
> Caskets of jewels and coffers of gold.
> Richer than I you can never be—
> I had a mother who read to me.

After we children went to bed—and we went to bed early—Mama read for her own enjoyment. She liked the Waverley novels by Sir Walter Scott, books on travel, and biographies. She especially enjoyed books on Arctic and Antarctic exploration.

Where was Papa? If he wasn't traveling, he was at church or board meetings most nights.

In high school, books by Charles Dickens rated twice as many points for the required book reviews as books by other authors, so I read Dickens: *David Copperfield, Oliver Twist, Nicholas Nickleby,* and *Our Mutual Friend.*

We had a radio but listened very little, except for "The Old Fashioned Revival Hour" and "The Lutheran Hour" on Sundays. Despite his reservations about the Lutheran church in general, Papa rated Dr. Walter Maier, longtime speaker on "The Lutheran Hour," as the best preacher of the day. They even became friends.

Ruth, Billy, Eunice, Alan

ONE TIME after Harriet and Lois had left for school, Papa took Charlie and me to Grandma Trappe's. That seemed strange since we never went there except on Sunday, but Papa didn't say why. Late in the day, when he came to pick us up, he said we had a baby sister! Mama was in bed when we got home, and Grandma West was cooking supper. They named the baby Ruth Atwater. I thought Atwater was a funny name for a girl. I liked my middle name, Louise, because it was also Mama's name.

Three years later William Judson was born. We called him Billy, never William.

When Billy was four and a half, we girls could see that Mama was assembling baby things. She made new flannelette diapers and kimonos. But there wasn't any talk about the coming baby. Whether it would have been like this in other homes, I cannot say. For sure there was no talk about where babies came from!

One night when we younger children were getting ready for bed,

Mama took a bath earlier than usual, and then she had to call Papa to help her get upstairs. And I heard her tell Harriet to call Mrs. Ball and ask her to come right away.

Naturally we children couldn't go to sleep, and soon we heard a strange man's voice in Mama's bedroom. It must have been Dr. Vincent. Then we heard a baby cry. Before long Papa came in Ruth's and my room and said we could go see our new baby sister. She had some dark hair, but not as much as Ruth had had. Lois suggested Eunice for the baby's name. She had a friend named Eunice, and it was a Bible name.

A couple of weeks after she was born, in January 1929, Eunice got bronchitis and had to be hospitalized in Portland. Mama stayed at the hospital in order to nurse her. We managed as best we could. We older five walked to school, and Papa took Billy to Grandma West's every day when he went to work. Mrs. Pollard, the wife of our hired man, came in to wash the breakfast dishes, make the beds (Mama hadn't trained us to make our own beds), and clean the house. What we all remember about those ten days is that our canary, Dicky, died. Starved to death without Mama to feed and water it.

After Eunice recovered from that illness so early in her life, she seemed healthy enough. She learned to walk at the usual time and was a happy toddler. All of her sisters and brothers doted on little Eunice.

Uncle Fred's first wife, Marie, contracted tuberculosis after their son, Alan Frank, was born, and she had to go to a sanitarium in California. Fred found it impossible to get proper care for the baby and for Patty, Marie's daughter by a previous marriage, and he asked for help from his family back in Oregon. Uncle Will and Aunt Hilda, who had no children, offered to take Patty; Mama, with seven children including baby Eunice, said she guessed she could manage another little one with Aina's help. Aina was our Swedish maid, who had been with us for two or three months.

Aunt Hilda went to California and brought back the two children on the train. By the time they arrived in Portland, she had had enough of both children. Alan, maybe 18 months old, was especially fussy, having been shifted from place to place and having had different caretakers. Aunt Hilda found Patty, age 8, to be "impossible" and shipped her back to California after a few months. Eunice was 15 months old when Alan came to live with us in the spring of 1930, not long after we had moved to the big brick house in Raleigh Hills. This was during the time that I was out of school for a semester between grade school and high school.

With two little ones to dress, change, feed, and generally take care of, Mama looked after Alan while I took care of Eunice. Alan was still on a bottle, which Mama didn't approve of. She thought a child should be weaned before then. Of course Eunice had never had a bottle, as Mama nursed all her babies. Mama probably moved too fast to get Alan off the bottle, but there weren't any child development or psychology books to read.

During that summer when she was a year and a half old, Eunice began to droop. Our parents took her to the best pediatrician in Portland. He could detect nothing wrong and only prescribed what I'm guessing were vitamins in liquid form. They didn't help. In the fall she was also given violet-ray light treatments. She didn't have obvious symptoms of any identifiable illness. She just got weaker and weaker until finally she couldn't walk anymore.

I don't know what Mama had to say about it, but Papa had some Christian friends come and anoint her with oil according to the biblical instructions in James 5:14. She didn't get any better.

By then I had started high school, and with Aina's help, Mama had to take care of Eunice and Alan and Billy, clean the big house, and do the laundry for our family of nine. Harriet was a freshman at Pacific University in Forest Grove.

On Armistice Day, November 11, 1930 (the old name for what is now called Veterans Day), a school holiday, Papa was starting breakfast—putting the coffee on to perk and making mush. While we children were getting dressed, Mama got Eunice from her crib in the sun room next to Papa and Mama's huge bedroom and laid her on her own bed. Then Mama brushed and braided her own hair, putting it up in a big knot in back with a few tortoiseshell hairpins. Then she turned to pick up Eunice and carry her downstairs. But while Mama was brushing her hair, an angel had come and taken Eunice to her heavenly home. Only Eunice's little weak body was left on the bed.

Mama went to the top of the stairs and called out an anguished, "Harry!" I was in the next bedroom and didn't know what was wrong. But something was obviously wrong from the way Mama called for Papa. Then she was kneeling by the bed and saying, "Safe in the arms of Jesus."

They should have called all of us children into the bedroom to say good-bye to Eunice and to cry together, but we just cried in our own rooms as soon as we knew. Papa called Mr. Pegg of Pegg Funeral Home in Beaverton, but I didn't see him come and take her body. I just knew it wasn't in the house, because I looked. I cried and cried and cried all morning until Aina scolded me and told me to stop—it wasn't going to help a thing. Papa called Harriet at Pacific University, and she came home on the next electric train.

I had never been to a funeral. My three grandparents were still living (Grandpa Trappe having died when Mama was just a girl). The funeral couldn't be at our church on account of Papa's never going inside a Lutheran church. And besides, the church was miles away in Portland, and the cemetery they chose (Crescent Grove Cemetery) was pretty close to our house. Papa bought a plot with space for four graves. Mama was buried there 20 years later, and Papa 20 years after that. Grandpa and Grandma West are buried nearby.

And so the funeral service was in our living room. The funeral home supplied the folding chairs. The room was filled with relatives, former neighbors in Bonita, and Red Rock Dairy employees. The little casket was in front of the fireplace. Our own immediate family sat in the library, out of sight of others, but where we could hear the Scriptures that were read and join in the singing. I do not remember the other hymns, but I do remember "Asleep in Jesus" because I had never heard it before.

It was only after the service that we filed by the casket for a final glimpse of our much-loved 22-month-old sister. She looked like a sleeping china doll surrounded by the baby pink lining in the casket.

I remember nothing of the committal service at the cemetery. Probably I was drowning in tears. Afterward our grandparents and aunts and uncles came back to the house for a meal, just like it was Fourth of July or Thanksgiving.

Seventy years later I can still say that the death of my little sister was the hardest blow I have experienced in this life. After I was married and had children of my own, I thought it would not be as difficult if one of them died at an early age, since I then had greater maturity in understanding the ways of God. Of course, I could have been all wrong in that supposition, but I was never put to the test, thank God.

As the years went by, there was no deception about the fact that Alan was really our cousin rather than our brother. Sometimes when he was disciplined as a small child he threatened to run away and live with his "real mother" in California. His real mother and Uncle Fred had divorced, but neither parent ever came to see him or even inquired about him.

When he started school, he was still called Alan Trappe, even though everybody (and certainly our family) thought of him as the youngest member of the West family. Since my parents had no legal claim to this towheaded boy they were raising, they decided when he was ten to adopt him. His parents were agreeable. In court the judge asked him if he wanted to keep Trappe as his last name or change it to West. He said he wanted to change it.

Still, he wondered about his birth parents, and his mother in particular. When he was 18, Alan made a trip to California to look her up. After that his doubts were gone, and he never contacted her again.

When he was an adult and living in California himself, he occasionally saw Fred and Fred's second wife but didn't think of him as his father. After all, he was a West, not a Trappe.

13

Vacations

MOSTLY, VACATIONS meant going to the Oregon coast and renting a cottage. (In New Jersey they say "shore," but in Oregon it is "coast.") One year Papa took us for a weekend at a seaside hotel, maybe at Bay Ocean. It created quite a stir among other guests to see such a large family—"and so well behaved!"—in the dining room.

Eventually Papa bought a vacation cottage at Neskowin. We called the cottage "WestWind." My parents particularly liked that oceanside community because it was quiet and noncommercial, unlike Seaside, Cannon Beach, or Newport. There was one store, a small cafeteria, one hotel, and a campground with a communal building for meal preparation, eating, and laundry. My parents had done tent camping earlier, but not in my memory.

There were rowboats for rent on the creek that ran through Neskowin. A large haystack mountain, Proposal Rock, was at the edge of the surf. It provided lots of climbing fun and exercise, but we would get scratched all over from the scrubby undergrowth.

While there was no lifeguard, there were green, yellow, or red warning flags to let bathers know the relative safety of going in the surf. The waves were normally quite high. The water was very cold (forget the Japanese Current, which is supposed to have a warming effect), but eventually one got numb and could stay in an hour or two. The hot sand felt good after that. We learned that it was almost impossible to go in the surf a second time after thawing out. The cold was even colder.

Papa never stayed for the two weeks that we children enjoyed to the hilt, but he would come for the weekend in between. He wouldn't go in the surf, so after going for a brisk walk, what was he to do? Mama and all of us children came armed with books and games in case it was too cool or rainy to be out on the beach.

Mama complained that she never could fill us children up when we were at the cottage. Since she couldn't bake bread in the little woodstove, we were forever going to the store to buy more bread.

An unforgettable pie was baked for us by the cook at the cafeteria when we brought in a bucket of red mountain huckleberries. We made a bargain with her: she could have berries to make a pie for customers if she would make one for us too. What had taken us hours to pick disappeared in a few minutes!

I had a summer crush on George Roth, whose family also had a vacation place at Neskowin. George's father was publisher of a newspaper in Salem. During the Depression, when I was in high school, Papa must have needed some cash, so he sold WestWind. Good-bye, George Roth. And good-bye, family vacations.

We took one vacation trip to the Wallowa mountains in the northeast corner of Oregon. The gorge created by the Snake River was more spectacular than the Columbia River Gorge so familiar to us.

In the summer a day trip around Mt. Hood was a must if we had visitors from the East. This was before the now-historic Timberline Lodge made it possible to drive right up to the snow line. The mountain itself would come into view only at certain points because of the forests, but still the trip had to be made. If smoke from forest fires obliterated the view entirely, we were more disappointed than our guests. It was "our" mountain, and we wanted them to see it at every angle. After all, we described weather in Portland in terms of whether or not one could see Mt. Hood.

Harriet, Lois, Charlie, and I climbed Mt. Hood with the Trails Club on one of their periodic climbs in July, 1932. The prior evening we drove from Government Camp through thinning stands of timber as far as the firefighters' road went, then walked quite a distance. We had supper and bedded down for the night in bedrolls made of army blankets. We got cold even with our clothes on inside our bedrolls. The climb started long before daybreak. We were energetic, and it seemed kind of dumb to take 20 steps and then rest. The Trails Club prided itself on getting every climber all the way to the top, and that's how they did it—with that slow, steady pace of 20 steps and then rest. The higher we went, the thinner the oxygen became. We were climbing on the south side, which is normally quite safe, so we were not roped together, but we did climb single file. If someone seemed to be slowing down, he or she was put right behind the lead guide.

We rested and ate lunch on the warm rocks 1,000 feet below the peak. Steam was coming through cracks from the mountain's hot innards. I finished my lunch and was still hungry. Someone offered me a tomato sandwich. I did not particularly like tomatoes and had never eaten a tomato sandwich, much less one made the day before and then jostled for hours in a knapsack. I won't say it was the best sandwich I ever ate, but I ate it and was grateful.

We all made it to the top, just like the club boosters said we would. It took ten hours. We were given little cards with our name and date to prove we had made the climb. There isn't much room on top, and we didn't stay long. Going down we could break rank, and Charlie and I got back to our base camp in two hours.

A few years later I climbed Mt. Hood on the steeper north side with another hiking club. It was a different story. We were roped together, and we needed to be. It was a strenuous climb and took ten hours. I had a narrow escape when a boulder that was inadvertently loosened came crashing down. It missed hitting me only because it hit another boulder and bounced over my head as I clung to a nearly vertical rock face.

A really memorable vacation for Harriet, Lois, and me was in the summer of 1926, when we went to California for a month with Papa and Mama. It was a chance for Papa to mix pleasure with business, as he was going primarily to check out and work through some problems at the Petaluma cheese factory. The mid-California market wasn't the same as the Portland market in terms of milk suppliers, consumers, or the competition. Not that I absorbed much of that at age nine, but I grew up listening to business talk—which may account for the fact that even today I may turn to the business section of a newspaper before looking at the main section. Conclusion: one's background does make a difference.

Papa bought a new seven-passenger Buick before we made the long trip to California, and it was outfitted with a cupboard to hold nesting cookware, enamel plates and cups, and basic food supplies. It sat securely strapped on the running board on the passenger side, and the cupboard door came down to make a small table. He also bought a new tent. We were going to camp!

Aunt Hilda and Uncle Will came to stay with the younger children—Charlie, Ruth, and Billy. Mama bought me two play outfits, and that was news. At that time she still made almost everything for us girls except our Sunday dresses. The Kute-Kuts were simple coveralls that buttoned down the back and across the back with a drop seat. The "Kute" part was the way the side pockets stood out. I loved those coveralls and lived in them that summer.

The first night we were in southern Oregon we found we couldn't put the tent up because there was no center pole! So much for Montgomery Ward; their stock, in the family's estimation, went down.

Enough people were hitting the road by 1926 that a new family business had evolved—namely roadside cabins. So, for lack of a center pole, we stayed in a number of those precursors to motels. Mama still fixed most of our meals and used that cupboard where everything fitted in just so.

Some hairpin turns through the Siskiyou mountains were so tight, and our car so big, that Papa had to back up to get around the turn. I wanted to get out of the car. What if a back tire went over the edge? WHAT IF? Papa noted in his diary that we covered 2,700 miles during that month's trip.

We had never been as hot as we were in Eureka—113 degrees. The little cabins we stayed in—and they were *little*—were bake ovens. Of course, in Oakland we got the Bay breeze. The San Francisco-Oakland car ferries were enormous, and we enjoyed riding on them several times.

There were trips to Golden Gate Park, Mt. Tamalpais, Stanford University, Sequoia National Park, Yosemite, and umpteen museums. I got tired of museums. I also got just plain tired. Mama wondered if they should have brought me along because I slept so much in the car when we were driving.

On our last day in Yosemite, we climbed to Glacier Point. That was the only way to get there in those days. Papa climbed out on the rock, and we girls screamed. Mama took pictures. Climbing used different muscles than gardening and standing at an ironing board for hours, and Mama was so stiff and sore the next day in Merced that she couldn't bear to step up on a curb. She walked in the street!

We also went to Crater Lake and the Oregon Caves in southern Oregon. The road to Crater Lake Lodge, closed in winter, had just been opened, and the snow banks were higher than the car.

All in all, we children were privileged to see so much West Coast scenery and have so many experiences during our vacations.

Once I went on a trip with Papa and another man to Seattle. It may have been for a Gideons convention. I stayed with the Lawrence Kane family at their summer home on Whidby Island in Puget Sound. Mr. Kane was a printer (Kane and Harcus Company) and a good friend of the family. He made trips to Portland a couple of times a year and always stayed with us.

There were three things about Mr. Kane that all of us West children remember: He always had PK (candy coated) gum in his pocket, he brought us little pads of colored paper that were wonderful for writing notes at school, and, above all, he told the most interesting stories at the dinner table.

For instance, there was a man at the mining camp who coughed and coughed. It bothered his fellow workers so much that they said he would cough his insides out if he didn't do something about it. One night the other workers figured out a way to scare him good and plenty so he would go to town and get help for his cough. They killed a rabbit and strung the guts out on their fellow miner's chest after he was asleep. At breakfast he appeared shaken: "It done happened just like you guys said. I coughed my insides out, but by the grace of God and a long-handled toothbrush, I got 'em all back in again."

Maybe it was Mr. Kane who gave us this string of words to punctuate: "That that is is that that is not is not is not that it it is." Grandma West loved things like that. She was a word person, worked crossword puzzles, played anagrams, and made puns.

Coming home from Everett and Seattle, we stopped in Olympia to see the new state capitol building. We got out of the car to admire it from the outside. It hadn't been officially opened yet, so there was no way we could get inside. But a workman came by and offered to let us in if we were interested. Papa and his companion were. We saw the two legislative chambers and other things of interest. Our guide seemed very knowledgeable, especially about how much this or that cost. Finally he led us into the governor's office. He even knew how much the draperies and the governor's chair cost! Then he said to me, "How would you like to sit in my chair even before I do?" I climbed up. Only then did we realize that our guide and informant was no less than the governor himself. That made a good story to tell at school.

In 1928 Papa and Mama went to England for almost the entire summer. There was an International Dairy Congress in London in June, and that was a reason to go, but not necessarily the primary reason. It was an unforgettable vacation trip for them. The dairy employees put on a bon-voyage party in our spacious front yard and strung Japanese lanterns overhead. They gave our parents new luggage.

Years later we learned that Mama wanted to call off the trip when she learned she was pregnant. But apparently Papa was persuasive. If former pregnancies hadn't interfered with her heavy load of household work and gardening, why not cross the Atlantic twice in luxury steamships and see England at leisure by touring in a rental car? We have letters that they wrote home and photo albums that show the famous sites they visited as well as humble thatched-roof cottages.

They had two months to discover England and Scotland by car after the Dairy Congress. But a week before they were due to sail from Southampton, Papa saw an ad that said, "Fly to Paris and Switzerland." He knew they would enjoy seeing the Alps, since the snow-covered mountains in the Cascades at home were favorite sights. So he bought the tickets first and then told Mama! Passenger flying in the States was hardly off the ground in 1928, so this was quite an adventure. We have pictures of both planes—the one from London to Paris, where they changed planes, and the one that flew from Paris to Zurich. Mama got airsick on that second flight.

And yes, they were glad for the few days in Switzerland, riding cable cars as far as they could go on the Jungfrau and other peaks. Then they returned to England by train and ferry.

Among the souvenirs they brought home was a set of colored plastic tumblers. We had never before seen anything made of plastic—lightweight but virtually unbreakable. These tumblers went with us on picnics for years and years.

Papa had arranged for a young, redheaded Christian high school teacher, Edna Sandblom, to stay with us six children. Both Harriet and Lois had had her for Latin and/or English. Six country kids used to considerable freedom would have been a handful for anyone, but for Edna, 24, who had grown up an only child, we were probably several handfuls. She took her duties very seriously. Harriet and Lois turned 16 and 15 that summer. I was 11.

Edna was particularly concerned for me, as I must have made life more difficult for her than some of the other children. She figured that I must not be a Christian. I wasn't, but neither was I looking for an opportunity to make "the big decision." One night, after reviewing my unacceptable behavior in a private session between the two of us, she asked if I wanted to turn my life over to Jesus. I felt trapped and could only say yes. However, nothing changed, and I was very relieved when our parents returned. Because we moved from Tigard a year and a half later, I did not have Edna as one of my high school teachers to confront me about my spiritual growth, or lack of it.

Edna gave me a devotional book when she left, making me promise to read it. I tried, but I never finished it, and I put it in Papa's part of our big built-in bookcase. I had read all of Louisa May Alcott's books from Mama's section, and I was reading Gene Stratton Porter's novels, like *Girl of the Limberlost.* The following summer I remember reading 50 books. I always kept a book under my pillow to read early in the morning, and during the day, a favorite spot for reading was a limb in the Gravenstein apple tree.

14

The Big Brick House

BIG CHANGES came in our lives late in 1929 and early 1930. Papa sold the Red Rock Dairy to Kraft Foods, we moved from Bonita (Tigard) to Raleigh Hills the first week in January, and the Depression started. It all runs together in collective West family memories.

The new house was very grand. Anyone would agree to that. Some said it was the finest house in Washington County. Seven bedrooms (count them again), three and a half baths, a full basement (we could roller-skate in it), the Philippine mahogany woodwork, hardwood floors, three fireplaces, the lift that brought wood up from the basement for the fireplaces in the library and living room, the laundry chute, the big cooler in the butler's pantry from pre-refrigeration days. On and on there were things to exclaim about. The two stairways between the first and second floors, the finished attic—for sure we could make a playroom up there.

The house, with three acres of landscaping, was on Scholls Ferry Road directly across from, and at a higher elevation than, the private Portland Golf Club. Our property was between the old road and the new, and we entered from the old road. A driveway cut through our property in front of the house and zigged in a Z shape below the house because of the grade. The driveway was marked with brick gateposts at both ends.

Though we were in Washington County, we had a Portland address (Route 5), Portland water (Bull Run), and a Portland phone. Portland is in Multnomah County. Papa's new business was in Portland, and we still attended church in Portland, but we lived ten miles out in the country. There was a well on the property, and in the summer water was pumped all night to fill an aboveground concrete tank for sprinkling the large lawn. It doubled as a small swimming pool if one could stand the cold water.

The Patullos, the builders and previous owners of the house, never had a garage, so they parked their car in a barn across the old road that bordered the back of our property. Papa decided to have a three-car brick garage built to house our three cars—a seven-passenger Buick, Papa's business car (maybe it was a Chevrolet), and the secondhand coupe he had just purchased for Harriet and Lois to drive to Tigard High School, the school they had been attending before we moved.

The construction of the garage left a graded slope that was ideal for a rock garden. It was professionally built under Mama's watchful eye. That meant an array of low, creeping plants that were not familiar to us previously. Mama's specialties at the Bonita house had been a rose garden on the south side of the house and a wide perennial border between the yard and the hayfield.

Mama kept a landscape man busy all spring. The overgrown shrubbery around the house (mostly laurels) was replaced with a variety of lower evergreen shrubs. There were grass walks through flower gardens, but Mama had a high white fence constructed to separate her perennial flower border from the vegetable garden. A gazebo was put in at the end of the walk.

Since Mama couldn't imagine not having her own fresh eggs, a chicken house with a small fenced yard was built on the lower corner of the property. It was far from our house and out of sight, but close to our neighbors, the Junors. Mr. Junor was the greenskeeper at the golf course. His brother, who lived nearby, was the golf pro.

A neighbor boy, Leonard Stark, was hired to do yard work. Since there was more than enough room, we had a large vegetable garden. This meant spading by hand as we no longer had a horse to pull a plow. Both Papa and Mama could beat anyone they ever hired at that backbreaking job.

Invariably, if Papa brought a man from the Union Gospel Mission to help with the spading, he never lasted a day. Papa would get up early every day before going to work and spade for a couple of hours while the ground was just right so the vegetables could be planted on time.

It was around this time that Aina Peterson came to work in the house. She had come from Sweden only a few months earlier, but at 18 had already married a fellow Swede. Aina lived with us during the week, but went home for the weekends. She could never get used to the fact that she was expected to sit down and eat with the family, even when we had guests. Only in America!

Harriet graduated from Tigard High School in May 1930, and enrolled that fall at Pacific University in Forest Grove, 20 miles west. Lois drove to Tigard High again the next year, while I started at Beaverton High School, in the district where we now lived.

Charlie, Ruth, and Billy went to the two-room Raleigh school on Scholls Ferry Road. Neighborhood schools were in vogue, and two-room schools were not all that far apart. Lois was May Queen at her high school's spring festival. Three years later I was a princess in the queen's court at a similar event at Beaverton High. Lois followed Harriet to Pacific University following graduation.

In addition to the outdoor work that first spring, improvements were made indoors. Oak flooring was laid over the original maple, which apparently had not been seasoned long enough, for there were cracks between the boards. In the dining room Mama installed inlaid linoleum in a small tile pattern. The interior decorator was unhappy about that, but Mama had her way. All our meals would be eaten in the dining room, and the linoleum would be easier to keep up.

The quite new made-to-order American Oriental rug from our old house had to be shortened (by cutting a section out of the middle) and rewoven. Oriental rugs were purchased for the entrance hall and the library, and glass doors were made for the library bookshelves. There were new draperies and glass curtains for all the downstairs rooms—quite formal compared to the chintz draperies in the old house. New furniture for the living room and library was chosen with the help of the decorator. Mama also purchased a chest for the entrance hall, and that became an ideal spot for her floral bouquets for many months of the year.

Before we got too used to having a maid and a yard boy, however, the Depression forced us to let them go. So we were back to doing all the work ourselves.

15

High School

I WAS terribly shy when I was young, and I was pretty much still in that mode when I started high school. The only high-school-aged person I had met since moving to Raleigh Hills nine months earlier was red-haired Eddie Posson. He came a few times to the afternoon Sunday school Papa had started at the nearby Raleigh School. It was obvious that he was not from a Christian family.

At school I signed up for English, Latin, algebra, and home economics. My English teacher was red-haired Miss Edna Sanford; Latin was taught by Mrs. Metzler, the principal's wife; Mr. Warren taught algebra. In home ec we had clothing one semester and cooking the second semester. We made simple cotton dresses after learning the intricacies of paper patterns. After that I was able to more or less sew for myself. Miss Kinnear didn't have high goals for the class, and we could pretty much do what we wanted. I did some embroidery projects when I could have been doing more advanced sewing. Overall, I made good grades, but I studied to get them.

It wasn't long before I was watching for Kenneth Taylor to enter the algebra classroom. And I've been watching for him to come through doors ever since!

Henrietta Hawley and another girl from town (Beaverton) chose to come back to school for a fifth year because jobs were nonexistent and they couldn't afford to go to college. They remembered my sister Harriet from their freshman year. If these "big" girls stopped to speak to me by my locker, I got teary-eyed because I was so shy. I haven't forgotten the embarrassment.

But I grew up that year in several ways. My dresses (all two of them) and one skirt grew too short, I could speak up in class, and I made new friends—boys as well as girls. In grade school I didn't particularly notice or care about boys. When "Fatty" Bilyou sent me mushy notes across the room in eighth grade, I didn't send answers back.

The last day of school before Christmas vacation my freshman year, I received gifts from two boys—Eddie Posson and Bob Denney. I couldn't conceal them as I got on the school bus with my algebra, Latin, and literature books. I sat near the front of the bus, but I overheard Kenneth Taylor teasing Bob Denney in the back seats. "You gave Margaret a present. I know because I saw you with that package before, and now she has it."

Though I gave no indication that I had heard, my heart stirred. It was more important to me that Kenneth had noticed—and teased Bob about it—than that Bob had given me something tangible.

I wondered what Mama would think. Did she know about boys liking girls enough at age 13 to give them gifts? I didn't worry about Papa's reaction. He didn't know about a lot of things that happened in the lives of his children. Mama probably wouldn't say anything to him either, I reasoned.

Years later I realized that Mama had probably said to Papa that night, "Our Margaret is growing up, Harry, in case you haven't noticed. The boys are noticing her, and she brought home Christmas presents today from two of them." Papa, being Papa, probably would not have asked what they were or from whom, but would have responded, "Then we need to pray more for her." There was no kidding in our family about boy-girl relationships.

Eddie's gift was a lace-edged blue satin handkerchief case. His mother would have chosen it at Meier & Frank, "Portland's own store." The box from Bob contained homemade candy—fudge, penuche, and divinity. Bob lived on a farm with an uncle and aunt and did chores to pay for his board and room. He wouldn't have been able to buy anything at a store.

There was a never-to-be-forgotten encounter with Papa about boys the summer I was 14. A mixed group of us from two or three families—including Harriet, Lois, Charlie, and me—was going to climb to Wahtum Lake above the Columbia River Highway and camp overnight. Chaperons were not necessary, but proper attire was, I learned in no uncertain terms.

The previous summer I had gone to Girl Scout camp and had had to get the regulation Girl Scout camping outfit, which consisted of an olive-green shirt and shorts. Since then the outfit had been in the bottom of a dresser drawer. This seemed like an opportune time to wear the comfortable shorts again with knee socks and hiking boots. As we were about to load the family car, Papa spotted me with several inches of bare leg exposed between my shorts and boots, and he pulled me aside. He said I could not go until I changed my clothes! And he proceeded to give me a lecture on modesty and told me about the fire that burns inside of men and boys when they see girls' legs.

He held up Grandma Trappe as a model of modesty. It could as well have been his own mother. They both wore dresses with high necks, long sleeves (even in summer), and skirts almost to their ankles. I was crushed but had no option but to change to a skirt that covered my knees. This was years before girls were wearing slacks or jeans. I didn't think Arnold Garnett, who was going on the hike, or any other boy would notice what I wore, but we never talked back or argued with Papa. You can see why we never got to see a circus. There was too much skin to be seen!

I usually attended evening basketball games or other high school events with Eddie, but it wasn't serious dating. His mother drove us in the Possons' big family car before he was old enough to get his license. My parents came to my graduation but almost no event before that. This was a grief to my brothers Charlie and Bill when they were in school sports.

Having a Portland phone meant it was a long distance call (10¢) to almost all of my classmates. Long distance calls were an expense that could be controlled. We children simply didn't make them. Consequently, there were no after-school calls to school friends to talk over assignments or boy-girl relationships or anything at all. And in the summer I didn't see or talk on the phone with anybody I went to high school with. They lived in Beaverton (and we never went there), Aloha-Huber, Bethany, or Helvetia. All miles away. The majority of us rode to school by bus. I did call Porter Underwood or Ed Posson occasionally, as they had Portland phones. Kenneth and Douglas Taylor also had Portland phones, but I *never* called them!

For the same reason that I didn't call my friends—the cost—I didn't ask to borrow the family car to go see them during the summer. In those little ways the Depression affected everyone: cutting out or cutting down on controllable expenses.

My sophomore year brought out leadership qualities in me. I was president of the class one semester and president of the Torch Honor Society. Neither organization did anything of note, but there was the usual slate of officers, and meetings were duly called to order.

I made a new friend my junior year when twins Lilah Faye and Hayes Boice came from eastern Oregon to stay with the McMinn family. As we became good friends, I would invite Lilah Faye to sleep over. Besides the usual girl talk about what was going on at school, we would lie awake wondering aloud how we could get those Taylor boys to date us! Well, she could have Douglas; it was Kenneth for me. Eventually Mama would call out from her bedroom for us to stop talking and go to sleep.

Our talk and wishful thinking didn't change anything. Douglas and Kenneth didn't pair off with us or with any girls for that matter. We wondered if their parents forbade them. If so, how old would they have to be before they could date?

Lilah Faye and I saw Kenneth and Douglas every week in the informal setting of the McMinn Bible Class on Saturday nights. The class had started my freshman year at the Gordon Fraser home in Beaverton. When the Frasers' house proved too small, Ray and Janie McMinn invited the group to their home on Canyon Road, even though their three children were not yet of high-school age.

This was before Youth for Christ, Young Life, or any of the other recognized Bible clubs had begun. It was not a club or the beginning of any movement, but a local effort started by a few concerned parents so their young people would be grounded in the Word of God. Strictly evangelical—the several teachers over a period of years were Scofield Bible devotees—but not particularly evangelistic. While we were encouraged to invite others, the group remained fairly stable. As the original young people grew up and went off to college, their younger siblings filled the chairs arranged in a circle every Saturday, during the summer as well as the school year. Not surprisingly, several marriages came out of that group: Arnold Garnett and Kay Denney; Bill Denney and Ruth West; Don Mortimore and Elaine McMinn; David McMinn and Martha Fraser; Kenneth Taylor and me. And all of those marriages have survived the vicissitude of the turbulent decades since. So our friendship—Kenneth's and mine—grew in that healthy climate of choruses and gospel songs, prayer, and Bible teaching.

Kenneth and I were not in any of the same classes at school after freshman Algebra until senior English with Mrs. Snyder. Once she reprimanded me in front of the whole class for turning around so much to make eye contact with Kenneth.

I took public speaking my senior year thanks to the example of

Kenneth, Douglas, Ivan Bierly, and others who were doing well in debates with other schools in the state. There was only one public speaking class, so Kenneth and I were together in that.

The issue being debated that year was: "Resolved, that the United States government should have a monopoly on radio broadcasting similar to that of the BBC in Great Britain." With our reading, note taking, and class drills, we were prepared to argue both affirmative and negative sides of the question. When it came time to assign team positions, Mr. Webb paired Kenneth and me. We won a number of debates in the district but did not get to the final state competition that year, as Beaverton High debaters had done the year before. But Kenneth went on to star on some notable debate teams during his four years at Wheaton College.

Kenneth and Margaret Dickman were candidates for student body president the first semester of our senior year. Never before had a girl been nominated. It was going to be a historical vote. Margaret was the oldest daughter of the Presbyterian pastor and his wife in the Bethany community north of Beaverton and was a good friend of mine. When it came time to vote, it was not an easy decision for me. But through talks I had had with Kenneth, I knew how important victory would be to his self esteem.

The vote was taken when I was in civics class. Mr. Hughes gathered up our ballots and took them to the principal's office. When he came back in the room he stopped by my desk and said, "Well, I see you betrayed one of your fair sex to vote for Kenneth." I was so angry at his invasion of voting privacy that it brought on a nosebleed, and I walked out of class. Margaret won the election. But in the second semester Kenneth was again nominated, and that time he won. All three of us were on the commencement program with short speeches.

Kenneth and I were both in the farce "Who Kissed Barbara?" put on by the Torch Honor Society. You can be sure Kenneth didn't really kiss the girl who played the part of Barbara. Any real kissing of a girl was still a long way off—both in his thinking and in reality.

Schools cut expenses to the bone during the Depression. Consequently, we didn't have "extras" like vocal music and art, and at Beaverton High there were no teachers for physical education and no sports for girls at all. There were teams for interscholastic competition in football, basketball, baseball, and track, and the athletes proudly wore their letters on their lettermen's sweaters. There was a band (of sorts), but no orchestra or glee clubs. The school paper folded, and finally school news appeared only in a column in the local weekly, *The Beaverton Enterprise.* What we missed most of all was not having a yearbook for the four years I was in high school. No photos of classmates to look at or a permanent record of sports and activities. And no experience of working with others on a yearlong project of editing, layout, and advertising.

I had another leadership role my senior year as I was president of the Girl Reserves. Unlike the boys' Hi-Y, which had a select group of members, Girl Reserves, at least at our school, were required to let all girls be members.

We put on a big indoor fair annually that was a lot of work and drew a large crowd. While decorating for the fair, another student and I moved an upright piano across the gym. We were pushing broadside, and the piano fell over on its back. Visualizing a piano-sized dent in the gym floor, if not an outright hole, I did not jump back but did my best to ease the fall. I got my fingers out in time, but the piano came down on my left foot and smashed my big toe. Kenneth was one of the students who came to Dr. Mason's office after school to see if I was badly hurt!

My best dress that year was black and long-sleeved, but a teenaged wearer could be relieved that it had a pale pink satin jabot. I had let my hair grow and wore it in a tight bun. My graduation dress was pale blue, floor length, with ruffles around the neck and armholes. I shared it with Lois, who wore it for a spring piano recital at Pacific University.

At graduation I still had floor burns on one arm from falling while roller skating with Kenneth at our class party. I told him he skated like a horse!

In my sophomore and junior years, I was excused early one day a week to attend confirmation class. It meant walking a few blocks to downtown Beaverton, catching the Greyhound bus to Portland, and then a long streetcar ride to Trinity Lutheran Church on the East side. I diligently used the time to do my memory work from Luther's Small Catechism. When we were through with instruction from Pastor Rimbach, we should be able to recite the answers to every question in the catechism with proof texts from Scripture. The class was a special one for the few of us in our church who were not enrolled in the Christian day school. Those schools were, and are, a distinctive of the Missouri Synod. After the confirmation class I caught a streetcar back to downtown Portland, walked to Papa's office at the appliance store, and rode home with him in time for dinner.

I was confirmed at Trinity Lutheran Church in April, 1932. And for me it really was a time for confirming my faith. Three years earlier—at Papa's urging—Harriet, Lois, and I attended an evangelistic service at the Sunnyside Congregational Church. The speaker was E. J. Pace, whose cartoons appeared regularly in the *Sunday School Times.* I do not remember his text or the gist of his message, but when the invitation was given all three of us left our seats in the balcony and joined others at the front of the church. I have the letter I wrote to Isabel Taylor, who had been my teacher at Bonita Sunday school, letting her know, "I'm saved."

An event occurred one summer in late high school that has colored—or discolored—my whole life. A neighbor, Ione Whiting, asked me to teach a class of boys at vacation Bible school. She and her sister Doris, both several years older than I, were talented teachers who had the Christian commitment to reach boys and girls. To me it was an assignment. I'm sure there was a teacher's handbook, but whatever it was, it was not enough for me to fill the class time. I did too much repeating and knew it. Each day I was in a torture chamber.

The two weeks dragged by. As a consequence I resolved never to be a teacher.

In college my home economics dean was very disappointed that I elected not to take education courses that would have prepared me for teaching home economics at the high school level. But I couldn't stand the thought of teaching. And I have never taught Sunday school. That is not a record to be proud of but rather ashamed of. But I just couldn't. I remember the agony.

16

After High School

THE DEPRESSION was worst during the four years I was in high school (1930–1934), and while life changed some, we Wests were still extremely privileged.

Papa had purchased our house on contract from the Patullos in 1929. A few years later, without a regular salary while the appliance business was getting established, it was necessary to renegotiate terms, but I don't know the particulars: The house would have been a white elephant, impossible to move had they foreclosed and taken it back. So we continued to live in the finest of homes, while Mama worried about paying the utilities.

As the Depression wore on, Harriet left college after two years and went to work in Portland in the office of Jantzen Knitting Mills, where our Aunt Mae worked. The following year Papa felt that he could no longer pay the college fees for Lois. She got a job as a maid in the home of the Smiths, a high-society couple in Burlingame, where she wore the black dress and little white apron that all maids wore in that fashionable suburb.

The Smiths had no children, but still Lois worked hard. Mrs. Smith had many silver serving pieces, and Thursday was silver-polishing day. If Mrs. Smith hosted a tea in the afternoon (as noted on the society page of *The Oregonian*), she invariably had dinner guests that night, and Lois was sure she more than earned her $20 a month (plus room and board).

She used some of her first earnings to have her hair cut and get a permanent. For years she had hated her long hair. This created quite a stir when she came home on her day off. There was no family law that said she had to have long hair, but still getting her hair cut (and a *permanent*) showed an independent spirit—even when she was 21!

Later, Lois was able to get work as an elevator operator at Meier & Frank, and she moved home again. She kept that job until she was married in June 1939. Tailored uniforms were provided, so Lois didn't have to buy clothes for work. Exposed to the best in merchandise day after day, Lois once exclaimed, "I see so much I would like to buy!" Mama's rejoinder was, "When I go to the store,"—and Meier & Frank was where she shopped almost exclusively—"I see so much I *wouldn't* want to buy!" I am like Mama in that regard.

When I learned that I shouldn't get my hopes up for attending college the fall after high school graduation, I decided to spend what little money I had saved for a different project. I would represent our church at the Walther League convention in St. Louis, Missouri. I won a spot in the Talent Quest with a melodramatic oration based on the hymn "The Church's One Foundation."

New trains, called Streamliners, were cutting travel time, and the *City of Portland* was put into operation during the summer of '34 between Portland and Chicago. Florence Udy, several years my senior, and I were Oregon delegates, and we traveled together. That made Mama more comfortable about my trip at age 17.

We bought coach tickets, and to save money, we packed whatever food we might need. We were cramped and had to sit up all night, which wasn't all that comfortable. Because it was such a novelty in speed and appearance, people turned out to watch this silver bullet of a train go through hamlets and crossroads. The whole train was a single unit, and cars could not be added or taken off depending on the volume of traffic.

We did not see Chicago at all as we were shuttled underground from one terminal to another for our last lap of travel. St. Louis was hot and humid. My one new dress for the trip was of yellow rayon with a long brown jacket—much too warm. Delegates were housed across the city in homes of Lutheran parishioners, so many of us were dependent on public transportation to get to sessions in the convention center.

I did not win a place in the oratorical contest—my first and last such attempt. A fellow named Ed from Buffalo, New York, who had met Harriet at a previous convention, took some interest in me, and I was flattered. The climax of the three days was the banquet with Dr. Walter A. Maier of "The Lutheran Hour" as speaker. I thought Ed was picking me up at the house where I was staying, so the other guests left without me. No Ed, nor any message from him. Finally, I called a cab and arrived after the meal was over. What a letdown! Because of my mental turmoil and disappointment, I scarcely heard Dr. Maier.

After the convention I traveled by train to Carbondale, Illinois, where my grade-school friend Lois Jones and her husband, Darrell Frewing, from an old Tigard family, met me. They were living in Murphysboro. Darrell had just graduated from Oregon State College in forestry and was supervising a CCC (Civilian Conservation Corps) crew building roads in this backwoods tip of Illinois. Lois was only 18, but marriage—at least marriage to Darrell—had seemed more important than finishing college. Their little house was just a notch above camping out, but they were happy. My exposure to the local people was an eye-opener. The women were barefoot. They had not traveled out of their immediate "hollers" and were more or less oblivious to what went on in the wider world.

I could not make good train connections in St. Louis on my return to "civilization" and had to stay overnight. Following instructions from my mother about what to do in just such a case, I called the home of a Lutheran pastor and asked if I could stay overnight! When I arrived in Chicago, I stayed with the family of a distant cousin of my mother's in Blue Island, a southside suburb. I went to the World's Fair a couple of times, including an outdoor concert in Grant Park. While they were cousins and church people, their lifestyle was not like ours at home, and I didn't feel all that comfortable with them, though they were very gracious.

The *City of Portland,* on which I had my return ticket, was out of commission for a few days getting repairs. Wanting to please me, my host family asked what else I would like to see or do. I said I would like to go to Wheaton to see Wheaton College, as I had several friends who would be enrolling there in the fall. They couldn't understand why anyone would want to go to college so far from home, or even go to college at all. It was even more incomprehensible to them when I explained about Wheaton College's pledge—no movies, dancing, drinking, smoking, etc. My girl cousins smoked, and movies were their favorite amusement.

There were only four main buildings on the Wheaton campus. Blanchard Hall, of cream-colored limestone and strange architecture, was at the top of a sloping campus dotted with very large trees. The only other buildings were the old gymnasium (now the art building), a red brick dormitory (Williston Hall), and Pierce Chapel.

On our drive between Blue Island and Wheaton, I was amazed by all the unprotected railroad crossings. To be safe, one really needed to "Stop, Look, and Listen," as the cross-arm signs everywhere cautioned drivers. While the situation has greatly improved in the 60 years since then, Illinois still leads the country in deaths due to accidents at railroad crossings.

I got homesick and decided not to wait any longer for the *City of Portland* to be up and running, and I exchanged my ticket for one on a regular train. Due to inexperience, I did not let the family know of my change of plans. Consequently, there was no one to meet me on my arrival back in Portland. When I telephoned Mama from Portland's Union Station, I choked up on the words, "I'm home. Can you come get me?" It was a lesson I never forgot, and since then I have always let the family know when to expect me so I would not look like an orphan beside my suitcase after fellow travelers had been warmly greeted and left the depot.

What to do next? The answer wasn't long in coming. The parents of Mrs. Smith, for whom Lois was working, were looking for live-in household help at their summer home in Bay Ocean near Tillamook. They had given up their Portland home and planned to live on the coast year-round.

I prepared meals, did the dishes and laundry, and cleaned house. And I still had time to myself for reading and letter writing. It was a time for rethinking spiritual commitments. When I wasn't working, I would find a sheltered spot on a sand dune to read. I received my first letter from Kenneth at the Smiths' Star Route address. Eleven pages. What a thrill! When his family vacationed with the Garnetts at nearby Twin Rocks, he was able to drive out to Bay Ocean to pick me up and join them one evening.

After six weeks I realized that the isolation was more than I could stand, and I asked the Smiths to look for a replacement. If I were home, I would be able to take evening courses at the University of Oregon's extension program in Portland. I got a catalog and decided on Psychology 101 and Oral Interpretation.

The McMinn Bible Class occasionally had summer picnics on the Tualatin River. There was one last picnic the night before Douglas, Kenneth, and Bob Denney broke up "this old gang of ours" by leaving for Wheaton College. What would the future hold? Sung around the campfire, the same songs we had sung so often tugged at our hearts: "Trust and Obey," "Beneath the Cross of Jesus," "Turn Your Eyes upon Jesus," and "All the Way My Savior Leads Me." Prayers for each other may have been brief, but no less earnest.

I was temporarily helping Lois at the Smith home, so that is where Kenneth drove me after the picnic. As we said good-bye, he gave me his Hi-Y pin! It was not the same as if he had given it to me during the school year, because now no one would know. But still, it was a gesture. There was hope. He cared for me. We promised to write. I couldn't sleep that night!

He kept his word. I could look for a letter every Thursday written on Sunday afternoon or evening. The Taylor boys had been brought up not to study on Sunday. College courses were more demanding than high school, but they continued to keep the Sabbath day holy by faithfully attending church and not studying.

I helped Mother in our big house. Even with Lois away, we still numbered eight. Cleaning, baking, canning, and ironing kept me busy. By then we had an electric mangle—a laundry machine for pressing fabrics—which we used for ironing towels and sheets but not linen tablecloths or shirts or dresses. I also studied for my night classes.

I dated some, but largely because I didn't know how to say no. I measured all young men by the stature of Kenneth Taylor, and none of them measured that high.

Mother offered my services when a young couple at church brought their first baby home from the hospital. I also helped the wife of Dad's business manager after she had had surgery. (By now we had dropped "Papa" in favor of "Dad," though it wasn't easy to make the change.)

I was called into service again when Mrs. McMinn had surgery. While she was in the hospital, and for several weeks after, I did everything—cooking, dishes, cleaning, laundry, mending, and straightening out some cupboards. Mrs. McMinn was fond of lemon meringue pie, which I made several times. She taught me to knit, and I made my first sweater. I made two dresses for her, which was a challenge as I had previously made dresses only for myself. Dad dropped me off at her house on his way to work and picked me up again on his way home. As a result of these weeks of help, I became a favorite of Janie McMinn's forever after. Consequently, I am the proud owner of a number of her oil paintings and antiques, which she gave me in later years on our infrequent visits to Oregon.

I got my first pair of glasses that year and wore them all the time. The next summer, when Kenneth first saw me with glasses, he expressed disapproval. Did I really have to wear them all the time? Couldn't I just use them for reading?

Except at the Saturday night Bible studies, we did not see each other. Kenneth worked long hours in the hayfields in order to make as much money as possible for the coming school year. His father's salary as superintendent of the United Gospel Mission was minimal.

It seemed awkward to see Kenneth after nine months. What should we talk about? Our experiences did not converge. I was hoping for him to say that while he had met some nice girls at Wheaton he still liked me best, but the summer came and went without so much as a hint that that might be the case.

Dad was able to send me to college that fall. It was Mother who suggested I might like to go to Oregon State College since I enjoyed cooking. OSC was known for its fine Home Economics department. While farther away than Pacific University in Forest Grove, where Harriet and Lois had attended for two years each, Corvallis and Oregon State were only 80 miles due south in the rich Willamette Valley.

If Kenneth wasn't going "to be there for me" despite going to different schools, why should I keep the illusion alive? I decided not to correspond with him that year. That way I would be freer to make new friends. He was disappointed but didn't put any pressure on me to change my mind.

17

Oregon State College

MOTHER WENT with me to shop for new clothes. I especially liked one olive-green tunic dress with a wide belt and bronzelike buckle.

My parents asked me not to join a sorority that first year without really specifying why. Since I knew nothing about them, it was no problem to agree that I wouldn't. They also did not want me to get a job, apparently lest I overcommit myself.

Mother drove me to Oregon State. I was assigned a room in Snell Hall, one of the two large women's dormitories. But the room turned out to be the dorm infirmary. It was no longer used for that purpose, and I had five roommates! The room itself was large enough for our beds and study tables, but it was not conducive to good study habits. And we were such a diverse group that none of us became best friends.

Right off I learned that I had arrived with a smaller wardrobe than anybody else, but I made the best of it. Sorority rushing soon occupied everyone's attention. Mailboxes were eagerly opened to see how many invitations had been received for teas or open houses. It was literally "all Greek" to me.

Things have been so open on college campuses since the revolution of the '60s that it's hard to believe the rules that were in force in the '30s in Oregon's state-supported schools. Doors in the women's dorms were locked at 10:00 P.M. Sunday through Thursday, and all the lights were turned out at 10:30 through a master switch! On Friday and Saturday nights, the doors were locked at midnight. In the evenings we signed in and out by the door and had to indicate where we planned to go—library, movie, etc. If a girl was ever discovered to have stayed out all night without permission, she was immediately expelled. Some California parents were known to pay the extra out-of-state tuition to have their daughters so well protected.

In our infirmary room we were on the honor system for lights out, as our lights weren't connected to the master switch. If we failed to turn them out, the housemother could see light under our door on her rounds and would tap a sharp reminder. But we had our own bathroom, and she couldn't see that light in case we wanted to study late!

Snell Hall had its own dining room. We could come and go for breakfast, but lunch and dinner had set hours, and we filed in and sat down when the bell rang. Meals were served family style at tables for eight or ten.

On Sunday mornings, I faithfully attended the Lutheran church just across the street from the engineering building. It was a small congregation, and almost no students attended, unlike the Methodist, Presbyterian, Baptist, and Catholic churches, all of which had student directors on staff and large programs.

During the winter term I took swimming lessons for gym credit, and in the spring I took canoeing on the Mary's River. Second semester I asked to be moved out of the infirmary room, and I roomed with Ruth Anderson, a sophomore girl.

Before I left for school, Dad had me read a book about the moral pitfalls lying in wait for college students. Social dancing would have been at the top of the slippery slope. There was a record player in our dorm lounge, and the girls would put on records and dance while waiting for the call to dinner. Occasionally someone would get me out on the floor, but I was not anxious to learn, and I lacked any sense of rhythm and was painfully ungraceful. I soon quit making a spectacle of myself. Smoking was also popular. Too many girls who didn't already smoke succumbed to peer pressure that year and got into the habit. We couldn't smoke in our rooms, but there was a smoking lounge.

Dad also saw to it that I signed up for a Bible-study correspondence course designed for college students. It was a day-by-day program with answer forms to be mailed weekly to a California address. I dutifully answered the questions but usually did the reading at one sitting on the day it had to be mailed instead of reading every day as intended.

Dad wouldn't know about my faithfulness or lack of it in that program, but he would hear from Gordon Fraser if I failed to appear regularly at a weekly Bible study held in a room in the Memorial Union. I'm guessing that the Bible study began the same year I started college and that Dad probably gave Mr. Fraser gas money to drive to Corvallis from Beaverton! And of course Dad would have backed up these efforts with his personal prayers for my protection from the wiles of the Evil One. A verse he frequently quoted in his letters to me was, "Keep thy heart with all diligence; for out of it are the issues of life" (Proverbs 4:23, KJV).

I was disappointed in not being able to take clothing courses that year, but there was a year's prerequisite called Color and Design. At the time I couldn't see any direct connection between the principles of art that we demonstrated on drawing paper and making clothes to be worn. So I had lessons in art whether or not I wanted them, and the clothing had to wait.

Having had two years of French in high school, I signed up for French 201. But after the "Bonjour, mademoiselle" as I came in the door, I was lost! The instructor spoke not a word of English, and it became clear that Miss Schaeffer had not been a good high-school French teacher, as we did not learn to *hear* and *speak* in French but only to read it. I quickly dropped French. How could I continue when I didn't know what the assignments were! I elected another class in English literature. I had done so well on an English placement exam that I was not taking the basic freshman English course.

I studied hard, and my grades showed it. I was elected to the Alpha Lambda Delta scholastic honor society at the end of the year. But more important to my way of thinking was being elected to Talons. This was a small (maybe 16 girls) but highly visible honor society of sophomore girls. They had their own sweaters like lettermen's sweaters, and they ushered at school convocations. I suppose the girls one year decided on the girls to follow them the next year, so basically it was a popularity vote. But the girls had to be from different sororities to spread the "honor" around, and there were only a couple of independents like myself. My sophomore year would be a good one!

Once during my freshman year I had a letter from Bob Denney, asking me to relent about not writing to Kenneth. Bob reported him to be pining away. But my German stubbornness prevailed, and I did not weaken. I endlessly heard "Smoke Gets in Your Eyes" on another Margaret's record player, with the line "When a lovely flame dies, smoke gets in your eyes." But for me there had never really been a lovely flame. Still I wished there had been, so smoke could get in my eyes!

In late fall an ad in our school paper alerted me to a performance of a passion play at Corvallis High School by a traveling cast. I decided to go, but none of my roommates were interested, so I walked the ten blocks alone. What came through to me, all aside from the professionalism of the actors, or lack of it, was the true humanness of Christ. The humiliation and pain he suffered was the same as it would have been for any man. On the way home, a fellow came up from behind and fell in step. "I'm Walt. How did you like the play? Have you ever seen it before?" With Dad's abhorrence of the theater, of course I had not seen it before and could make no comparisons.

Walt and I shared a little more about the play and then proceeded to get acquainted. He was a sophomore from Montana, a fraternity man, and his slight limp was from a hunting accident. He walked me to Snell Hall, which was farther than his fraternity house, and before leaving he asked if he could have a date the following weekend. I was agreeable. Would a movie be all right? It was. I had not promised my parents that I would not attend movies (probably an oversight on their part) when I promised not to join a sorority.

Walt and I spent a fair amount of time together on weekends the rest of the year. Sometimes a walk into the country, or just sitting in a comfortable lounge in the Memorial Union, if not a movie. Going to school dances was out since I didn't dance.

When he brought up the subject of marriage, I explained I could never marry him because he wasn't a Christian. To him, being a Christian meant "being good enough," but to me it was acknowledging that one could never be good enough and, by faith, relying on Christ's death as a penalty for one's own sin. I never urged Walt to make that decision, but I prayed he would.

One night as we stood outside the dorm entrance just before the doors were locked, Walt said, "What's with this fellow back East you are always thinking about? Does he kiss you like I kiss you?"

"No, he's never kissed me at all."

Involuntarily, he pulled back to look at me as if there might be something wrong, something he hadn't seen. He exclaimed, "Never kissed you! What's wrong with him? I . . . I . . . " But he was so nonplussed he couldn't continue.

That gave me something to think about that night. Certainly my feelings for Kenneth had nothing to do with physical closeness, and I didn't even fantasize about his kissing me. I would never be able to explain it to Walt. I couldn't even analyze my feelings to myself! I just knew that I automatically compared any boy or young man I met with Kenneth, and so far nobody else measured up. What if nobody ever did?

Sophomore Year

"OUR BOYS" came home from Wheaton in June of 1936 full of stories about the revival on campus. Kenneth suggested that I transfer to Wheaton. I replied, "But they don't have Home Economics, or I might have gone there in the first place."

"You already know how to cook, so why do you have to take courses in it? Isn't studying the Bible and being in a good Christian atmosphere more important?" he countered. He was eyeing my rosy fingernail polish but said nothing about this new sign of worldliness.

Every Saturday night he brought up the subject. I began to weaken after I thought about the possibility of just going for one year and then transferring back to OSC. The costs were high, considering what I would be giving up: the year of being on the popular Talons squad, the chance of going to China as an exchange student my junior year. Of course, there was no guarantee I would be chosen as one of the two students to go, but by not being on campus that sophomore year I would forfeit all chances of being considered.

Dean Milam, of the Home Economics school, had taught in China, and she kept the exchange program alive with the university where she had been. Two students came from China one year, and OSC sent two over there the next year. By the end of our freshman year, Dorothy Harstad and I were thinking it would be something to aim for.

There was no indication from Kenneth that I could count on his dating me, so why did I weaken late in the summer and send in my application to Wheaton? I sent it so late, in fact, that there wasn't time to learn whether I had been accepted before I was boarding a train with Marian Little, Ray Little, and Robert LeTourneau—other students from Portland. Kenneth and Douglas would have to find a way to go by car (maybe with Bob Harrah) and not squander their hard-earned summer wages on train fare.

While they didn't ask me to do so, I promised my parents I would work to make up for the additional cost that year. I'm sure Mother had misgivings about my going ("It's all because of that Kenneth Taylor putting pressure on her!"), but Dad was probably relieved. The Christian atmosphere would strengthen my character. I left the fingernail polish at home, but not my lipstick! During the summer I had had my hair cut and also got a permanent.

When I arrived at Wheaton College, I was assigned a room several blocks from campus at 714 N. Scott Street. A Swedish couple, Mr. and Mrs. Lindblad, and their daughter, Aina, crowded into a couple of rooms in the back of the first floor in order to take in as many girls as possible. I think there were 11 of us ranging from my freshman roommate to several graduate students. We never did form a cohesive, caring unit.

In addition to a required course in Bible (I took New Testament Survey), I signed up for courses that would fit in with my major back at OSC—general chemistry (ugh!), history, and literature. I had lit courses both semesters from the legendary Elsie Storrs Dow. Carl F. H. Henry was in one of those literature classes.

I got a job in the dining hall of the "new dorm"—so new that it didn't have a name yet. (It was later called Evans.) I worked at the steam table and on the dishwasher, a steamier job, for 30¢ an hour.

I had to study harder than I did at OSC to get good grades. I could only count on seeing Kenneth during daily chapel, where my seat was on the main floor toward the back of Pierce Chapel and his was in the balcony. Attendance at chapel was compulsory, and attendance was taken.

Since Kenneth wasn't about to date me (or any other girl, apparently), another boy took up the slack. We studied together, went for walks, and sat together in the balcony of College Church of Christ on Sunday evenings. To others it looked serious in the manner of Christian college budding romances, and maybe it was. Until Thanksgiving weekend, that is. After returning from Chicago, where we had dinner with his grandmother, Chuck didn't call anymore and actually seemed to avoid me. I was mystified as to the sudden ending of our congenial friendship, but the damage went further than that. I had been "Chuck's girlfriend" in the eyes of other fellows, and after that nobody else even walked me home from the library. Any social life with the opposite sex dropped to near zero.

In order to avoid loving Wheaton and its wholesome Christian atmosphere too much, I had not joined one of the four women's literary societies, reasoning that it would be easier to transfer back to Oregon State at the end of that year. That was a mistake. I missed a lot by not being involved in the Friday night meetings. There were four corresponding men's societies and periodic joint social events. The literary societies were a hangover from the nineteenth century, but still flourished in Wheaton's "We don't go to movies, etc.," climate. Kenneth was the president of his society. I studied on Friday nights!

Not going home for Christmas vacation was harder than I had anticipated. Christmas celebration for our family was tradition from first to last. Grandpa and Grandma West came for breakfast, followed by the reading of the Christmas story from Matthew and Luke's accounts. Dishes were hurriedly washed. Our freshly cut fir tree from a hillside not too far away would have been put up and decorated just the day before. The candles on the tips of the branches were lit and made a beautiful sight, the tinsel twisting from the warmth. Of course by now we had strings of electric lights, but I liked to remember the candles from my childhood. Presents were passed out. Gifts from our parents would include books, games, toys, or puzzles, but rarely new clothes. Those we got seasonally as needed.

Before I could start reading a new book, it was time to leave for church—the Lutheran church (I can't remember what Dad did). Then we went across town to the East side to Grandma Trappe and Aunt Mae's for the traditional dinner. In addition to the beef roast, potatoes and gravy, and vegetables, there would be homemade pickles served in cut glass dishes. Homemade bread and jam, too. Cherry pie for dessert. And always stuffed dates rolled in granulated sugar and chocolates.

We numbered ten around the table unless Aunt Anna and cousin Dorothy were there. Uncle Will and Aunt Hilda and Uncle Ted and Aunt Marie would stop by later. Aunt Mae would get us girls started on the latest craft. Yarn flowers made into a corsage and worn on a winter coat. Bead flowers. I once made a clutch purse of needlepoint canvas covered with patterned stitches. Aunt Mae's gifts were always a delight. I remember the little Eversharp pencil on a ribbon to be worn around the neck, a gold ring with an emeraldlike stone, my first bottle of cologne with a carnation in the bottle, and my first suede gloves. Then I could curl up and read a new book until it was time to go home.

Every Christmas as far back as I could remember was just like that. They were happy memories of the way our family celebrated Christmas.

Most of the girls at 714 Scott had gone home, and others had flu. To sit in a chilly bedroom and open gifts from home all alone hardly cheered me up. Mother had made me flannel pajamas, and Kay Markovich, my best friend in high school, sent a box of apple candy from Washington State. Apple candy (I had never eaten it before) was better than no candy at all, but I would have preferred some chocolates—even the cheap chocolate drops one got in the dime store. Later in the day, Kenneth and I were invited to dinner at the home of Dr. and Mrs. Moule. I suppose the faculty saw to it that those of us left on campus had invitations to one home or another. Dr. Moule was a Bible prof with a face as long as the prophet Jeremiah's.

Long-distance telephoning was still an extravagance when greetings could be sent with a three-cent stamp, or one cent on a postcard. So there were no calls between home and Wheaton even on Christmas Day.

Dad paid me a visit during the winter. It was 20 degrees below zero at the time—much colder than it ever got in Portland. He was asked to speak in chapel. All I remember was that he made some innocent reference to Peoria, which brought a laugh from students. Even then, "But will it play in Peoria?" was a put-down.

Daily chapel was something I really appreciated that year. To worship with hundreds of like-minded young people was uplifting. There were inspirational talks by outside speakers as well as by President Buswell, other faculty members, and local pastors. Billy Graham didn't come to Wheaton as a student until a year or two later, but there were other student preachers, like Don Hillis and John Ballbach, who could be heard at "the Tab," which held services in the Masonic Temple.

Students who weren't involved in ministries that took them off campus on Sundays mostly flocked to Wheaton Bible Church and College Church of Christ, both of which were close to school. I, however, walked alone a block or two farther to St. John's Lutheran Church on Sunday mornings, where the early service was still in German. I didn't attend that one, except once when I was anxious to take Communion and it was only being offered in the first service. God could and did meet with me in an "unknown tongue." No one in the congregation ever invited this lone student home for a meal.

The second semester, I asked to move closer to the campus if it were possible. It was, and I moved to the Engelsman home on Franklin Street, on part of the property where Edman Chapel now stands. My roommate was Vivian Weld, a senior from Hemet, California. My reason for moving was to pick up a pattern begun at OSC—going to my room for a nap rather than to the library if I had a free hour in the afternoon between classes. I seemed to need more sleep than others, and I preferred studying in longer, unbroken periods in the evening.

By late January I could read the handwriting on the wall. I would not be going to the Washington Banquet—the Big One of the year for which dates were made weeks in advance! Why had I ever come to Wheaton? Why? Because in the dim past of the previous summer a fellow named Kenneth Taylor had urged me to. He hadn't said, "But don't count on me to take you to the Washington Banquet come February; I still plan to be careful not to get linked up with any one girl." So I could always hope. As it turned out, Kenneth did go to the banquet, but with another girl. It was hard to concentrate on my studies that night!

Three more months to go! I didn't count on the complete letdown that would come with spring break. The campus was deserted. Everybody had gone home—their own home or someone else's. I scrubbed the bathrooms in Williston Hall and cleaned a couple of houses to earn money to buy food for the two meals I allowed myself each day. If I had eaten three meals a day, I probably would have felt better! There wasn't even a hint of spring in the air.

At home the borders around the big yard would have been bright with daffodils, narcissus, and hyacinth. The red camellia by the back door would have been in bloom. Oh yes, and gold forsythia. Mother would already have had colorful bouquets on the chest in the front hall and on the dining room table. She never entered a flower show in her life, but if she had, she would surely have won some ribbons.

What did I take with me when I left Wheaton in June? I took two verses: Mark 10:45 (KJV): "For even the Son of Man came not to be ministered unto, but to minister, and to give his life a ransom for many" (Mark 10:45, KJV); and "But these are written that ye might believe that Jesus is the Christ, the Son of God; and that believing ye might have life through his name" (John 20:31, KJV).

Dr. Stone had us repeat the first verse every day in Bible class during the first half of his Life of Christ course, and the verse from John every day the second half. Since those words are eternal truth, the repetition was not mindless but engraved that truth deeply on our minds. At least on mine.

19

An Eventful Trip

AT THE END of the semester, I got a ride home in a new Buick that Bob Harrah, a junior, had picked up at the factory and was driving to Seattle for his father. Other passengers were Mary Soltau, an MK, and Sandy Campbell. Bob's brother, Cal, was driving a carful of students to the Northwest in a second new Buick. What luxury! So much better than sitting up on a train coach.

It was ironic that fellows and girls could drive that long distance together, for when we were on campus we could not ride in cars at all. Period. Never, unless it was necessary for Christian ministry. Of course, students didn't have cars, but we weren't permitted to ride with townspeople either.

Rules like that were left behind as I shook the dust of Wheaton, Illinois, population 7,500, from my feet. I hoped never to see the place again, and I assumed I wouldn't. Not that it was a wasted year—not at all. The credits I would transfer to OSC were with good grades. The five hours earned in general chemistry weren't the best, but they were good, thanks to Bernard Peterman, my lab partner, who was a real help.

We drove all night the first night and the next day, taking turns driving. Cruising at 70 miles per hour felt about right if the pavement was in good condition. There were no speed limits. The second night we decided to stay in roadside cabins and get a good night's sleep. We agreed to meet the other car in a certain town around 10 P.M.

We got there before Cal's car. Mary and I went to bed after opening the window to try to get a breath of moving air. We were roused by a male voice outside calling loudly: "Bob Harrah, message for Bob Harrah . . . Bob Harrah." Obviously the caller, whoever he was, didn't know what unit Bob was in, and he was risking waking every tired traveler in the place. What could the message be? We wouldn't be able to go to sleep until we knew.

Eventually Sandy rapped on our door. The message was a heavy one. Cal's car had been in an accident at a railroad crossing; the car, that big, new, shiny Buick, was totaled. We were to go on and not wait for Cal. That was all. We were a sober foursome the next morning, not as rested as we had hoped to be. So many unanswered questions. Had anyone been hurt in the accident? Why had this happened? We drove all day across Nebraska and into our third night with only the minimum number of rest stops needed for a bite to eat or to change drivers.

Sandy was driving when I went to sleep in the backseat. Mary was in front with him to help him stay awake and Bob was in back. I woke up when Sandy braked hard and brought the car to a stop. What now? It was all black outside, no lights. Sandy opened his door, stuck his head and shoulders out and shouted into the darkness, "Taylor, is that you?"

It *was* Taylor—Kenneth—hitchhiking his way back to Oregon. It was the cheapest way to travel. "Climb in. Man, what a coincidence to meet up with you out here in no-man's-land."

I moved over to the middle to make room for Kenneth. He said he had been trying to sleep in the sagebrush, as the prospect of picking up another ride in the middle of the night was nil. But the mosquitoes were fierce. Then he had a strange compulsion to get back on the highway and hail the next car. The first car never slowed down, but Bob Harrah's car was the second.

When Kenneth tells this story he always says, "It was cold lying on the ground on the Wyoming plains, but even colder in the car when I got in next to Margaret!" The fellows talked briefly and then drowsiness put the three of us in the backseat to sleep. I was careful not to let my head fall over on Bob's or Kenneth's shoulder!

Help! We're in a crash! The car ground round and round, skidding in loose gravel on the shoulders. Mary and I screamed. With no seat belts we were being tossed back and forth, and Kenneth put his arms around me. Would we survive? The turning stopped and the car slid down an embankment without turning over.

The fellows were able to open doors on the passenger side after ascertaining that no one was really hurt. Just shaken up and still shaking. They climbed up the bank to check on the other car, for obviously we had sideswiped. Mary and I stayed in the car, crying with relief.

They were college students in the other car, too. And like us, they weren't hurt. One or both of the drivers must have fallen asleep for us to have collided on a straight highway on a clear night. When the fellows came back to our car, we gave thanks to our heavenly Father that none of us was hurt. A few more inches of impact, and it would have been a different story for the drivers and the passengers directly behind them. Maybe for all of us.

Eventually a patrolman came, interviewed us for his report, and took us to the nearest town, which was Wamsutter, Wyoming. We ate breakfast in the little cafe, then we rented a cabin for the day while we waited for help. Mary couldn't stop crying. I sent a telegram home, something like, "ACCIDENT NOT HURT STOP SEND MONEY FOR TRAIN FARE."

Bob had to get in touch with his father to report the awful news of this second accident involving his second son. It was then that we learned that a Wheaton student had died following the first accident. Our minds reeled. Why Tim and not one of us? Why two accidents anyway? Why? Why? There weren't any answers. Mary kept crying.

Eventually Kenneth and I went for a walk. Somehow, being away from school and out here in the middle of nowhere, we could talk and act like we were best friends. We were tired, and it was hot, but the cabin was hotter. And going over and over the scenario of the night just past didn't turn up any answers. But if I closed my eyes I could still feel Kenneth's arms around me. Tight around me.

The fellows borrowed a car and drove Mary and me 40 miles to Rawlins, where we boarded a westbound train around midnight. We were so exhausted physically and emotionally that having to sit up in coach seats was no problem. Sandy elected to stay with Bob until the insurance adjuster had come and finished his report. Kenneth continued hitchhiking.

That time, I remembered to wire ahead what time I would arrive. It was so good to be home with Mother, Dad, and my six siblings. Ruth, Billy, and Alan had grown so much!

It wasn't long until Harriet's wedding. She was marrying lanky, sandy-haired John Baden, a Lutheran parochial school teacher from Houston. I hadn't met John yet, since I had missed his visit at Christmastime when they became engaged. Harriet wasn't going to be an old maid after all! Lois and I were her attendants. I had never even gone to a wedding before, much less been in one.

Kenneth and I were on better terms that summer than ever before. Not that we saw a lot of each other. While I was at home (summer jobs were still hard to come by), Kenneth again worked long hours in the hayfields. When we said our good-byes in the fall, it was with promises that we would write, and a hint that maybe I would even come back to Wheaton for his graduation. This just three months after wishing I would never see the place again? Well, it wasn't the *place* I wanted to see but the *person*.

Junior Year at Oregon State

BACK AT OREGON STATE for my junior year, I lived in the other large women's dorm, Waldo Hall. My roommate was Tess Varney from California.

Now I was into the food and clothing courses that had first attracted me to major in Home Economics, but there was also organic chemistry, followed by biochemistry, physiology, and bacteriology, as I was on the B.S. track.

I did not join a sorority, though I could have. After my year at Wheaton, it was no longer appealing. Being in a Greek letter society was not essential for enjoying college life. To continue to be an independent was all right. I was elected to two honoraries at the close of my junior year: Omicron Nu, the Home Economics honorary, and Phi Kappa Phi, similar to Phi Beta Kappa.

I dated some but nothing serious. Walt, my friend from my freshman year, was no longer in school. Lettie Warrington and another girl had gone to China as exchange students. That was okay, for I was writing to Kenneth every week!

When I was home during spring break in March, I tried to be casual in mentioning to Mama (we were standing in the driveway in front of the house) that when school was out I would be going east for Kenneth's graduation. I had saved money from waiting tables in the Memorial Union to make the round-trip by train. I knew in my heart of hearts that she did not approve, but I was going anyway.

"You know I don't think it's a good idea. Look at it this way, Margaret. If it were your turn, would Kenneth come across the country to see you graduate?" I hardly needed to answer but managed to mumble, "Probably not."

My voice was low, but inside another voice was screaming, "No, No, NO," and I saw myself as the fool I was. With just that one sentence, Mama made me hate myself. But I hated Kenneth more because the answer was no. He was not prepared to make the statement concerning our now eight-year friendship that such a trip would be. To him we were friends, nothing more. I was still hoping our friendship would blossom into romance and real love—the kind to last a lifetime. If he wasn't prepared to make that statement now, he probably never would be.

Before that week was over, I went to the attic and found the packet of letters he had written me from Wheaton his freshman year. I threw it into an evening fire in the fireplace. Our friendship was now ashes as far as I was concerned.

I wrote Kenneth what I supposed would be my last letter—that for reasons I couldn't put in words I would not be coming to Wheaton for his graduation after all, and furthermore, not to expect any more letters. Period. *Finis*. Life would go on, a repetition of two years before when I had tried to put him out of my thoughts. I had been unsuccessful that time. I would try harder, apply myself to my studies even more. Maybe even become a missionary when I was through school. Not for undying love for my Savior, but for undying love for a young man named Kenneth Taylor. Maybe 10,000 miles would quench those feelings.

Later, I purchased and mailed him a leather-bound pocket New

Testament for a graduation present. I wasn't looking forward to seeing him as summer approached. Then I thought of an escape so I wouldn't have to. Instead of using my money for a trip to Wheaton, I would go to Houston as soon as school was out. Perhaps it was a suggestion from Mother that Harriet could use some help that started my thinking about the possibility. She and John were expecting a baby in July, and she was finding Houston's heat and humidity debilitating.

As soon as I got assurance that they would welcome me, I bought a train ticket for Houston, using the money I had earned waiting tables during the school year. The money I earned so I could go to Wheaton now took me in another direction!

I had never experienced such heat as welcomed me along with John and Harriet's warm hugs and kisses. Now I could understand why Harriet had been laughed at two years earlier when she went to Houston for a Walther League convention and got off the train carrying a summer coat. It was even reported in the convention paper!

Harriet and John lived in a garage apartment, something not known in the Northwest but quite common in the South—living quarters over the garage (in this case a three-car garage) of a larger home. That put them right under the limbs of big shade trees.

John grew up in Kansas, but for ten years he had been living in Houston, where he was church organist and choir director at a Lutheran church. He also taught the upper grades in their parochial school. Apparently he was acclimated, but Harriet just wilted in Houston's heat. Summer showers seemed to be frequent. The trees dripped rain, and the people dripped perspiration. Twice-daily showers were a necessity. I got used to two baths a day, but not to the cockroaches that were everywhere. I had never seen cockroaches before. Ants were a problem, too.

There wasn't a real second bedroom, but there was room for a couch for me to sleep on. I pretty much took over doing the laundry and cooking to enable Harriet to wait out the last two months of pregnancy. I learned to drink iced tea and eat watermelon like a native. Watermelons were so plentiful that grocery stores threw one in for free if you bought enough groceries.

I received one letter from Kenneth during the summer but did not respond. After all, I was actively trying to forget him. He did not say anything about flunking the MCAT exam that meant he would not be going to medical school. I learned about that later.

Margaret Elaine Baden was born July 27, 1938. As one of her sponsors, I held her for her baptism two weeks later. What a precious privilege and responsibility.

I stayed in Houston as long as possible, allowing just enough time to get my wardrobe in order before returning to school for my senior year. The Sunday I was home, I saw Kenneth while I was sitting in our family car outside the Portland Union Bible Classes waiting for some of the family. But I did not get out of the car to speak to him.

21

Senior Year at Oregon State

FOR MY SENIOR YEAR, I moved back to Snell Hall, where I had lived my first year. I roomed with Tess again.

Having elected not to take education courses, which would have prepared me for teaching, I took a number of institutional Home Ec courses, not knowing how I might use the information. An important part of the senior year for all Home Ec majors was "practice house." Six girls moved into a private residence with a faculty adviser and played house just like little girls everywhere. But it counted for half our credits that term. A girl would be assistant cook one week, then cook for one week—including making the menus and doing the grocery shopping. Household cleaning occupied a third week, laundry another week, and two girls divided the days and nights taking care of a real, live baby. The babies came from a foundling home in Portland.

Used to passing tests with flying colors, I decided to give myself one at Thanksgiving. Instead of having Mother drive down to pick me up, I asked her to let Kenneth have our family car to do the chauffeuring. Inwardly she must have groaned, but she acquiesced. I knew he did not yet have a steady job.

It had been 15 months since we had been face-to-face. The test was to see if I could treat him like any other boy I had known for eight years—like his brother Douglas or Bob Denney or Elman Johnson.

"Hello. Thanks for coming," I said with what I hoped was warm indifference. He picked up my bag, but we didn't touch each other! We didn't shake hands—too formal. Nor did we give each other a hug, as generations of young people have since greeted longtime friends. That "hands off" policy was bred in us.

Before we even got to Linfield College in McMinnville, where we picked up my brother Charlie, I knew I had flunked the test—no way was I treating Kenneth "just like any other boy." So with this encounter I lost ground. I would have to go back and try harder not to like him so much! Mother drove me back to school after the long weekend.

During Christmas vacation I worked at Meier & Frank for a second year, in a special gift-wrapping section. Charlie told me he had heard that Kenneth was going to go to graduate school at Oregon State beginning with the winter quarter. I was angry. How could he do that? Whatever he was going to study, there were other colleges—lots of colleges. Why did he have to choose the one where I was? He wasn't playing fair. How could I continue my campaign of *trying harder* (to forget him) if he might be crossing a quad the same time I was? Or if I might see him in the library?

As it turned out, I didn't see him very often. The home economics building was very close to my dormitory, and the science building where he was taking classes was a long way across campus. Once, when it was time for the library to close, he asked if he could walk me back to the dorm. I could hardly refuse.

The quarter ended in March, and we were back in our respective homes. One afternoon Kenneth called to ask if he could come over that evening. I said no, it wouldn't be convenient because we were having dinner guests. Well, couldn't I leave when dinner was over? Again the answer was no. Well, then he would come at ten o'clock.

Surely the guests would be gone by then. What had gotten into him? Ten o'clock? Self-respecting people were getting ready to go to bed at that hour.

No use upsetting Mother. I didn't tell her until Dr. and Mrs. B. B. Sutcliffe had gone that Kenneth wanted to see me and would be coming at ten. She must have wondered, just as I did, why he couldn't wait until the next day to make an appearance. But Mother was a woman of few words, and she kept her counsel.

These occasional meetings were awkward. We went for a drive but said little. At a lookout point on Terwilliger Boulevard, Kenneth stopped the car and turned to me with the big question. Could we start dating again? If I had been of a different disposition, I might have laughed aloud. Was he dreaming? Start dating *again*? When had we ever dated? Once to the senior play our last year in high school when his mother came along. Canoeing a couple of times on the Tualatin River after a picnic of the McMinn Bible Class. A couple of dates that year at Wheaton College, and seeing each other a few times the following summer. We hadn't ever seriously dated, and that was the whole problem as far as I was concerned. So how could we start dating *again?* We weren't kids anymore. In a few days I would be 22.

I was slow to answer his question, trying to absorb the implications—or what I saw as implications. And my answer finally was, "Not unless you have marriage in mind." He said he probably did. Whew! This was heavy. Now that is exactly the way it happened. In Kenneth's version, he says he told Douglas he was going to propose to me that night. If that was a proposal, it was pretty unromantic. There was nothing about love or wanting to spend his life with me. I said I would need more time before giving him an answer, and we drove home.

My sister Ruth was asleep, but I nudged her awake when I got into bed. "How would you like to have Kenneth for a brother-in-law?" "Okay, I guess," was her sleepy reply. In the morning I asked her not to breathe a word about what I had said the night before.

I felt the need for adult counsel but did not know where to turn. Janie McMinn would say, "It's about time. Kenneth's been awfully slow to see what a wonderful girl you are. I was afraid he would let you get away." I needed someone more objective. Then I thought of Mrs. Sutcliffe, who had been at our home the night before. She was probably the wise wife of a wise pastor, although she and Dr. Sutcliffe had no children. I made an appointment to see her at their Portland apartment. While she didn't know Kenneth and me as individuals, she knew our families.

I rehearsed the ups and downs of our friendship: how I had known for at least five years that I loved Kenneth, and how I always compared other young men with him, and how they never measured up. And even though he didn't know yet what he wanted to do with his life, since he was unable to get into medical school, he was earnestly seeking God's will. I must have said I was willing to risk the unknown as long as it was with Kenneth. After prayer she gave me her blessing.

The next day I gave Kenneth the good news that the answer was yes. We could start dating—forget the "again." But since we weren't engaged, we didn't tell our parents anything.

The first Friday night after we were back on campus, I was babysitting, and Kenneth came over. He wanted to sit by the fireplace and talk. I wanted to study, and I did, or tried to. Walking back to the house where I was staying that quarter, it came out that I was going bicycling the next morning with a fellow student. Kenneth protested. "But we're not engaged," I countered. "So what's wrong with that?"

Apparently he couldn't tolerate my going out with other fellows under this new agreement, not even for an early-morning bicycle ride. The upshot was, "Well, let's get engaged!" I was willing, and as we stood by the door to say goodnight, he gave me a kiss. Finally.

With that taken care of, Kenneth lost interest in school, dropped out, and went back home! He asked me not to write him more than once a week, so as not to alarm his parents. He felt they weren't prepared for the fact of our engagement. I think the problem was that he himself wasn't ready to be engaged, but neither did he want to lose me to someone else. It wasn't until much later that I learned he came to Oregon State only because Bob Denney told him I was dating a fellow on campus and that it looked serious. I don't know how "private eye" Bob got that information. Ted, a senior from southern Oregon, had started walking me home after Walther League meetings Sunday nights at the Lutheran church. He gave me a myrtle-wood cross on a chain that Christmas. I still have it, but our relationship wasn't serious enough for me even to remember his last name!

What a strange way to prepare for a life together! And if he couldn't tell his parents, I couldn't tell mine.

With no dates after that bicycle ride, I was able to apply myself to studies and make straight A's that last quarter. I graduated with the highest GPA of anyone in the School of Home Economics, and my name was inscribed on a brass plaque in the hall of the home ec building.

My parents and Lois came for my graduation. It was a big day, as I was the first person in the West family to have earned a college degree. Unbeknownst to them, Kenneth came too, and I asked if he could join our family after the ceremony for the picnic lunch Mother had prepared. We ate on the banks of the Mary's River.

22

My First Job

I WENT to work almost immediately at the Northwestern Electric Company in Portland, as did several of my classmates, for $100 a month—about the same wage as teachers were getting then. Mostly it was a public relations job, and each of us had the use of a company car. We made appointments with women who had purchased new electric ranges to see if they had any problems or questions. Sometimes we checked the oven by baking a small cake using a cake mix. This was a novelty, as cake mixes were not yet available in grocery stores.

I rode to and from work with Dad. I carried my lunch in order to save as much money as possible. I paid Mother $20 a month for my board.

My classmates who took jobs at the electric company were from out of town, so they rented apartments. Before long they were entertaining men from the company for dinner, even top executives who were married. I suppose the men told their wives they had to stay downtown on business. My impression of another woman in our department was that she was kept on because of the availability of her house and herself during the day. It certainly wasn't because of how many customers she called on. And our supervisor, an unmarried woman in her forties, was quite obviously a weekend alcoholic. I certainly was disillusioned about the ways of the world.

During that spring (1939), C. Stacey Woods of the Canadian InterVarsity Fellowship had contacted Kenneth and persuaded him to join their fledgling staff. In the summer he could be a counselor at a boys' camp on a lake north of Toronto, and during the school year he was to establish Bible study groups in high schools across southern Ontario. Consequently, Kenneth left for Pioneer Camp almost as soon as I started to work. But first we (or really Kenneth) told our parents we were engaged. My mother's response was, "I'm sorry to hear it!"

Kenneth never said anything about an engagement ring, and I didn't even hint about wanting one.

We were back to writing letters again. After six months' separation he was able to come home for a few days at Christmas. I gave him a pullover sweater that I had knit.

There were holiday parties and places to go in the evenings as Kenneth had been a popular leader in the youth group at "The Classes." Too soon his vacation was over, and he was gone again. No more social life for me. Maybe, just maybe, he could come home again in June before summer camp.

Even if he wasn't planning on our actually getting married sometime, I was. I bought sheets, towels, a sewing machine, and a set of silverware. Then he began writing about the possibility of going to seminary. Not just any seminary, but Dallas Theological Seminary,where Willard Aldrich, the youth pastor at The Classes, and some of Ken's Wheaton classmates had gone. Most seminaries have a three-year degree program, but Dallas required four years!

Kenneth could continue to work for InterVarsity Fellowship in Texas, traveling to colleges on weekends to organize Bible study groups of Christian students. Not a word about getting married.

Didn't he want to be married? Wasn't he trying to move mountains to make it possible? Obviously not. Further education first, though he wasn't sure for what end, as he had no desire to be a pastor.

He did come home for a week in June, but there were no parties in June, and as far as I was concerned, it wasn't such a joyous time. Without being together more, we weren't progressing in our personal relationship, though we didn't recognize that at the time. We both came from families where feelings weren't expressed, so we didn't share thoughts and dreams. We had been engaged for 15 months, but our conversation and our correspondence were not much different than if we had been casual friends. Surely marriage would change that.

But there was one unforgettable experience on Saturday of that week. June was the best month for climbing Mt. Hood, something Kenneth had never done, so this was his chance. My brother Charlie and his friend Rachel agreed to accompany us. Climbing the south side without a guide is relatively safe. Hundreds do it every year.

When we got as far as the sulfur springs below the last steep pitch, Rachel said she was too tired to go farther, and Charlie said he would stay with her.

And now comes the part that is hard to explain. Many years before, mountaineers had installed a cable to insure a safe climb from there to the peak. Why would anyone in his right mind, already weary after hours and hours of climbing, even think of making it on his own? But Kenneth thought if we veered off to the right it would be shorter. Why didn't I say, "Are you crazy? You've never even been up here before. Let's go where we have the cable to hang on to." No wonder they say love is blind!

So I followed his suggestion and climbed the steep ascent ahead of Kenneth. Finally I could go no further. There were no more ledges for handholds. And when I looked back to retrace my steps, I froze. One misstep and I would fall. Probably to my death. Then a cloud blew over. A cloud at that height means snow. Now I couldn't see to descend even if I had the courage. Kenneth had disappeared. He had said he would try to reach me from the top, though I couldn't imagine how. I recalled newspaper stories of people dying on Mt. Hood. How long could I stay immobile in this one spot? The cloud blew over. Now the headline would read, "Climber sees fiancée fall to her death. Unable to help."

Eventually Kenneth reappeared below me, no doubt pumped with adrenaline. He had gotten to the summit by the cable route but then had no clue as to where I was below him. I hadn't responded to his calls, not having heard them. He reasoned with me. "Just one step at a time. Come down just the way you went up." And somehow, seeing him brought fresh courage, and I took one step down and then another. So God spared my life again.

And then Kenneth was off to Quebec, where he and Charlie Troutman would be running a summer camp.

Since he wasn't writing anything about our getting married, about looking forward to that blissful estate, or what we might do to make it happen, it looked like it would be up to me. As far as I could see, it was only a lack of money that was keeping us from making vows of lifelong fidelity to each other.

If I could get a job in Dallas, we could get married. It was as simple as that. With my two-week vacation after a year of employment, I would go to Texas. I wasn't so bold as to announce to the family that I was job hunting. I went to Houston to visit Harriet, John, and their two children—John Peter Baden III having been born on June 11. I went by train. I remember nothing of my visit with them, but before my time ran out, I went to Dallas.

At the seminary I met John and Johanna Voget Munro, who invited me to stay with them after I had spent one night in a seedy hotel near the train station. Both John and Johanna had attended Wheaton. I contacted the local gas company to see if there were any prospects for work similar to what I was doing in Portland at the electric company—something related to home economics. There were no openings, and prospects for the future were slim. They told me if I lived in the area, they would let me know if something opened up. But I wasn't going to move to Dallas in hopes of finding a job.

Johanna had been working at the seminary, and she took me to meet Dr. Lincoln, who managed the office in addition to teaching Bible courses. He couldn't promise, but he thought there might be an opening in the fall for someone half-time. I explained about my fiancé coming in September and how we could be married and come as newlyweds if I had the security of a job. Kenneth would be working for InterVarsity Fellowship on weekends with a salary of $50 a month.

It would be office work—of sorts. Yes, I could type. It was ironic that, having taken home economics in college so I wouldn't have to work in an office, my eyes were lighting up at the prospect of a "maybe" office job. Just maybe. Dr. Lincoln would let me know if things worked out.

I went back to Portland and wrote Kenneth that there was nothing firm about a prospective job. Just a "maybe" at the seminary.

Late in August I received a letter from Dr. Lincoln. There *would* be a half-time job, paying $12.50 a week, if I were still interested.

I dashed off a letter to Kenneth, addressing it in the care of Tom and Barbara Lindsay in Wheaton. Tom had been Kenneth's college roommate. He and Barbara were going to drive west on vacation, and Kenneth was planning to come with them. Of course Tom and Barbara would be full of the joys of married life, and it would rub off on Kenneth as they traveled over several days.

The three of them arrived at our house late one afternoon, since Tom and Barbara were going to stay with us. Kenneth took off to see his parents, freshen up, and be back for dinner. Nothing was said about my Important News, which he should have thoroughly digested by now.

During dinner with my parents and siblings, the talk was about their cross-country trip, summer camp, and what Tom and Barbara should see in the Portland area during their brief visit. Surely a hike up Larch Mountain and a trip to the coast. When it was time to say goodnight, I went out on the porch with Kenneth for another kiss after our nearly three-month separation.

"Didn't you get my letter?" I was finally able to ask.

"What letter?"

"I sent you one in Wheaton. I heard from Dr. Lincoln! He has a job for me! We can get married next week!" I ran it all together. It was too much for Kenneth to take in. He did not whoop, holler, or turn handsprings. He was due in Dallas the very next week! How could we get married in just a few days? But there was no time to talk then. Tomorrow was another day.

Our Wedding

TOM AND BARBARA were all for a quick wedding when we talked about it the next day. They were only sorry they couldn't stay long enough to celebrate with us.

I was already envisioning a small wedding at our home with just our families and a few friends. I would wear the lace dress that Harriet and Lois had worn and come down the open stairway to be met at the foot by Kenneth. We would proceed to the living room, stand by the fireplace, and . . . and . . . .

But Kenneth surprised me, now that he had had a few hours to think about it. We should have a church wedding by all means, and invite everybody. Now it was my turn to ask, but how can we? There isn't even time to mail invitations—invitations that weren't printed yet. Even if it were at a church, which church, and when? Elaine McMinn and Don Mortimore were being married the next Friday, and "everybody" was already invited to their wedding. My sister Ruth was one of Elaine's bridesmaids, and Charlie was in the wedding, too. The Classes still met in the Behnke-Walker Business School auditorium, so their wedding was to be in the Calvary Presbyterian Church just a few blocks away.

I gave a week's notice at Northwestern Electric, but under the circumstances they told me not to bother coming to work that week! The sales department put on a hasty farewell party and gave me a Sunbeam Mixmaster. Our first wedding present!

In order to get to Dallas in time to find a place to live, our wedding had to be no later than Thursday. Friday was out because of Don and Elaine's wedding. It was our good friend Mrs. McMinn, Elaine's mother, who came up with a possible solution to the dilemma. Rather than upstaging Don and Elaine's wedding, couldn't we wait one more day and have a double wedding with them?

Elaine and Don were agreeable, so that is what we did. We just stepped into a ready-made wedding. All of the decisions about where, when, and what (like flowers and music) had already been made. Bob Denney's mother was making the bridal bouquets with flowers from her and Janie McMinn's gardens. She would just make two more bouquets. The male soloist was going to sing "Because" and "O Perfect Love," two favorite wedding songs at that time.

We would have to forgo a reception as there wouldn't be time. We would board the Southern Pacific night train right after the ceremony—as soon as I could get out of my dress. In order to save money, Kenneth and I would have gone to Dallas by bus, but Dad came to our rescue with train tickets. All we had to do was get our wedding license, have our medical exams, buy wedding rings, buy me (hopefully) a wedding dress, order wedding announcements, and phone our unsuspecting relatives about the time and place.That meant a busy few days. There was one premarital counseling session, of sorts, with the pastor, Dr. John G. (Jack) Mitchell.

First of all, however, we had to give Tom and Barbara a taste of the Northwest. We did the promised climb up Larch Mountain, and it almost did them in. They have never forgotten the experience. Then we had to go to the coast. We went to Land's End Beach for the weekend. I got a cold from our chilly walks. Tom and Barbara left for California as soon as we got back home.

Church weddings, at least in our circles, were simple affairs at that time. There was no rehearsal. To give balance to the wedding parties, Elaine and Don relinquished Ruth and Charlie to be our attendants in addition to Gerry Shipley and Doug Taylor, whom we invited to be maid of honor and best man. Gerry was teaching at a distance and would arrive at the church just in time for the wedding. I would have my bridesmaid's dress from Lois's wedding for her to wear.

Since it was the very end of the summer season, wedding dresses were in short supply in Portland's department stores. (This was long before there were special bridal shops). I could fall back on Harriet's dress if necessary, but it was much too formal when compared with Elaine's dress. What I found was a chiffon dress with short sleeves, a mandarin collar, and insertion bands of narrow lace for decoration.

Despite Mama's original unhappiness about our engagement, she was as helpful as could be that week. Of course there was no time for anyone to host a last-minute bridal shower. There wasn't even time for news to make the rounds about the double wedding.

The night before the wedding I finally received an engagement ring! Kenneth had told me he purchased one in Canada, with a platinum setting, but a friend was bringing it across the border. Since it was platinum, the wedding ring we chose that week needed to be platinum, too. I would have preferred yellow gold!

Our wedding was on Friday, the 13th of September, 1940. Obviously we weren't superstitious.

With the first strains of the wedding march, Dr. Mitchell entered from the side, followed by the men for both parties. Then Elaine's attendants processed down the center aisle, followed by Elaine on her father's arm.

We were still giggling in the foyer because when Gerry stepped into the dress I had brought for her it dragged on the floor. Someone found a piece of string that we tied around her waist; then we pulled up the extra length in a blousy effect. Our laughter dispelled last minute jitters. As the march music continued, my sister Ruth went down the aisle, followed by Gerry (would the string hold?). Finally, Dad, erect as always, escorted his third daughter to the marriage altar.

The Kenneth who was waiting for me had a blond mustache and did not look like the Kenneth I had known for ten years. When he arrived from summer camp in Quebec, I told him I did not like the addition. Apparently he didn't hear me. Later I asked him to please remove it, but he didn't. As it turned out, that was a portent of things to come through most of our married life. If and when we have had differences of opinion, Kenneth has won the day. He would say that's just the way it is—the wife submits. Don't argue. Not that I was given much to arguing—I would just be angry inside. Did he never read, "Submit one to another"? In recent years there has finally been much improvement along that line.

It wasn't long before he himself tired of trying to keep the mustache evenly trimmed and got rid of it, but it was too late for me to be consoled. He had had it at our wedding when it really mattered to me.

The wedding began at eight o'clock, and the train pulled out of the Union Depot, a few blocks away, at nine-thirty! There were quick good-byes in a side room at the church to our parents, my grandparents, a few aunts and uncles, and at the station to a few friends and siblings.

Good-bye, good-bye. Good-bye, Portland. Good-bye, Mount Hood. Good-bye, Oregon. Good-bye, childhood. Clickety-click, clickety-click, the train picked up speed.

At breakfast in the dining car the next morning, we ordered only tea and toast for the sake of economy. Then the steward came along and asked if we were Mr. and Mrs. Taylor. When we acknowledged that we were, he said breakfast would be courtesy of the Southern Pacific Railroad. So we reordered a full breakfast!

We spent two nights at a hotel in San Francisco en route to Dallas, again thanks to my dad. It was unseasonably warm for mid-September, so why did I wear my one new dress of blue wool when we went to the

World's Fair on Sunday? Probably because everything else was packed and in the baggage car. I came as close to fainting as I ever have.

On the train we worked out a tentative monthly budget for our combined income of $100 per month, beginning with a tithe of $10. It would be tight, but "love would find a way."

An oversight that we regretted was having no wedding pictures. Two years later, when a seminary couple was married in the lounge of the dormitory, I put on my wedding dress, and we posed for pictures in the same setting. I was disappointed with the result; we never tried again.

24

Beginning Married Life

We knew we were too late to obtain married-student housing on campus, so after our arrival we spent three days following up every lead within walking distance. We needed a furnished apartment since we were in no position to buy furniture. Some were too expensive for our limited budget. What we finally settled on was a one-room dwelling with a tiny kitchen and a shared bath on the second floor of a house on Adair Street, near the big Baylor Hospital.

The closet wasn't very large, but between us we did not have all that many clothes. I was used to a walk-in closet, however, and this definitely did not fit that description!

Laundromats had not yet come into existence. People commonly sent laundry out if they did not own a washing machine. We could not afford to do that, so I washed our clothing by hand in the kitchen sink and did sheets in the bathtub. I could not leave them soaking because we shared the bath with two nurses. Clothes needed to be taken down from the outdoor lines as soon as they were dry so that no one would walk off with them.

I had to keep food expenditures down to $20 a month. While there were just two of us, it was not cooking for two, but more like cooking for four. Kenneth had an enormous appetite. After eating the first plateful he could not have named what he had just eaten—that only tamed the hunger pangs.

As modest as our surroundings were, we entertained—provided that the ingredients for dinner cost no more than one dollar. We could entertain two people for dinner at a tiny table if one person sat on the bed. We even had Jack Mitchell, the pastor who had married us, as a dinner guest when he came to the seminary as a special Bible lecturer.

Books on marriage must assume that two people of the opposite sex who are used to sleeping alone can adjust to sleeping together without a problem, as they don't address it. But Kenneth had trouble adjusting to sleeping with another warm body, especially a female body, even when said female was his wife! So before very many weeks, he borrowed a single bed from the seminary. Our tiny apartment was now more crowded than ever, though the bed was less so.

While we had known each other for ten years and had been engaged for 18 months, we had not had a courtship in any sense of the word. We were not relaxed and comfortable with each other. I think it is safe to say that Kenneth did not know what girls were like. For one thing, I cried very easily. That first year I shed buckets of tears, though usually when I was alone. The girl Kenneth married had to be an angel, and I was no angel. Of course he knew I wasn't an angel, or he would have had an easier time deciding to marry me.

In one respect, he confused *his* bride with the bride of Christ. I should not have a "spot, or wrinkle, or any such thing" (Ephesians 5:27, KJV). On closer inspection Kenneth found I had several spots (moles) and one "such thing"—a lipoma, which is a lump of fatty tissue—in the middle of my back. I had to have them surgically removed! (The wrinkles came later.)

Where else, in addition to my appearance, was I failing? In conversation with others, as it turned out. Too often he would say, "You shouldn't have said that" about something I had said in the company of others. Yet it had not been something hurtful, and I could not see why he considered it wrong.

Even our devotional life was strained. It was not easy for me to pray aloud in the first place, so I wasn't at ease with Kenneth, always afraid I was missing the mark as he listened in while I talked with God.

He failed to realize that men and women don't think alike and consequently may not express themselves the same. I became very cautious about opening my mouth in his presence. So, it wasn't long before my personality changed. I was no longer the life of the party—not that we were going to any parties.

But I was at fault, too. Those two years in college when I was trying to forget him took their toll. To make forgetting easier, I thought about his faults or shortcomings and exaggerated them in my mind, overlooking all the good qualities that attracted me to him in the first place. That kind of negative thinking about my dear husband didn't automatically "cease and desist" following my promise to "love, honor, and obey as long as we both shall live."

Apparently Kenneth found his fears about marriage unfounded, because before long he was asking, "Why didn't we get married sooner!" I was the wrong person to ask. On the other hand, he still had lingering doubts about the long haul. Could romance be sustained year in and year out? Would we still be attracted to each other in five years? ten? twenty? Kenneth inadvertently revealed his doubts when he expressed surprise at seeing the couple who lived across the hall from us holding hands when they were out walking. They had probably been married two years! Well, he still wants to hold my hand, and I his, after 60 years!

I fault his parents for giving him such a negative view of marriage. They modeled lifelong fidelity, of course, but the union of male and female that God had declared "good," and that he meant for a lifetime of good, seemed to have turned mediocre for them. Was it the serious personalities that they brought to their marriage, their being older (he was 40 and she 30) than the typical bride and groom of their time? Or was it the poverty they shared through 32 years of marriage that snuffed out the *joie de vivre?* Perhaps the combination. A revealing fact is that Kenneth does not remember his mother ever smiling, much less laughing.

Kenneth will object to my commenting on the Taylor family's poverty. After all, they never went without food—but there must have been a lot of homemade baked beans, of which there is nothing cheaper, and always oatmeal for breakfast. Was it only for economy that there wasn't more variety, or was it lack of imagination or just getting in a rut?

Our family had plenty of oatmeal, too, with Guernsey cream that came from the pitcher in globs, but other days it could be Cream of Wheat, Wheatena, graham or cracked wheat cereal, cornmeal mush, or piles of pancakes or French toast. And breakfast always included fruit: fresh berries in the summer, fresh grapefruit in season, and canned fruit the rest of the year—peaches, pears, applesauce, cherries, plums, or rhubarb.

Maybe other boys wore patched shirts in high school during the Depression. If so, I didn't notice theirs, but I felt sorry for Kenneth. But Kenneth must not have been completely unaware of the family's poverty in his growing-up years, because he told me when we were in high school that he wanted to be rich and famous when he got older. To achieve those goals, he was going to be a doctor. He aimed to follow his brother Doug in that calling—except that Doug cared for neither wealth nor fame, but only to serve Christ in some benighted country such as Tibet.

Kenneth's father was very careful to tithe, as a notebook of his reveals. Not only was a tithe of cash income set aside, but the tithe column also listed a tenth of the estimated value of used clothing, such as a coat he was given. God, who also keeps accurate accounts, will reward Kenneth's parents generously in the final reckoning.

Kenneth never got to medical school, but that did not put an end to his desire for wealth and fame. Those unworthy goals were later cast aside when he gave himself to the Lord to be used anywhere, in any way, after reading *Borden of Yale '09,* a life-changing experience he has written about in his book.

Kenneth traveled to Texas universities on weekends to set up chapters of InterVarsity Fellowship that united Christian students in Bible study and prayer. There was not as much emphasis on evangelism as in later years; it was more a way for students away from home to hold on to their faith in a secular setting. He traveled by bus or in cars borrowed from other students. I seldom went because of the added expense. Charles Troutman was introducing IVF to college campuses in Michigan that year, so Kenneth and Charles were the first two IVF secretaries, as they were called, in the U.S. Others were working in Canadian schools, all under the direction of Stacey Woods.

My work at the seminary was with typewriter (manual, of course), mimeograph (also manual), and graphotype. That machine made lead address plates for mailing lists: donors to the seminary, the alumni list, and subscribers to the theological quarterly, *Bibliotheca Sacra.* I cut the stencils and ran off copies of exams, entered changes of address on the mailing lists, and stamped addresses on the seminary bulletin and *Bib Sac* for mailing. It was not hard. I worked alone in a couple of rooms in the basement of the men's dormitory, and my hours were flexible. And I always got paid, which was not true for the professors, whose salaries were sometimes late if the mail did not bring in enough cash. Days set aside for prayer concentrated more on current needs than the spiritual ministry of alumni!

Wives of married students were not permitted to attend classes, much less enroll as students. We could, however, attend the special lectures by Bible teachers who came in for a week of concentrated exposition on a given book of the Bible. Those teachers included Harry Ironside, Roy Aldrich, Jack Mitchell, and Norman Harrison. Dr. Louis Sperry Chafer, founder and president of the seminary, did teach an evening class for women one semester on the book of Romans. It helped give me an assurance of salvation.

That first fall we received wedding gifts by mail for a number of weeks. We received several luncheon-size cotton tablecloths, really too big for our tiny table, and silver napkin rings. We received a couple of chenille bedspreads, but no blankets or additional sheets to supplement those I had bought. We had the worn blankets Kenneth had taken to college. They looked (and were) pretty skimpy on our double bed. A few years later my mother sent me a new blanket for Christmas—the only new blanket I had for years and years. As our family grew, my sister Harriet shared extra used bedding with us.

Most of our gifts arrived in the form of cash—$3.00 or $5.00 checks. We added these to my meager savings in a local bank, to be used for household items when needed. Our little apartment came complete with dishes. We would buy our own later. I "made do" rather than have every convenience of my mother's kitchen, even using a glass milk bottle as a rolling pin for rolling out pie crusts.

Very quickly Alan and Gerry Hamilton became our best friends. Like us, they had not come to seminary directly after college but had had some experience with Child Evangelism Fellowship. Gerry assisted Dr. Lincoln in the seminary office. The Hamiltons lived in their own trailer, which was parked at the rear of the seminary property. Ted and Mary Lou Benson, friends from Wheaton, were also on campus. Ted managed the dining hall that year.

My sisters Harriet and Lois had married fellow Lutherans (Missouri Synod), so they continued in that tradition. I had decided that if I married a non-Lutheran, I would be the one to change denominations and not repeat what my parents had done—attending different churches. When Kenneth was in town, we attended Sunday morning services at Scofield Memorial Church in downtown Dallas, which was not unlike The Classes in Portland. We usually walked the mile or more, even though carfare was only five cents. In the evening we attended a Southern Baptist church that was nearer.

I probably would have given our tithe to the church we attended, or to the seminary or InterVarsity. Kenneth was for evangelism via the printed page (tracts), and he has written about our effort along that line in sending tracts to postbox holders. It was years before he felt any financial obligation to a local church, despite his father having held pastorates when he was young. And what Kenneth wanted to do, in this area or any other, *I* wanted. If I dissented, I was overridden, so what was the point of speaking up?

If we could do it over again, we would never have agreed to be separated the first summer after our marriage. I don't think I agreed at the time—Kenneth made the plans, and I had to follow through. When he realized that he had a growing interest in journalism, it seemed to call for summer school. Northwestern University in Evanston, Illinois, was rated one of the top schools in that field. Probably he could find a job somewhere in Chicago to work for his board and room, but that left me out in the cold. There was no work for me at the seminary during the summer. One possibility was to go home to my parents, but it might appear as if we were having problems, and *that* was to be avoided. Kenneth came up with the idea of my working and/or counseling at the girls' Pioneer Camp in Ontario, not far from the boys' camp where he had been the two previous summers.

Did we have more problems communicating with each other than other young couples did, or more than our parents had had when they were first married? We should have had marriage counseling, but that was an unknown commodity, just as it had been in our parents' and grandparents' day. We muddled through and learned from disappointments.

25

Canoeing

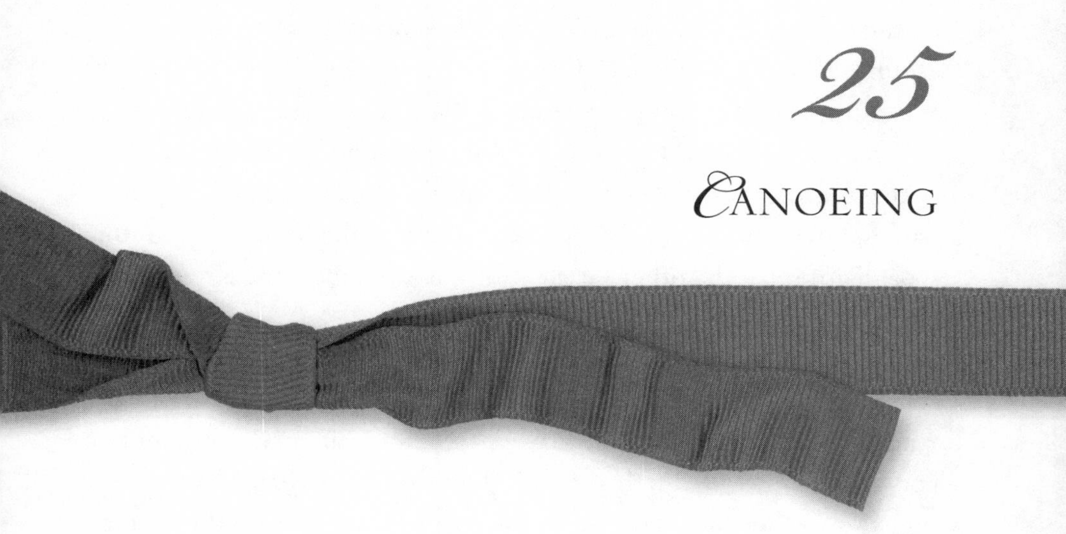

WHEN I TOOK CANOEING for PE credit at Oregon State, the classes were taught on a shallow secondary river. I later learned that canoeing on open lakes with wind and waves was a different experience.

Why was I canoeing in open water if there was a wind? I was following my young husband. If he had said, "Let's fly to the moon," I would have hung on to his coattails as we went up through the clouds.

We were in Toronto early in the summer after our first year in Dallas, and Kenneth suggested, "Let's go canoeing." Ferries took other pleasure-seekers out to an island in Lake Ontario, but paddling a rented canoe appealed to Kenneth. We had canoed together on the sluggish Tualatin River as teens, so the idea of canoeing brought back romantic memories.

As for me, I would never forget the time Kenneth deliberately came alongside in another canoe and dumped me and Bob Denney. It was such a juvenile thing to do! If he cared about me at all, why hadn't he asked me to go in his canoe? And if he was jealous, how much better to take steps to resolve the situation instead of thinking, "I'll show them."

Kenneth and I paddled out to the island without incident, warmed by the sun and the exertion. We beached the canoe and walked around the amusement park but did not spend any money. When the sun went behind a cloud, we realized that the afternoon would soon be over and we should head back. We pushed off and shivered a little as there was an offshore wind. Was this the same placid lake we had paddled three hours earlier? No, it was one of the larger lakes in the world! And like the other Great Lakes, it could become a raging sea that sends huge freighters to its bottom.

Well, we made it back to Toronto's waterfront and the rental stand, or you wouldn't be reading this. But we paddled hard through rough water, keenly aware that we had neither life preservers nor any container with which to bail water. Did the Coast Guard have an eye on us? Whether they did or not, the one whose eye is on the sparrow had his eye on us. He had a plan for Kenneth Taylor, and he wasn't going to let him drown—or die in a car or plane crash or succumb to a heart attack—until he used him to make his Word more readable for millions of people.

From Toronto I went north to Pioneer Camp on Clearwater Lake while Kenneth went back to Evanston (just north of Chicago) to begin summer school at Northwestern University. While I wouldn't earn any money as assistant cook and cabin counselor for several 15–16-year-old girls, my living expenses were paid during those two and a half months, and I could be with some wonderful InterVarsity Fellowship staff women who modeled the Christian life for me.

Camp life was quite unstructured, and my girls and I spent a lot of time cutting young trees and building a large tepee, covering the framework with large pieces of bark. The process of building it was more important to us than how we might use it upon completion. Actually, it was an ideal place for overnights—it was not far from the camp itself, and it provided shelter instead of a lost-in-the-woods feeling to city girls.

Quite a number of our campers were from England, young girls whose parents had sent them to the safety of friends or family in Canada—away from the *blitzkrieg* that was pounding London during 1941. Those girls needed a lot of mothering.

The waterfront was perhaps the most important part of Pioneer Camp, with lots of opportunity for swimming, diving, and canoeing. The water was frightfully cold, so being *on* it rather than in it was the more bearable. The girls had to get over their initial fears. They were sure that the slightest motion would capsize a canoe and that they would immediately find themselves in deep water.

Overnight canoe trips were scheduled for all but the youngest girls. Eventually I was asked to take eight "middlers" (ages 12 and 13) on such a trip. With our sleeping bags, matches, rations for four meals, and a map of the connecting lakes, we set out in three canoes. Two girls paddled and one rode in each. Back at camp they had practiced changing positions while in the water to give relief to a tired paddler, but it was still scary.

Confidence grew, tired muscles were rejuvenated, our picnic-style meals were satisfying, and we were having such a good time that after the day and night out, we didn't want to return. "Can't we go farther? This is so much fun." "I never slept out under the stars before." "Call Cathy [Nicol] and see if we can't stay out another night. Please?" To tell the truth, I felt the same way. Why go back so soon if we could explore another lake, continue to learn cooperation, and improve our handling of the canoes?

We stopped at a village and called the camp director. Cathy was agreeable: "Don't go too far. Remember you have to paddle back!" So we bought food for another three meals and were off.

The next day, on our return trip, I headed the lead canoe into the middle of one of the lakes. My goal was simply to take the shorter route rather than hugging the shore, but I was breaking a cardinal rule of tripping with novice canoeists. After all, a storm can come up with little or no warning.

And suddenly a storm did arise—complete with thunder, lightning, and rain. The lake's gentle ripples became small waves. Canoeing on the Mary's and Tualatin rivers in Oregon was no preparation for this.

We would have to turn our canoes and head for shore, but that meant the waves would hit us broadside and we could more easily capsize. Instead, I headed my canoe at a 45 degree angle so we could cut diagonally through the waves while making slow progress toward shore. Would the two canoes behind me be able to stay in line, or would the girls panic? I was so intent on watching the churning water that I could hardly afford to turn my head. Finally we all made it to shore.

It was an experience none of us would want to repeat, and it had been my fault—jeopardizing the lives of eight young girls. After resting in the rain with some tears on our already wet cheeks, there was no option but to get back in the canoes. There were no roads or houses in sight. Never had we paddled so close to shore, though by then the squall was over and the water was calmer.

The camp leaders were joyful as we put our paddles up on the dock. Someone else would have to unload the soggy sleeping bags and camp gear. We were exhausted.

"We had a special prayer meeting for you when that storm came up," they told us.

"Thank you. We needed those prayers. God heard and answered." Then I had to confess that we had been in the middle of the lake. And now that they were back at camp with the prospect of a hot shower and dry clothes, the girls were eager to share their adventures.

26

Second and Third Years at Dallas

THEN THE SUMMER was over, and Kenneth and I, strangers again, were back together. We made a quick trip home to Portland to see our parents and siblings, driving a used car Kenneth had purchased with money my dad had sent. He would resell it in Portland, and we would return to Dallas by train. What Kenneth bought was a jalopy, not my Dad's idea of a used car! Douglas had finished his third year at medical school, as had John Frame, with whom Kenneth had shared some experiences during the summer. They were well on their way to careers as medical missionaries. Kenneth had one year of seminary behind him and now a few journalism credits, but where was he headed? He couldn't really say. He was counting on God to show him in time.

We began the second year of seminary in one of the apartments for married students on campus. Again it was just one room and a kitchen and bath, but at least it was a private bath. A Murphy bed pulled out of the wall when it was time to retire. I continued with my mail and mimeograph job.

I preferred calling my husband Kenneth rather than shortening it to Ken, but from seminary days onward other people have usually called him Ken, and I finally succumbed.

Ted Benson left the seminary midyear, freeing up his job of supervising the dining room, which he recommended to Ken. The dining room job paid a small salary, and it entitled us to a larger, rent-free apartment. We also got free board, as we ate with the unmarried male students.

Ken learned about going to the market to buy a quarter of beef and to the farmers' market for fresh fruits and vegetables. The cook and his wife did not need much supervision. They were experienced, and we were not. The school budget did not allow for anything but the plainest fare. And the men couldn't afford to complain too loudly, for their schooling was free.

America had now joined the war, and Ken's father wrote about job opportunities in the shipyards in Portland. At the end of the school year, we went home for the summer—but not together. I was happily pregnant, and my conservative obstetrician did not think a cross-country trip by car was advisable during the first three months. So a few weeks after Ken left, I rode to California with another student couple and then took the train to Portland.

We stayed with my parents in their big house. Charlie and Ruth were both married and had established their own homes. My brother Bill was finding parental strictures too onerous, and he was staying at the nearby golf club where he worked. Ken worked the midnight shift and drove to and from the shipyards in our family car.

A couple of times we drove to Cloverdale on the coast where Dad Taylor was pastoring a small church. The parsonage didn't have an extra bedroom, and I remember sleeping, or trying to sleep, on a pew in the church! I think the best part of that job was the occasional gifts of Tillamook cheddar cheese from parishioners! Tillamook cheese is made only in that one coastal county of Oregon, and at that time one of the small factories was in Cloverdale, just across the highway from the church. These days, Janet knows that a gift of Tillamook cheese will always be appreciated when she comes home from Oregon. Ken is as fond of good cheddar cheese as his father was.

When the summer was over, we told our families good-bye and took the train to Dallas. I gave up my part-time job at the seminary, as I was now well along in my pregnancy.

Early in the morning on December 4, 1942, we walked to the hospital when my labor pains became regular. Those were busy days in maternity wards everywhere, and a private labor room was not immediately available. During the night a disheveled girl wearing a bathrobe came in with her sister. Her water had already broken, and she was in pain and frightened about what lay ahead. Not only did she not have a doctor, but she also did not have a husband and could not or would not give a name for the father of the baby soon to be born. That was my first introduction to a situation that was rare then, but has become rampant since the sexual revolution of the '60s.

Ken could not stay with me, so I was alone for most of the 24 hours that I was in labor, as the nurses were too busy to check on my progress frequently. Finally I called out in desperation and was immediately wheeled to the delivery room. Moving from the gurney to the delivery table brought on the last big push, and I heard a nurse say: "Beautiful! Just the way it should be. It's a girl." Then another nurse pushed an ether cone over my nose, even though it was no longer necessary! Consequently, I was out cold before I could see the baby. That was natural childbirth without planning or specific training and without a doctor in attendance, though he was in the hospital waiting to be called.

I was in the hospital the customary ten days, and glad to be there, for I was completely exhausted from the long, hard labor. When Rebecca Louise (Becky) and I went home those few blocks, it was by ambulance, and I was carried upstairs on a stretcher! I had not been out of bed to walk yet, but only dangled my feet over the edge. It was expected that I would continue to stay in bed while I "recovered" and that I would have help with the care of the baby. I was not to go up or down stairs for six weeks! I write these details only to show what great changes have come about for mothers during and after childbirth. Customs were already changing in the North, but this was the South, where "the way it's always been done" was harder to change.

I did have help from the neighboring wives, especially Eloise Portman, who had several children of her own. Ken was jealous of "the girls" hovering over Becky. She was his baby, and he had not held her for the first ten days. Neither had I, as I nursed her while lying in bed, and between feedings she was in the nursery.

Still, being the father of a new baby was not enough to keep Ken from participating in a trip to Mexico over the Christmas vacation. He was going with fellow students Alan Hamilton, Harold Good, and Tom McKinney. It was not for sightseeing south of the border but to see missionary work firsthand. They left just a day or two after I was home from the hospital.

I was unhappy that Ken bought a camera for that trip, even though it wasn't a new one. Sure, it would be nice to take pictures on the trip, not to mention of our first baby. But since it behooved us to watch our pennies, how much more the spending of dollars—and that camera cost dollars. Well, maybe my reaction was due in part to postpartum blues, something that neither of us had dealt with previously!

I do not remember the hospital charges, but the doctor had a special rate of $100 for seminary wives—including all the prenatal visits and delivery. Put together, the charges were a substantial drain on our savings—most of the money we had received as wedding gifts.

What a lonesome Christmas I had without my husband of two years! It would have been hard enough *with* him, as I still missed the West-Trappe Christmas traditions of my childhood. If Ken had any such happy Christmas memories, it was never apparent to me. I deduced, correctly or not, that there had been very little in the way of gift-giving or holiday decorations and feasting in the Taylor home, and that he had learned not to get his hopes up for anything special under the Christmas tree.

Ross Cornell, a friend of ours from Portland, was stationed at a nearby Army base. He called just before Christmas to ask if we could spend some time together on Christmas Day. When he learned that Ken was away, he suggested that he and Virginia could take me out to dinner. I agreed, but only if he could carry me up and down the stairs! To be with these good friends from The Classes was a wonderful encouragement while I was regaining my strength and feeling deserted by Ken. Eating in a restaurant was a very rare treat. Baby Becky, three weeks old that day, never made a peep during the dinner hour.

On his return from Mexico, Ken brought me a finger-tip white wool jacket with bright wool embroidery on the back. I enjoyed wearing it for several years.

We bought a crib, a playpen, a buggy, and before long, a high chair. All new. Despite our limited resources, we weren't into buying secondhand yet. People tend to follow the way they were brought up, and my family had bought everything new. One exception to the "all new" was a used wringer washing machine. I was still doing our laundry by hand, and I couldn't see washing diapers that way. Even with a washer it involved plenty of hand work, as I had to fill the washer with bucketfuls from the kitchen sink and then empty it the same way.

When Becky was four months old and we were beginning to settle into a routine, I had to tell Ken I was pregnant again. It was just a fact. I couldn't think through all the implications. His response was, "You can't be. People don't have babies that close together." I knew better. Just ask any woman, and you will hear about the aunt who had babies ten months apart or the neighbor who had two babies in the same year. My own sisters Harriet and Lois were only 13 months apart. Becky's little brother or sister would join our family sometime around her first birthday.

It was a hot summer, as all summers are in Texas—just five years after the hot summer in Houston when I was "running away" from

Kenneth. Now we were a family with one child and a second on the way!

While he probably could have found a factory job that summer, Ken did editorial and pasteup work with Alan and Gerry in producing three monthly issues of the *Child Evangelism* magazine. He thoroughly enjoyed it.

Toward the end of the summer, Stacey Woods wrote to ask Ken if he would like to edit *His*, the magazine published by InterVarsity Fellowship. Would he?! Yes, but he had another year of seminary, and the job would mean moving to Chicago. There were plenty of seminaries in Chicago, but mostly liberal. Northern Baptist Seminary was an exception. The wheels in Ken's brain soon became railroad wheels taking him north. He went ahead of me and Becky to find a place for us to live.

Dr. Chafer was away for the summer, speaking at conferences, so there was no opportunity to tell him good-bye and explain our reason for leaving Dallas so abruptly.

As soon as Ken had found an apartment near Northern Baptist Seminary, he sent word for me to come. I flew—for the first time in my life. It was a night flight, and the windows were blacked out for wartime security, so I couldn't see anything. Howard and Hazel Goddard drove Becky and me to Love Field (our stuff having been shipped), and Ted Benson met us at Midway Airport.

CHICAGO, 1943–1944

WHAT KEN had found was an apartment of sorts in an old dormitory of a defunct German seminary on Washington Boulevard. Originally it would have been a suite for single men—three rooms and a bath, all opening into a long dark hall. The only thing that had been added was a gas range in one room to turn it into a kitchen. All of the rooms were dark and dingy. Ken has written in his book that my first reaction on seeing the place was to burst into tears. I wasn't alone in my reaction. My parents visited a few months later, and Dad told me years later that my mother, too, cried when they got back to their hotel.

There was no kitchen sink, and no cupboards or counters either. The washbowl was in the hall outside of the bathroom and was most inconvenient for washing dishes. There was no drain board, so I had to put a dish drainer on a chair and carry a few dishes at a time from the kitchen table. So we washed our faces, brushed our teeth, and washed dishes in the same bowl.

The heat was erratic and could not be regulated at all. Since all of Chicago was still heated with coal, fighting coal dust was a losing battle. Curtains were dirty in a week. What a contrast to the clean country air of Oregon's Washington County where I had grown up, and even to Dallas with its gas heat when heat was needed.

I couldn't put Becky on the floor to crawl. It was too dirty and, soon enough, too cold as well. Periodically I lifted her from crib to high chair to playpen to a walker in which she could scoot up and down the hall.

We had shipped our wringer washer from Dallas, and it went in a dingy basement room. Fortunately, Becky was so docile that I could sit her on a tabletop with an empty bottle and a handful of beans while I did our laundry. She had no toys.

We got acquainted with Paul and Freeda Kaufman, who lived upstairs in the same building, but we made no other real friends that year. Ken walked to Northern Baptist Seminary for classes, and he took the elevated train to the InterVarsity office on Wacker Drive and to Moody Church on Sunday. I stayed home on Sunday, as well as every other day, except for prenatal visits to my obstetrician, whose office was on Michigan Avenue.

Paul Kaufman drove me to Wesley Hospital when I went into labor. Freeda took Becky out to Wheaton, where Mary Lou Benson had agreed to keep her. We were very much dependent on friends.

This time I was completely "out" and unaware of the baby's birth. It was a boy, and we named him John Alan after our friends John Frame and Alan Hamilton. John was born on December 8, just three days after Becky's first birthday.

My hospital roommate was Jewish. She had conscientiously refrained from smoking while pregnant, but now she was making up for lost time. We were decades away from being aware of the dangers of secondhand smoke. She was on the phone a great deal with her mother, her sister, and her friends, especially regarding the celebration around her son's circumcision. I had no one to call, and Ken was my only visitor.

I think I stayed in the hospital for ten days again, and I was in some-

Wedding picture of my parents, Louise Trappe and Harry A. West.

Grandpa and Grandma West in their sixties.

Grandma West, Mama, and Grandma Trappe.

Mama holding me at three months.

Me at fifteen months.

Side view of the Bonita house where I was born.

Me at six years old.

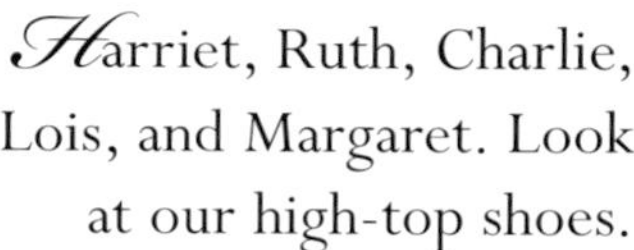

Harriet, Ruth, Charlie, Lois, and Margaret. Look at our high-top shoes.

Going to California, 1925. Harriet and me in front of our seven-passenger Buick.

Mama and Papa.

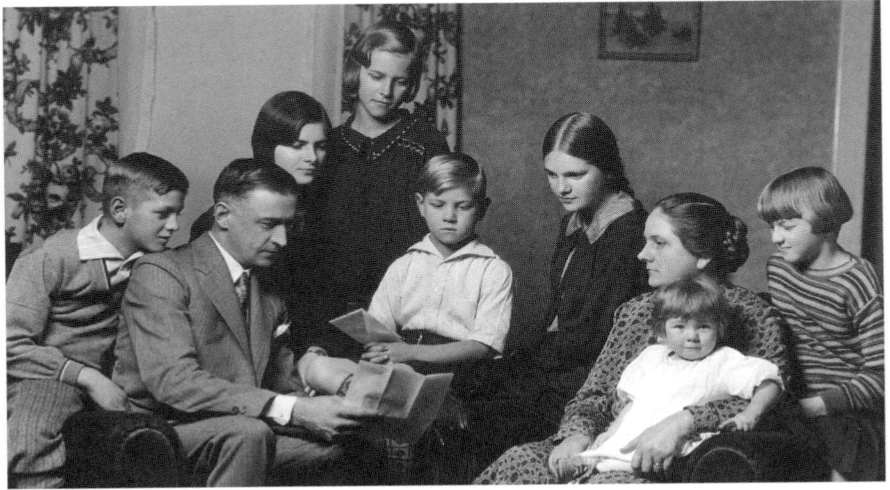

West family, November 1929. Charlie, Papa, Harriet, Margaret, Billy, Lois, Mama holding Eunice, and Ruth.

The big brick house in Raleigh Hills where we moved in January 1930.

My high school graduation picture, 1934.

In my wedding dress, but not taken until two years later.

Front porch of our old house at 1515 E. Forest Avenue. Eventually, it became the bedroom for John, Peter, and Mark.

Our Christmas card picture, 1955. Mary Lee was the baby.

The twelve of us in 1963.
Back: John, Marty, Becky, Peter.
Middle: Gretchen, Alison, Mary Lee.
Front: Mark, Janet, Margaret, Ken, Cynthia.

Working a puzzle with Gretchen, Alison, and Mary Lee.

At CBA convention in Denver, 1971, when the Living Bible was launched: Gretchen, Alison, Mark, Mary Lee, Margaret, and Ken.

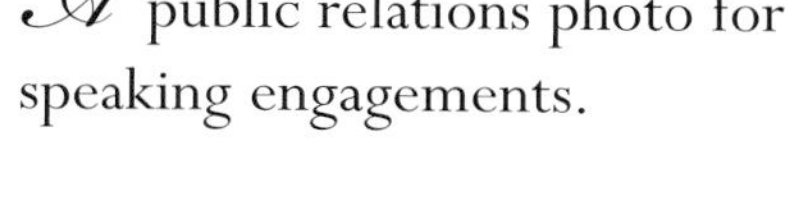

A public relations photo for speaking engagements.

Our new house at 1515 E. Forest Avenue.

With my brothers and sisters in 1986: Alan, Bill, Charlie, Ruth, Margaret, Lois, and Harriet.

Our summer house in Sawyer, Michigan.

Whitewater rafting with Nancy Hawley and granddaughters Kristen, Margaret, and Rebecca. The latter two are covered by water.

Up high for a better view of Jerusalem.

With all ten children, summer 1998. Becky, John, Alison, Marty, Peter, Janet, Mark, Mary Lee, Gretchen, and Cynthia.

what better shape when baby John and I went home—by car this time, not ambulance! And I had to forget the old prohibition about going up and down steps for six weeks. Our apartment was on the first floor, but the washing machine was in the basement. Naturally, I had to do a load nearly every day with two babies in diapers.

There was no thought on Ken's part or mine of his helping me in that area. Woman's work was woman's work—the same as it had been in our parents' homes, and for generations before that. All the way back to the beginning? Was that what God intended when he made Eve a helpmeet for Adam?

Mary Lou loaned us a large baby basket, so we did not have to buy a second crib immediately. But paying the doctor and hospital bills nearly depleted our dwindling savings.

John was a fussy baby. He did not take to nursing naturally, and it soon became evident that he had colic. We could count on his crying in distress about an hour after every feeding, and the feeding itself could take an hour. I would be crying too out of helplessness and weariness.

When I went to Wheaton to bring Becky back the day before Christmas, I had to take John with me on the streetcar and the Chicago, Aurora & Elgin train. John had a crying spell on the train, and sympathetic women gave me advice on what to try that I wasn't already trying. Our pediatrician assured me that changing from breast-feeding to a bottle would make no difference as far as colic was concerned, so I kept on with nursing.

When Mary Lou brought Becky downstairs from her nap, I did not recognize her after three weeks of separation! Such a big baby after handling seven-pound John! She still had very little hair and wasn't walking. It was another two months before she walked.

To give John some relief from the gas pains of colic, I learned to keep him on his tummy on a hot water bottle with the basket bed propped up so that his feet were higher than his head.

When Freeda was visiting with me one day, she discovered when changing John's diaper that he had an inguinal hernia. This was causing extreme discomfort, so his screaming was not just due to colic. As a nurse, she knew what to do. She made a temporary truss out of yarn wrapped around a coin and held it in place with a tight band.

The baby-sized truss we got from a medical supply company was made of rubber tubing and was easy to clean—a necessary feature as it was worn under his diaper. Trips to the doctor were not easy, as we took the "el" and then walked to his office. With the truss in place, the hernia did not rupture anymore. John wore it until he was 20 months old, when he had corrective surgery. Nowadays doctors would operate as soon as the problem was discovered.

When the kitchen was too cold, I put the enamel baby bathtub on the oven door when giving baby John his bath. I made quick trips to the nearby A&P grocery store when both babies were asleep. It was not open in the evening. I could not expect any help from Ken, who was carrying a full load at the seminary, writing his master's thesis, and working half-time at InterVarsity.

After Ken's graduation in May (which neither of us remembers), we were anxious to move out of the city. Wherever we went, it would have to be on a commuter rail line so Ken could get downtown to his work at InterVarsity.

Ken had been exempt from the Army draft as long as he was in seminary. Graduation changed that, so in order to qualify as a chaplain in case he was called up, he checked to see if Central Bible Church (an outgrowth of the Portland Union Bible Classes) would ordain him. It would, and he made a quick trip out west by train for that purpose.

Before he left, we knew that I was pregnant again. The baby would be born the following January.

During that year our good friend Gerry Hamilton died in Dallas from a heart problem. Plenty of people—still in their twenties—were dying in the war, but at home? As we mourned with Alan, we remembered that God does not take lightly the death of one of his saints.

28

We Move to Wheaton

KEN'S BOSS, Stacey Woods, gave us the welcome news that he and Yvonne would be away for the summer, so we could rent their home in Wheaton on the corner of Lincoln Avenue and Gary Avenue. Three months should give us ample time to find another place for our growing family. What luxury to leave the grime of Chicago and live in a beautifully furnished suburban home where the children could play on the floor or in the yard.

It was a three-quarter-mile walk from the Woodses' house to the Wheaton train station. And the same distance for me to push the baby buggy with Becky and John when I went grocery shopping at the A&P, or if I needed any notions from Estenfelders or Woolworth's, both on Front Street just across from the station. We opened a checking account at Gary-Wheaton Bank, which was also on Front Street.

We began attending College Church of Christ, pastored by Evan Welsh. The Dick Schnebergers lived in the house next door. Dick taught an adult Sunday school class at College Church. The pastor of the Wheaton Bible Church also called on us, hoping we would join there.

Ken was happy to be working full-time at the InterVarsity office in Chicago, developing the monthly magazine *His*. It contained devotional and theological articles in addition to news from college and university chapters around the country.

Though we scanned papers carefully, there were never any houses listed for rent in Wheaton, Glen Ellyn, Lombard, or Villa Park. Without a car we had to be within walking distance of a commuter rail line. The prospects for getting a car on Ken's salary were nil! As for apartments, they were practically nonexistent in the suburbs in the '40s. Some larger homes had been subdivided to accommodate more than one family, but vacancies were not advertised, as they were often illegal according to zoning ordinances.

In late summer God saw our need and answered our prayers "above and beyond what we could ask" (Ephesians 3:20). Pastor Welsh's mother was vacating her home at 502 E. Seminary and was moving with her companion, Irene Johnson, into the church parsonage. Evan's wife had recently died, and Mother Welsh would live with Evan to help care for his daughters. Evan called to say her house was available to us.

It was a two-story, four-bedroom stucco house just across the street from the lower campus of Wheaton College. By renting three of the four bedrooms to students we could afford it. We elected to have girls, five of them. There was room for Becky and John's cribs in a small sunroom off the master bedroom, and we didn't need any other furniture or furnishings, not even dishes, as Mother Welsh left everything. Having to share the one bath with the students was inconvenient at times, but not impossible. One girl, Grace Rohmer, worked for her room. I had her do cleaning and babysitting. Now we were closer to the train station and stores and only one long block from church.

We joined College Church in late fall (1944), but on the Sunday when new members were presented to the congregation, Ken wouldn't let me attend. I was "too big" with our third child. Eventually—of necessity—he got over those funny notions about me and pregnancies. But not over the "hurry up and get thin again" admonitions after each birth!

We were only a block from our good friends Ted and Mary Lou Benson, and we visited them frequently. And that fall we attended Comrades Club after evening church, a group for singles and young marrieds. Ken Hansen never let me forget that at the first meeting I introduced myself as Mrs. Kenneth Taylor. Well, I was proud of that title. Still am.

Seemingly the only option for baby care when I would have to go to the hospital in January was for Mother Taylor to come from Oregon. She was willing, and we sent her money to come by train. We couldn't afford for her to have a Pullman berth, so she had to sit up nights, but she didn't complain. She slept on the sofa in the living room when she got to our house.

Even after her arrival there was the problem of how to get to the hospital. My doctor sent his patients to a hospital in Aurora, 20 miles away. Pastor Evan Welsh came to our rescue again. He said that we could call his assistant day or night for a ride to the hospital. When the due date was imminent, our neighbors, the Barrons, said they would leave their door unlocked so we could use their phone during the night if necessary. It was, and the assistant pastor drove us to the hospital. Ten days later I came home with our second daughter, Martha Ann. Mother Taylor did not stay long after that.

Two pleasant years went by in that house. The rationing due to World War II affected everyone to some degree, but we did not feel it all that much. We had books of stamps for sugar, shoes, and gasoline. We saved all our fat trimmings and turned in full cans of fat at butcher shops.

Sometime during 1946 my mother visited us. I assume my dad was attending a national Gideons convention in Chicago. She was pleased to see how well I was managing with three little ones. Little did we dream that that would be her last visit.

In late summer Mother Welsh let us know she would be moving back into her home. Evan was marrying his secretary, Olena Mae Hendricksen, and moving to Detroit. The housing situation had not improved—nor had our bank account—so we were in no position to think of buying. A large enough house for our growing family (I was pregnant again) might have cost $12,000.

We decided that John should have surgery to repair his hernia before we moved. Ken drove him to Elmhurst Hospital the night before the surgery. He has never forgotten how John screamed from his crib in the totally unfamiliar surroundings when Ken turned to go. Parents were not allowed to stay with hospitalized children in those days. Fortunately that is no longer true. That bitter experience was sweetened some when Evan brought us a check for $100 from the church's benevolent fund. We would have had a hard time paying for the surgery without it.

Ken had left InterVarsity Fellowship by this time and was working for Clyde Dennis at Good News Publishers. Their offices were also in downtown Chicago. Good News was making a name for itself in the U.S. with its fast-growing line of attractive gospel tracts. It was hoped they could be translated and used in other countries, and Ken was hired to develop that side of the business.

Clyde and Muriel Dennis, with their three little children—April, Lane, and Jan—had found a place to live in Lake Geneva, Wisconsin, and they reported that there was another house available on the same property. Lake Geneva was the next-to-last stop on the northern spur of the Chicago & Northwestern Railroad. The house was a mile from the train station. It was a long commute to Chicago, but if others were doing it, Ken could too. But we would be able to stay only for the nine off-season months. In the summer the rent would escalate astronomically.

29

LAKE GENEVA

I HAVE A BOOK called *Lake Geneva, the Newport of the West,* which has pictures of the mansions that ring the lake and a brief history of the families (mostly from Chicago) who built these summer mansions between 1870 and 1920. All the properties had distinctive names. Our address that year was Snug Harbor, Lake Geneva. No other address was needed. And until the lake froze, our mail came by boat.

But times had changed. Many family fortunes did not survive the Great Depression, and the next generation frequently could not maintain the opulent (for that's what it truly was) lifestyle of their parents and grandparents. The summer houses were sold, and properties were subdivided to make room for the middle class. Snug Harbor no longer belonged to the Borden family.

The current absentee owners even rented out the big house and the boathouse. The original owners had had yachts for transporting family and guests from the train station (sometimes even a special train!) to their own docks. Those days were now gone, along with the staffs of servants. Snug Harbor had several cottages on the slope above the lakeshore that had accommodated the hired help, and it was in one of those cottages that the Dennis family was living.

The three-bedroom house we moved into was originally the guest house. The large rooms had hardwood floors, and the push-button panel by the phone was evidence of the bygone era. Buttons were labeled "main house," "livery," "kitchen," "boathouse," etc. Now the wires were disconnected, and we were on our own. I couldn't ring for lunch to be brought up and served on the porch, or for the phaeton to take me to town, or even for a saddle horse just to go riding!

The house was still furnished, so we did not have to make an investment that way. Good thing, for the rent itself ($80 a month) was a bit of a hurdle, especially with the added cost of fuel oil for the furnace. Also, the monthly commuter ticket cost more than it had in Wheaton. We just moved with our two cribs, two high chairs, the playpen, and the baby buggy.

But we did have medical insurance now for the coming baby, and that was a comfort. In addition, Ken had taken out a family income policy that, in case of his death or permanent disability, would support me and the children until the youngest was 18. This was insurance "above and beyond" what a wife could wish for. Almost above and beyond our budget, too. The only way we could pay the premium was to pay it in monthly installments.

Through subsequent years, as I addressed the monthly check to Central Life Assurance Co., Des Moines, Iowa, I dared not let myself think about what that money could be purchasing if it were available for food and clothing. But that insurance policy was sacrosanct, next to our tithe. It gave Ken great peace of mind, and the three children it originally covered eventually became ten. Even if Ken died, I would not have to reenter the workplace.

The feminists, having had it their way for a generation, are discovering that the satisfaction of "making it" in the business or professional world does not compensate for missing out on raising a family, and now it is too late. Now many working women have a husband and children in addition to a nine-to-five job, so the old adage "Woman's work is never done" still applies. What I was doing during the daytime—laundry, ironing, housecleaning, grocery shopping, meal preparation, attending to the needs of a baby or of a two-year-old in the "no" stage, and always "being there" when the school children came home—today's working woman has to do on the way home from work, or leave to others in the day care center, do during the evening, or simply leave undone. When is there time to renew her mind, body, or spirit? I could write more on that subject, but you can see where I am coming from.

What can be compared with helping to mold a child's character over a period of some 16 years? In the words of Scripture, "What shall it profit a man if he gain the whole world and lose his own soul?" It applies to our children's souls, too. Two paychecks do not make it easier to bring up a child in the fear and nurture of the Lord. I am very grateful that our daughters and daughters-in-law have put family before career. And at this point the granddaughters are making the same choice.

I walked to town on Saturdays to buy groceries, using the well-maintained path along the lake's edge. I had to be careful not to buy more than I could carry a mile in two shopping bags, so I couldn't purchase sugar, flour, and shortening the same week. Milk was still delivered door-to-door. Occasionally I went shopping with Muriel Dennis, who had a car, but that was the exception.

Monday through Friday the children had been fed and were in their Dr. Denton sleepers ready for bed by the time Ken walked in from his long day, so basically he only saw them on weekends.

Who would stay with the children when I went to the hospital for the birth of number four in October? Apparently it would have to be Mother Taylor again if she were willing. Fortunately she was, but I think she came out of a sense of duty rather than joyfully. It took all the money we could squeeze together to pay for her round-trip train ticket. Coach again, but she did not complain. It was traveling. She had a yen for traveling but had done very little.

She was a grandmother, but not grandmotherly. There was no swooping up the children to cover them with kisses. She did not bring them any treats such as balloons or suckers, nor did she ever send anything for Christmas or their birthdays. I think that all her married life there was simply no money left after the necessities were taken care of. But neither was she creative in making something out of nothing. She didn't help Becky and John make stick figures out of acorns stuck together, or sailboats from walnut shells filled with wax from the last jelly jar to hold a paper sail on a match stick.

An inconvenience for me was having to go outdoors and lift up a cellar door that covered the stairs leading to the cellar, where the furnace and washing machine were. That meant I could not keep an eye on the children when I was doing the laundry. Clothes were hung to dry on lines strung on a porch. Of course in winter they froze before they dried.

It was a beautiful fall. As the trees dropped their leaves, we got a better view of the lake beyond the big three-story Snug Harbor house. October came and went, as did most of November, and still no baby. Apparently I had miscalculated. Mother took the children for walks along the lake. A few friends from Wheaton drove up on Sundays to see us during the fall, but there was no opportunity to make new friends that year.

While we were in Wheaton, I had been seeing Dr. Mary Breme for this pregnancy. Her office was over the drugstore in Warrenville. Ted and Mary Lou Benson had recommended her after she saved their baby Marilyn's life. Without a car, getting to Warrenville meant going on the Chicago, Aurora & Elgin electric train. Now a call to Dr. Mary confirmed that she would be willing to induce the birth. So Ken borrowed Clyde Dennis's car to drive me to Community Hospital in Geneva, which explains why Peter was born in Geneva, Illinois, though we lived 80 miles north in Lake Geneva, Wisconsin.

Peter Waldo was born November 26, 1946. Waldo was a family name. Ken's great-grandmother was a Waldo. In her obituary it says she could trace her family back to the tenth century.

Ken brought Becky with him when he came to bring Peter and me home. It was her fourth birthday—December 5. She was pleased to be able to hold her eight-pound baby brother part of the way. Mother Taylor left almost immediately. Duties back home called her. I am reminded of Dr. Chafer at Dallas Seminary telling us about the hymnal with a misprint in the line, "Where duty calls or danger, be never wanting there." It read, "Where duty calls or danger, be never waiting there!"

Mother Taylor died of a stroke the next spring, April 22, 1947, even though she was getting medication for her high blood pressure. It was a week before her 63rd birthday. Ken could not go back to Oregon for her funeral because it would have meant borrowing money, which was unthinkable. It was nine years since his graduation from college, and he still hadn't paid back the $600 (the equivalent of a year at Wheaton College) he had borrowed from his parents during his college years. From this distance in time it is hard to realize how *big* that debt really was. In later years Ken regretted not going to his mother's funeral regardless of the cost.

Our fifth child (Janet) was conceived about the time of Grandma Taylor's death. The book of Ecclesiastes reminds us there is a time to be born and a time to die. Don't we really have to look at Scripture for answers to the mysteries of life? "The Lord gave and the Lord hath taken away; blessed be the name of the Lord" (Job 1:21, KJV).And we have never doubted that "children are an heritage of the Lord" (Psalm 127:3, KJV). So even though we were trying not to have another child in the months after Peter's birth, it wasn't many months before I was pregnant. I do not remember that we were unhappy—just surprised. We really wanted more children, but ideally we would have delayed a little longer, especially in view of the uncertain housing situation. We would have to move again by June 1.

We were happy to learn from Dr. Paul Wright (a chemistry prof at Wheaton) that his house on Irving Avenue, just a block from the college, would be available for the summer while he and his family went to the Black Hills. When we had to leave Snug Harbor before the Wrights' house was available, Gertrude and Clarence Nystrom took all six of us in for ten days or so. That was an unforgettable demonstration of Christian hospitality—an example we have tried to follow.

We moved into the Wrights' house with our cribs, high chairs, and playpen. The baby buggy gave out that summer. During that summer our friend Alan Hamilton was finishing his doctoral program at the University of Chicago, and he had four rooms of "student furniture" to sell. We agreed to buy the lot sight unseen for $200. There were twin beds, two chests of drawers, a breakfast table and four chairs, a couple of living room chairs, a lamp, a coffee table, and a big oak flattop desk and swivel chair. All this furniture was stored in the Wrights' roomy walk-up attic until fall, when we assumed we would need it. No car yet. We were within easy walking distance of College Church, and I pushed the buggy downtown for the weekly grocery shopping.

I saw Dr. Mary in Warrenville a couple of times during the summer. It was late summer before I wrote my mother about being pregnant. She had already heard a rumor to that effect and "hoped it wasn't true!" Mothers have a way of being concerned for their daughters.

30

Winona Lake

WITH AN ENTIRE SUMMER to look, we could surely find a house to rent in the western suburbs. But not much had changed during the year since we had last looked. We didn't have money for a down payment, so buying a house was out of the question.

Toward the end of the summer, when we had not heard of a single house to rent, we wondered if I would have to go home to my parents with the four little ones while Ken rented a room and continued the search. But how could we do that? To impose on my parents—especially without knowing how long the arrangement would last—would have to be our very last resort.

Then an acquaintance, Carl Nill, told us about a summer hotel in Winona Lake, Indiana, that he had just purchased and planned to remodel into apartments. Winona Lake was not within commuting distance of Chicago as Lake Geneva had been, but it was a lot closer than Oregon, and we could still be a family—at least on weekends.

Without benefit of an inspection trip, we moved to the Garfield Hotel in Winona Lake. It was strictly a summer hotel that was used by people attending Bible conferences in Winona Lake. Though it was adjacent to the conference grounds, it was surely the last choice for conference attendees. There was better housing right on the conference grounds, and some local people rented out bedrooms during the summer. We had never been to Winona Lake before, and after that year we never wanted to go back!

We were told that our rooms contained beds and dressers and chairs, so we only moved the cribs, high chairs, and playpen, leaving our recently acquired furniture in the Wrights' attic.

Our "apartment" was four separate hotel rooms at one end of a hall on the second floor. The hallway was boarded off with a door in a makeshift partition to make a semblance of an apartment. The four children slept in one room with a double bed and two cribs. Ken and I had a double bed in another room across the hall. There were no closets in any of the rooms, only a dresser and hooks on the wall. For a stove we had only a two-burner hot plate, which meant no baking—no cookies, cakes, muffins, or pies—as long as we lived there. That was a hardship, as I loved to bake and loved to eat what I baked! There was an icebox—by which I mean an old-fashioned icebox that was kept cold with real ice—but after the weather got cold we stopped buying ice.

The hotel was tolerable in the fall but became less so as cold weather came on. There was no heat in the two rooms we used as bedrooms. Our landlord finally got us a coal stove for the "living room," but of course I was not used to heating with coal and wasn't always successful in keeping a fire going all night. There was a portable kerosene heater in the kitchen, but we felt it was too dangerous to leave it on all night. Both the kerosene and coal had to be carried up a long outside stairway that had been built as a fire escape. One could have nightmares thinking about a fire in that place.

Becky did not start school that fall, as the Winona Lake school had no kindergarten. I should have compensated by teaching her the alphabet and numbers, but I didn't. I believe I was such a poor mother that year that I would gladly erase it from my memory.

Ken had left Good News Publishers during the summer and was now working at the Moody Bible Institute as director-in-training of the Moody Colportage Department. So he still had to commute to Chicago, but now we lived 115 miles away! Ken would leave at 4:00 A.M. each Monday to walk to Warsaw to catch the New York Central train, and he returned on Friday night after the children were in bed. He stayed with a fellow employee, Ray Hill, during the week.

I cried every Monday morning as I crawled back into bed after Ken left. Just the mechanics of living with four young children—then five—kept me busy during the day, but the evenings were pretty awful.

What I remember especially is that we had no books to read, except the Bible. There must have been a library in Warsaw, but we didn't use it. Any books we owned had been packed and left in the Wrights' attic along with our furniture. Apparently I did not mention this frustration to Ken, or he might have been able to bring me and the children some Moody Press books. But he didn't see this gap in our family life on his own.

There was a local bus between Winona Lake and Warsaw, which I took on Saturday when I went grocery shopping while Ken stayed with the children. Also on Saturday I would do his laundry, and on Sunday I ironed his six white shirts, which were *de rigueur* at Moody. This was long before "wash and wear" fabrics. Since there were no laundry facilities at the hotel, we bought our first automatic washer, a Bendix, and we made monthly payments on it. The Bendix was front-loading and tended to "walk," so it had to be bolted to the floor. It made the place shake if a load was unbalanced. There were no domestic clothes dryers at that time, so I strung clotheslines in a large dormitory room next to our four-room "apartment" for drying clothes. It was also a good place for riding tricycles in bad weather.

A family named Zahlout—Al and Verna, with five young girls—lived half a block away. Al was a violinist who gave concerts in churches and supported his family from the special offerings that were taken. Verna and I were congenial, but since Al was home most of the time practicing the violin, I didn't go often and crowd their small house with four more children.

A couple of tenants who were on the first floor when we moved to the Garfield soon found other places to live, and we were alone in this building with many empty rooms. The wind whistled through the halls on windy days. The bathrooms were quite a distance down the hall from our four rooms.

Getting a car became imperative. If a child was sick, I was dependent on neighbors to get to the doctor, and for my prenatal visits I had to leave the children with Verna and take the bus to Warsaw. Very likely a neighbor would have to take me to the hospital in January when the baby was due. Furthermore, the New York Central had only one eastbound train each day, but Ken wanted to come at a moment's notice so he could be with me at the hospital when the baby was born.

In December he found a local farmer who was selling a Dodge sedan that had only 28,000 miles on it. Further good news was that we could buy it for $200. We had that much in our bank account, but not much more. The bad news was that it was 20 years old—cars had changed a great deal between 1928 and 1948. Ken bought it. For the first time ever we could load the children in a car and go for a ride in the country. Only we didn't. There wasn't time with all that had to be done on Saturday and Sunday and the little ones' naps. Besides, the weather had turned cold, and there was no heater in the car.

I could send Becky down the hill, past Mrs. Billy Sunday's house, to the post office to check our mailbox with its simple combination. There would be a weekly letter from Dad Taylor, who was still adjusting to life without Mother, but most days there was no mail. I looked forward to the round-robin letters from my mother and sisters and tried to keep my contributions upbeat. It was not easy. The sameness—the same gray thoughts on gray days—was wearying. When and where would it end?

Even though the war was over, it took time for factories to switch from making war matériel to items for domestic consumption. As a result, I couldn't buy more gauze diapers. Peter was wearing the last of our old supply—two at a time. Mama was able to purchase some white flannel, and she made square diapers for our coming baby like those she had made for her own eight children. She also made baby kimonos with decorative blanket stitching down the front edges and ties of bias tape. It was such a practical outpouring of motherly love.

We had no money to buy Christmas gifts for the children, but Betty Boardman sent a never-to-be-forgotten Christmas box with coloring books and new crayons and scissors. Betty and her husband, Don, had been classmates of Ken's at Wheaton. Frances Ferries, our former neighbor on Seminary Street, sent new clothes for the children.

With the first really cold weather in December we had some frozen pipes, so I called a plumber. Before coming out from Warsaw, he wanted to know who would pay. He was leery of absentee landlords. I assured him we would. We paid and then subtracted the amount from our next rent check. Naturally the pipes froze again, but during a January thaw I discovered that a broken pipe on the second floor was sending a fountain of water in an arc over the open stairway balustrade down to the entrance hall and lobby below. I figured all that water would do a lot of damage. Something had to be done, and I couldn't wait for a plumber. I remembered him complaining that the shut-off valve was under the building at the far end of the crawl space. I was familiar with the crawl space, as our coal supply had been shoveled inside to keep it dry.

I would have to find that valve and shut off the water. So I grabbed a jacket and a flashlight and went under the hotel, crawling on hands and knees through cobwebs and over the musty dirt. I finally located a pipe and followed it to the valve. I don't think I was afraid, but it surely was not a pleasant experience. When I was back upstairs in our apartment and had dusted off my clothes, I called the plumber because now all the water was off. Same question: Who is going to pay?

When he came, he called up from the bottom of the back stairs. I opened the door at the top of the stairs and stood there, the children crowding around me, explaining what had happened. He was horrified.

"Lady, don't you ever do that again," he said emphatically. "What if something had happened to you under there?" (I was nine months pregnant and must have looked twice as pregnant from his vantage point, looking up the steps!) "What would the children do if . . ." He couldn't finish. It was too awful for him to contemplate. "If it ever happens again, just let the whole place float away!" And he repeated himself for emphasis.

I agreed to let the Garfield Hotel float, as I began to realize I had probably done a foolish thing in leaving the children while trying to protect somebody else's property. Then the plumber went under the hotel again to cut off only the water to the broken pipe—but that meant that the bathrooms lost their water supply.

The water heater was in the hotel kitchen below us, so we always had hot water for doing dishes, for the children's baths (in the kitchen sink), and for the washing machine. But for the next five months I had to take sponge baths in the kitchen and carry a bucket of water down the hall to the bathroom when the toilet needed flushing.

The second week in January, we bundled up and drove to Fort Wayne to meet my sister Harriet at the train station. She was taking five-year-old Becky and 13-month-old Peter back to Detroit on the next eastbound train as my due date was getting close.

That still left John, just turned four, and Martha, nearly three, needing a place to stay while I would be in the hospital for a week. I couldn't ask the Zahlouts, for they simply didn't have room. I finally asked two families in the Free Methodist church where we attended if they could each take one child. I hoped and prayed that the second great commandment, "Love your neighbor as yourself," would motivate them, and it did. Unfortunately, I can't give those families proper credit here, for I do not remember their names!

The next Monday Ken drove the old blue Dodge to Chicago rather than take the train. When I left for the hospital in the middle of the night, I called him, and he was able to leave immediately. Al Zahlout left his sleeping children to drive me to the hospital. Verna, who was spending the night with me "just in case," stayed with sleeping John and Martha, and in the morning she took them to the homes where they would be staying.

The fifth hospital and fifth attending physician for our fifth child! It was a small hospital, actually owned by the doctor. I was completely anesthetized and remember nothing of the birth. Ken arrived before the birth and remembers all too well. For the first time he was allowed in the delivery room. He has written in his book about the baby, being held back until the doctor finally arrived, and that the baby was not breathing when she was born, and how he prayed for the life of our little one. God graciously answered his prayer and spared our baby's life.

We discussed whether we should stick to Bible names, but we decided that wasn't necessary. True, the first four had Bible names, but we hadn't chosen them for that reason. They were names we liked and could agree on. We chose Janet Elizabeth, so she does have a biblical middle name. Elizabeth was also Ken's paternal grandmother's name.

My only memory of the week in that little country hospital is of loud caterwauling under my window one night. It was not a tomcat, but a mental patient who had gotten outside but couldn't find her way back. She might have frozen to death in her nightgown and bare feet.

I cried when Ken came to take me and baby Janet home. I thought I was crying for the baby, who would have such inhospitable surroundings for the first weeks and months of her life, but I was really crying for myself. We were going back to four dark, drafty rooms with paper curtains and no pictures or carpeting. Rooms that didn't connect to each other except through the hotel hallway. A bare light bulb hanging from the ceiling in each room. The balky coal stove. No bathroom. Baby Janet would be unaware of any of that.

We had to keep our wraps on while we got the stoves going, for with no heat in that uninsulated building, it was as cold indoors as out. When the "apartment" was warm, Ken went to pick up John and Martha.

One bright spot that illuminated the darkness was the baby shower by mail from my friends at College Church in Wheaton. They waited until after Janet's birth so that the gifts would be most appropriate. Betty Boardman sent a hand-smocked dress. How could I ever repay such love?

Two weeks later we drove to Fort Wayne again to pick up Becky and Peter at the train station. Peter had learned to walk while at Aunt Harriet's. Would I be able to keep him in the playpen anymore?

We probably had a babysitter more than the two times I remember in those nine months (but then again, maybe we didn't!). Once we were invited to someone's home for dinner, *sans* children. It was my first time to eat chiffon cake. And in the spring we went to see the play *Mama Knows Best* at the Warsaw High School. A boy who lived with his grandmother in a house next to the Garfield Hotel had a part in the play.

Spring was never more welcome! The three older children could finally spend some time outdoors. On one of those occasions they failed to latch the safety gate behind them, and 16-month-old Peter got out on the landing at the top of the stairs and fell 12 or 15 feet to the hard-packed ground below. I heard Peter crying. The sound was coming from a distance, so I raced to the living room window. Yes, the crying was coming from outdoors.

I knew I mustn't panic. When I got to the top of the fire escape stairs, I could see Peter on the ground below. I stumbled down the steps and picked him up. Getting back up the stairs was harder, my knees wanting to buckle. I put him down on the couch and checked as well as I could for broken bones. None as far as I could tell. Just a tiny cut on his upper lip where a tooth had punctured it.

Peter's crying wakened baby Janet in her basket and she started to cry. Big sister Becky had followed us up the stairs, concerned for her baby brother, though not taking all the blame for failing to latch the baby gate. She picked up Janet while I continued to hold Peter.

When his crying subsided, I was finally able to call the doctor. "Our 16-month old fell from the second floor to the hard ground. Except for a cut on his lip he seems to be all right. Should I bring him in?" He didn't think it was necessary. Just keep him awake and watch his eyes. I agreed, though I wasn't sure what I was supposed to detect in his eyes.

"Thank you, dear God, for your holy angels, who must have cushioned the fall."

Ken was somewhere in the deep South, visiting rural schools that used books from the Moody Colportage program, so I couldn't call him to tell him how Peter's life had been spared.

Peter was too young to consciously remember the fall, but he professes to have an extreme fear of falling. Apparently that event was programmed into his subconscious mind. And in subsequent years, Peter was kept from serious injury or possible death in bicycle accidents, falls from trees, and having a huge cable spool run over him. Our times—Peter's times—are in God's hands.

In late spring all five children had regular measles, probably picked up at Sunday school. That taxed my nursing abilities! There was no rocking chair to rock even one sick child.

If I were to live life over again and couldn't purchase a rocking chair, I would beg or borrow one. Babies and rocking just naturally go together with lullabies, even half-forgotten ones. I always had to create my own rocking motion by sitting on the edge of a chair. It just isn't the same.

Sometime in 1947 my dad gave us $1,000 to help us meet our housing needs. It was a help, but not enough for a down payment on an existing house, even a very modest one. Out of desperation, Ken succumbed to an offer to finish a house that would be framed in Northlake, a new suburb that was developing west of Chicago along

North Avenue. He put down the $1,000 from Dad. But the deal fell through months later when he went to Northlake and found that the house had not even been started.

To tell the truth, I wasn't sorry about the failure, at least not after we got our money back. I hadn't seen any evidence that Ken was handy with tools—not that we had more than a hammer, screwdriver, and pliers. "Where there is a will, there is a way," but neither of us had any experience in putting up wallboard, painting, or papering, and the house would have to pass inspection in order to qualify for a mortgage.

Did I have unreasonable expectations because of the truly fine home I had lived in during my teen years? Perhaps. And where would we live while Ken was working on the house? Another limiting factor was time. By the time he got home from work, ate dinner, and drove to the worksite, he would have three hours at most. And I wouldn't be able to help because I would have to stay with the children.

Neither could I let my husband down and say flat out, "It won't work, so why even try?" I was supposed to be a helpmeet, a builder-upper, not one to tear down. Male egos are as fragile as bone-china teacups. Drop one and the handle comes off every time! (At that stage of our married life, though, the illustration was more theoretical than based on experience. We didn't own *any* china, much less bone china, and we were using the heavy restaurant dishes from the hotel kitchen.)

It was with great relief that we learned that the Wrights' home in Wheaton would again be available for the summer.

31

Wheaton, Here We Come Again

IN JUNE we happily left Winona Lake for Wheaton, taking the cribs, high chair, playpen, tricycles, and the Bendix washer. Now we even had a car to park in the Wrights' driveway. I could finally drive to the bank, post office, and grocery, but I still went only once a week—on Saturday, never taking the children with me.

With an entire summer to look, plan, and pray, we hoped we would find the answer to our need for more permanent housing and get more stability in our lives.

But Ken's looking, planning, and praying was not confined to our family's needs. There was his challenging work at Moody Literature Mission (his new, up-to-date name for the old Moody Colportage Department). His vision was broader than just inexpensive Christian literature in English. What about our neighbors to the south in Mexico and Central and South America? Were their needs being met for Spanish teaching materials, doctrinal studies, and storybooks for children? A visit in person seemed the logical way to find out, so Ken made a trip in the summer of 1948 that took him to Mexico, Panama, Costa Rica, Honduras, Colombia, and Ecuador.

We began seriously thinking of buying a house if the $1,000 that my dad had given us would be sufficient for a down payment. At a Sunday night fellowship group in College Church, we got acquainted with Doug and Virginia Muir, who were also looking for a house. Could we, and should we, pool our resources? They had two little girls and did not want to spend another winter in a small house trailer out in the country. But there was almost nothing available, especially at the low end of the scale that our two families could afford.

Then we found a large two-story house on Pennsylvania Avenue at the western edge of Glen Ellyn for $15,000. If we bought it together, the Muirs could live on one floor and our family on the other. Not an ideal situation, but we were willing to settle for the less-than-ideal. I checked out the Glen Ellyn school Becky and John would be attending. We were cautioned against signing any papers until the five families who were occupying the house had moved. Nobody could guess how long that would be.

Labor Day was coming, and nothing was settled—in fact, it was very unsettled. The Muirs were living in their trailer, so a delay was not so crucial to them, but Labor Day meant moving day for us. This was the fourth September out of the previous five that we were uncertain about housing, and we were wondering if the Lord heard our prayers. And with each move there had been an additional child.

The Lord answered our prayers through friends, as he often does. When we had no place to go and needed to move out of Doc Wright's house, Ted and Mary Lou Benson said we could set up our beds in their basement, and that is what we did. It meant moving trunks, old bicycles, and other things we might use again. The beds were jammed together between the furnace and the laundry tubs and under the clotheslines we used on rainy days. It was a small house, hardly large enough for Ted and Mary Lou and their six young children, but they had enlarged hearts. "When God's children are in need, be the one to help them out. And get into the habit of inviting guests home for dinner or, if they need lodging, for the night" (Romans 12:13, NLT).

There was only one bathroom for 12 of us, not counting our babies still in diapers. And only one kitchen range and one refrigerator, so there was no choice but to cook as if we were one family and eat together. Since it was Mary Lou's kitchen, she did most of the cooking.

One week of doubled-up living would have been tolerable—something we could laugh about in later years—but one week became one month, then it was two months, with still nothing finalized on our house deal. Ken was gone from 6:30 A.M. to 6:00 P.M., so he missed most of the stress. He even took a ten-day trip to the Pacific Northwest for Moody Literature Mission to see how to widen distribution of inexpensive Christian books among Native Americans.

Ted was the executive director of the Alumni Association at Wheaton College. His office was just a block away. He did the grocery shopping since Mary Lou didn't drive. Ted could roll with the punches from our combined 11 children, the eldest of whom was nine!

While no progress was being made in vacating the Glen Ellyn house, we learned of a property in Wheaton with two houses at the same price. Furthermore, it was within walking distance of both the College Avenue train station and Holmes School, where Becky and John were attending. Since neither the Muirs nor we could qualify for a conventional mortgage, it was gratifying that the Fueszes, who were retiring and moving to Florida, were agreeable to selling on contract. We overlooked the shortcomings of the houses and agreed to buy. But there was a hitch when it came to the final closing—the Muirs had not come up with money for a down payment. We went back to the Bensons with heavy hearts.

This new uncertainty about when their hospitality and extreme generosity could be terminated was more than Mary Lou could take. She was pregnant with their seventh child, and one day she picked up her two youngest boys and took the train to Chicago to stay at her parents' home. When would she come back? We were the cause of her despair, but where could *we* go, when we were already in the basement, literally and figuratively?

Ah yes, the Garfield Hotel in Winona Lake—still there and still empty. I found another Holmes School family to take Becky in. She was behind her classmates in first grade and couldn't afford to miss school. How long would we be there? Nobody knew. Ken took his sleeping bag to work, prepared to sleep in an anteroom. I loaded the old blue chariot with bedding, the other four children, and a box of Pablum, the basis of their diet. I was terribly unsure of how I would cope, but preserving our friendship with Ted and Mary Lou was more important than my convenience. Ten-month-old Janet rode in a canvas infant seat hooked over the front seat. What we did on arrival and how long we stayed—a week or more than a week—has been completely erased from my memory!

Then came the good news: Come back! The final papers were ready to sign. Doug Muir had been able to get a loan from Herman Fischer of College Church to complete his down payment.

We moved on Monday of Thanksgiving week (1948), bringing the cribs and highchairs from the Bensons' basement and the four rooms of "student furniture" from Paul Wright's attic. For a few dollars we purchased with the house an old refrigerator, a still-older upright piano, a beat-up studio couch, and a couple of dressers with peeling veneer and balky drawers. We couldn't afford to be choosy.

What a memorable Thanksgiving! After eight years of marriage and repeated moves, we could settle down and stay put. The huge yard with its big trees was a bonus. We shared our thanks to God with friends at a traditional Thanksgiving dinner. Also thanks to another family who gave us their extra set of dishes. Our first dishes!

1515 East Forest Avenue

WE SUBDIVIDED the property on Forest Avenue as best we could. Ken and I took the old house, which was larger, and the Muirs got the newer house, which had been built for a Fuesz daughter during the Depression. Our share of the $15,000 cost came to $6,300.

The two houses were close together, separated only by the gravel driveway. There was also a large dirt-floor garage with attached sheds in the back, and three chicken houses. The Muirs tore down the chicken house on their property right away, but we kept "the red shed" and "the white shed," though there was no thought of having chickens. Without a basement, we used those sheds for assorted storage through the years.

Ken would tell guests that the only reason we didn't have a cow was that I refused to milk it. And who would supervise five young children in a firetrap of a house while I was out in the barn? Actually, it was never a serious consideration. The Welches up the street did have a cow, and the Holmstens across from them had a few sheep. This was within the Wheaton city limits, one block from President Street!

The state of euphoria at having a house of our own—our very own, not shared with another family—was tempered somewhat by its obvious limitations. We hadn't thought there would be a house in the city limits that did not have a furnace, or that *we* would live in it if there were! While we had no idea how old the house was (perhaps 80 years), the last owners had lived in it for 18 years, and they had survived without central heat. We would too.

I had never seen such a bare kitchen. There was a potbellied coal stove in the middle of the room, like one might see in a Norman Rockwell painting of an old country store. There was a sink in one corner, an ancient gas range in another corner, a refrigerator, and an enamel-top table under the window—but not a counter, cupboard, or shelf anywhere.

Between the sink and range was an open doorway into a bit of hall with access to a walk-in pantry, a bathroom, and a little closet containing the water heater. There was just room in that hall to install the Bendix washer without closing off access to the pantry. It would drain into the kitchen sink.

There were two other doors in the kitchen. One led into the combined living/dining room, and one to the enclosed side porch. The rear entrance to the house was through that side porch, but it wasn't visible to anyone parking in the driveway or in the gravel parking area behind the house. One had to go around the corner to find the back door. When coming in or out through the porch, there was an inescapable odor of fuel oil. One end of the porch had been partitioned off, and in that closed area was a 50 gallon drum of fuel oil. The spigot dripped, and it was evident that the container that caught the drip had periodically run over, so the soft wood floor was soaked with oil.

A positive feature was that the porch had space for an indoor clothesline for the almost daily loads of laundry for our family of seven (with two in diapers). Another plus was that the woodwork throughout the house had been given a fresh coat of white enamel paint. Also the wallpaper in the living room and bedrooms seemed to be new. The linoleum on the floors was definitely not. The ceilings of the first floor rooms were of patterned pressed tin, like in some of the old stores on Front Street. They got dingy from the stoves and were not easy to wash between paintings.

The living/dining room (maybe 24' x 11') had an oil stove for heat. There were four large windows, but three of these opened onto the enclosed porches, not the spacious front and backyards. The fourth window looked out on the Muirs' house across the narrow gravel drive. Consequently, the room was fairly dark, and even on sunny days it didn't receive any direct sunshine. At least Mrs. Fuesz had left heavy lace curtains on those windows, for which I was grateful.

There wasn't going to be any available cash for "fixing up." We would have to buy a half ton of coal right away. It would be stored in one of the chicken houses in the backyard. There wasn't much fuel oil left in the drum, either.

The master bedroom was over the living room and of the same size except for a walk-in closet across the end. A faded cloth curtain hung in the closet doorway. The big oak desk that was part of our student furniture went in that bedroom under the south windows. There was a small oil-burning stove for heat.

The other two bedrooms were small, and we had to walk through a corner of one bedroom to enter the other. There was a tiny closet over the stairs in one bedroom, but the other bedroom had no closet at all. It did have a register opening in the floor so heat from the kitchen below could waft up into the bedroom. The opening also served as a wireless intercom: "Breakfast is ready, hurry down!"

The first family member to visit us was my sister Harriet from Detroit. Harriet was one to speak her mind. When she came into our living room, she looked around, put her hands on her hips and pronounced, "Well, Margaret, what you ought to do is tear it down and start over."

Later, we learned that the house may have been a remodeled barn.

That might explain the lack of uniformity in the windows. No two rooms were the same, as if windows had been purchased from a demolition company and holes were cut to fit. The indoor wood trim around doors and windows had no finishing details—corners not even mitered. Of course, both Harriet and I realized that our standards may have been out of line with reality because of the fine home we had lived in during and after our teen years, with its polished hardwood floors, Philippine mahogany woodwork, and every convenience of the day.

Not only did this house have no basement, but it had no proper foundation either. The corners of the house were supported by concrete blocks, and sheets of tin were wrapped around the base of the house as a sort of camouflage. So in winter the air *under* the house was as cold as the air *around* the house, and that cold air came up through the walls and center partition. In winter my feet were numb all the time because of the cold floors.

Our lots were 635 feet deep—the equivalent of two city blocks—and behind them was a large field. In our front yard were a number of mature shade trees, a few fruit trees, and clumps of lilacs. Behind the houses the property was open. Except for garden plots and a small area of grass, we allowed the deep backyard to grow up to tall grass. There was too much to mow with a hand mower, which was all we had.

In the first six years of living in that old farmhouse, three more children were born, and we needed more space. So in 1954 we changed the enclosed front porch into bedrooms for the three boys, and the side porch into a dining room. That same year Ken installed a "crawl space" furnace from Sears Roebuck under the house. He lay on his stomach under the kitchen floor and loosened the dirt with a trowel. When he had filled a bucket with dirt and clay, the older children dragged it out and emptied it. We had already moved the coal stove from the kitchen to one of the sheds during the summer. Now it didn't need to come back. Happy day! The oil heater in the living room went to the junk man, too, but we kept the one in our bedroom. Even with the furnace, the children's rooms weren't heated.

When we had been in the house for a few years, a family in the church called to say they had bought a new sofa but the old one was still serviceable. Would we like it? My answer was yes, without asking about style, color, or fabric. We only had the worn studio couch we inherited with the house. With the "new" *pink* sofa, as it turned out to be, we could sit with comfort and not have a cold back. The studio couch was moved up to Ken's and my bedroom where it had more years of service as a second bed.

Table lamps were not an option for two reasons. One, we had no end tables. Two, a lamp wouldn't have lasted a week because of constant knocking over. We did have one heavy floor lamp, and eventually I was able to get two hanging wall lamps with S & H green stamps. They survived ball throwing in the house—even if windows did not.

After we had gone through a couple sets of breakfast chairs (the second set being tubular steel with vinyl seats that we rescued from the curb after the neighbors threw them out), Ken learned that Moody Bible Institute was selling off excess classroom chairs for two or three dollars each. He bought a dozen. They were sturdy oak chairs, but they had been taken out of circulation for a reason. They were well worn, and the edges of the seats were rough and chipped.

Some had numerals stenciled on the back for attendance purposes. Sometimes guests thought *we* had put the numbers on so our children would know where to sit—the number five child in the number five chair, etc. But we had more than one number five chair. Those chairs never did die of old age. We still have a few of them (they're great for standing on when hanging wallpaper), as do our daughters Marty and Mary Lee, who found the chairs (then free for the taking) good seating when they started married life.

Home improvements, as noted in our 1959 Christmas letter, "include tiling the kitchen and back hall floors and tearing down the garage and attached sheds. Margaret appreciates the additional landscape now in view from the kitchen window. One can see squirrels, rabbits, and pheasants, as well as smaller birds."

33

Louise Clara Multnomah West, 1889–1950

We had only been in our house for a little over five months when word came that Mama's exploratory surgery revealed advanced lung cancer. That explained why she had been troubled so long by a cough. She had had a radical mastectomy seven years earlier, and now cancer had again reared its ugly head.

The family said that if we wanted to see Mama we probably should come right away. If we waited until summer, it might be too late. I called five families we knew. Could each family keep one child of ours while we went to Oregon to see my dying mother? They all could.

We flew out on a DC-3. Papa and Mama met us at Swan Island Airport. They had had a long wait as we had made an unscheduled stop in Montana and were late in getting to Portland. This was our first time to see the four-bedroom house they had moved to a number of years earlier. It was well-suited to their needs. Alan had graduated from high school and was doing his stint in the Army.

To my shame, I have to say we did not spend that much time with Mama. We had not been home for seven years, so we were invited here and there by friends for lunch and dinner, and we didn't have sense to decline. Nor did we talk with her about death or heaven when we *were* together.

We visited Dad Taylor, too, who had been living alone since Mother Taylor's death two years earlier. Lyman was away at college.

The last night of our visit, we had dinner at the Union Depot with Papa and Mama before boarding the eastbound train. It is one thing to hug and kiss your mother good-bye when you know you may not see her for a long time, but it is quite another when you know you won't see her again this side of heaven. But I didn't cry until we were safely on the train.

Mama's strong body didn't want to give up, and she lived another 16 months. She died at home September 24, 1950, at age 60. Like Ken when his mother died, I did not return to Oregon for her funeral because of the cost involved.

My father was much comforted by her testimony, which he found in her desk. He had copies printed to be given out at the funeral home, and it was read by her pastor, the Rev. Mr. E. Eichmann, at her funeral:

> It looks now as if I might be spared the lingering and agonizing pain that is the usual fate of cancer sufferers, but be that as it may, come weal or woe, I can trust the Lord for grace to accept cheerfully, as from Him, whatever He sends.
>
> His grace and mercy that are new every morning will go with me all the way, even through the dark valley of the shadow of death, and I shall dwell in the house of the Lord forever.
>
> He has forgiven all my sins, and I am accepted in the beloved. (Ephesians 1:6)

Dad finally went to a Lutheran church, as the funeral service was at Trinity Lutheran. At Mama's request, the pastor based his message on the text "accepted in the beloved." Dad was surrounded by many in our family, including Grandma Trappe, who survived her daughter by several years.

Mama was a woman of few words, a faithful wife, a hard worker, and a gardener *par excellence.* She had unassuming faith in her Lord and lots of common sense.

I'm sorry that our children grew up without having known their grandmother, but maybe they can see some of her in me—except that I'm not a gardener.

On August 21, 1951, Papa married Edna Sandblom, the red-haired teacher from Tigard High School. She was a wonderful wife for Papa until his death in 1973.

34

MARTHA

LIKE ME, Martha probably can't remember learning to read. She learned at such an early age and so easily.

Whatever Becky and John could do, Martha could do, and often at an earlier age. As soon as she could walk, she was running. Consequently, there were more bumps and falls as things just naturally got in her way. She loved to climb, too. If we had owned chandeliers, she would have been swinging from them at 18 months.

We were living in Winona Lake, where there was no kindergarten, when Becky turned five. When she started first grade in Wheaton, she had not been introduced to reading, and (to my great shame) she could not count to ten. But she could mother a baby in grand style. So Becky had to catch up with book learning in first grade, and she did.

I am sorry that I bought into the education theory of that day that "teachers know best" and that parents should leave the teaching to them. What rubbish! Everything a child learns from the day he is born is taught him—by example if not by precept. Even neglect is a form of teaching, which today's educators seek to make up for through programs like Head Start.

John was learning about words in kindergarten. At home Martha just naturally learned from her big sister and brother. The first book she learned to read as a four-year-old was *Three Little Kittens*. A skeptic listening to her read it could have said, "She has it memorized and knows when to turn the pages." Of course she had it memorized. Young children want their favorite books read to them over and over again until parent and child both have them memorized, and even then they want them read again and again. And the parent who omits a repetitious line or tries to skip a whole page will be soundly corrected!

It was with that book that Martha learned to identify printed words with those she knew by sound and had in her head. And if she could read one book, she could read others, and she did—dozens of them. In that pre-kindergarten year, I brought home many books from the Wheaton Public Library to keep her occupied.

Martha couldn't start kindergarten the year after John, though she was 13 months younger, because her birthday was in January. Becky and John, with December birthdays, were among the very youngest in their classes. At that time children could start kindergarten if they turned five before January 1.

When she did start kindergarten, I was bringing even more books home from the library for Martha to read. She was certainly reading at the fourth-grade level, if not beyond. And she had learned simple arithmetic, too. It was obvious there would be no challenge in first grade. Obvious to me, her mother. But could I buck the school system?

I knew that Miss Johnston, the principal of Holmes School, was adamantly opposed to children's skipping grades. So I did the unthinkable, especially for me, and went over her head. During the summer following Martha's kindergarten year, I made an appointment with the superintendent of schools. He listened sympathetically to my plea that she be allowed to start in second grade in September; that she was two years behind John in school because of their birth dates but only one year behind in age—and in many ways ahead of him because of her disposition.

He emphasized that if a child were ever allowed to be double-promoted, he or she would have to rank at the top of the new class, not be dragging in any area, and be able to socialize at that level. I assured him that Martha would qualify in every respect. I'm sure I sounded like a pushy parent, but I only wanted what was best for her, and she wasn't going to find it in the first grade.

He made no promises, and I did not hear from him or his office. Consequently, Martha was enrolled in first grade on schedule. But it wasn't long before she reported that a man came to school and took her out in the hall and "played games" with her. Then he came back another day and asked if she would like to visit second grade. She would. The next thing she reported was that she was going to *stay* in second grade. Miss Johnston never mentioned it to me in writing or orally when I saw her at school! And I never heard of another student skipping a grade at Holmes School.

As I was sure she would, Martha excelled academically all through school. In addition to being active in our church's high school youth group, she was on the YFC Quiz Team and was Fox Valley Quizzer of the Year when she was a senior.

Immediately after her graduation from Wheaton College, Martha married Ken Thomson, whom she had dated since her senior year in high school. After Ken's graduation from Trinity Evangelical Divinity School, they moved to Washington, D.C.

After a few years a social worker friend asked Martha and Ken if they could take in a young sister and brother who were being neglected because their mother was ill and their father was an alcoholic. What might have been a temporary arrangement became permanent, and Lee and Joe Mason have been a part of our family ever since.

35

PETER

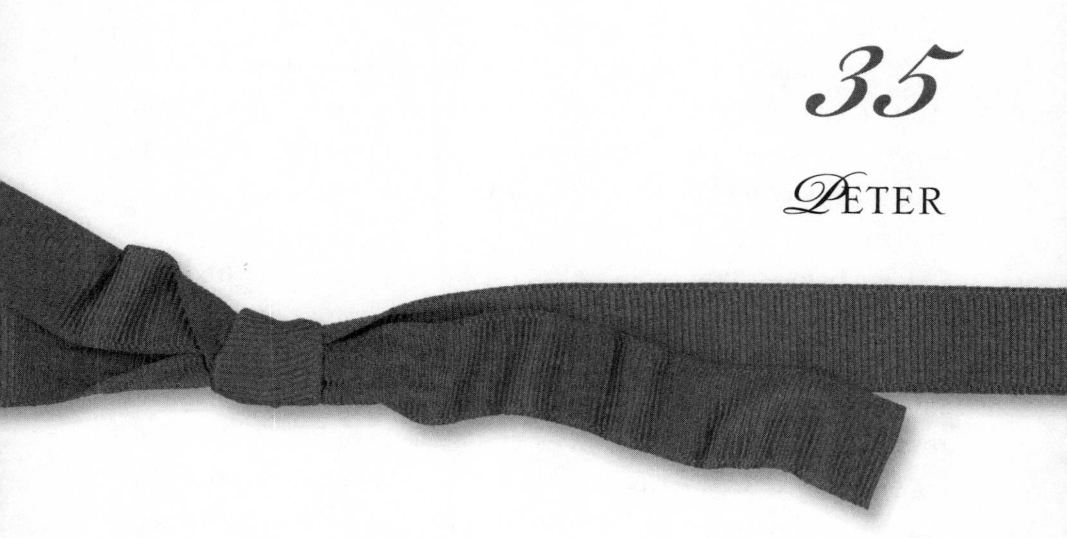

DR. JAMES DOBSON'S book *The Strong-Willed Child* was published in 1978, much too late to help us with Peter. His strong will was very evident even in infancy. As soon as he could roll over with ease, he took delight in getting away from me when I was changing his diaper. Since putting on a diaper with pins requires both hands, I learned I would have to do the operation on the floor and put my knee in his abdomen to keep him in position. You might think he would tire of this after a few dozen times, but this went on as long as he was in diapers, which was a long time. I had never heard of a child going to kindergarten in diapers, but I was afraid it might come to that.

Did he behave the same way for Ken, too? Well, Peter was only our fourth child. Ken wasn't into changing diapers yet!

Peter and I had it out with his naps when he was two and three and refused to stay in bed. He was spanked over and over. Once, he came downstairs, ruler in hand, and said, "Spank stick, spank." I spanked.

The spring that he was in kindergarten, Peter burst in the back door. "Look, Mommy!" What would it be this time? a finger painting? a snake skin? a dead bird? I turned to give him a hug and look at his offering. Tulips! A fistful of big red tulips. "I picked them for you," he said. We had no tulips in our yard.

Of my conflicting emotions, it was disappointment that won out. "How could you, Peter? Didn't you know you were stealing? Those flowers belonged to somebody else." I wish I had said, "They're beautiful. Let's put them on the dining room table. Did a lady say you could pick them?"

Long before this incident, I had established a pattern with Peter. I would punish or lay blame first and then ask questions. That's terrible—never giving a child the benefit of the doubt, tearing down rather than building up. But he was guilty or disobedient over and over, in ways that his three older siblings had not been.

When we think we have heard every childhood memory of our combined children, a new one comes up. One summer when seven of our grown children were together, they talked about how cold it was when they were children, walking the mile to and from Holmes School or delivering newspapers or eggs. Peter told about the time it was so cold on his paper route that he knew he couldn't keep going, so he decided he would lie down in the snow and die. He had read that snow could actually make you feel warm. He would die warm, but his parents would forever be sorry that they had made him take the paper route that cost him his life. Thankfully, he found that he didn't get warm, so he got up and shook off the snow. We didn't hear whether or not he finished the paper route that day.

Peter had a congenital heart problem, or perhaps it developed when he had rheumatic fever and endocarditis his senior year in high school. Dr. Mary sent him from Community Hospital in Geneva to a cardiologist at Presbyterian-St. Luke's in Chicago. Whatever the irregularity, it must have been something unusual, for Peter reported that a steady stream of doctors and interns listened to his heart. Surgery was not recommended, but he was told he should plan to lead a sedentary life so as not to put too much strain on his heart.

He had to have a physical the next year when he entered Southern

Illinois University. After a doctor put a stethoscope to his heart, the verdict was "no phys. ed. for you." Peter wrote us, "They won't even let me play Ping-Pong." Later, when his number came up in the Army draft, he was classified 4-F because of this heart problem.

Peter transferred from SIU to Greenville College in hopes that he would meet God there and have his life turned around, as he had seen happen to his older brother John. God knew all about that desire, and he graciously answered in the fall evangelistic services. Peter's life, all doubts removed, has never been the same.

Not only did he meet God that first year, but he met Sharon Potts, who understood him as no one else ever had. Less than two years later, they were married and established a Christian home. They could write a book about answers to prayer in their lives and those of their three sons.

After he was married and farming in Wisconsin, Peter compensated for his heart problem by lying down in the field when he got too tired. At the same time, he was exposed to the concept of faith healing in a house church that he and Sharon attended. But Peter assumed that it was God's will for him to live with this limiting heart condition, and he did not seek healing. But the Lord had other plans. On October 28, 1971, Peter wrote me only the bare facts: "Tonight the Lord gave knowledge of my condition to a preacher who doesn't know me. He prayed and thanked God for my healing, and I accepted it." Later Peter told us that this visiting preacher had said, "There is someone here tonight with a heart condition whom the Lord would like to heal." Then he prayed. Peter did not have to move to the "healing seat" or in any way indicate to others that he was that person.

Dramatic confirmation came the very next day. After he moved a refrigerator down the steps to their basement, he came back up all excited. "Sharon, I'm not even panting!"

Ken was on a lengthy overseas trip at the time. In his Bible reading on October 28, he was especially struck with Jesus' instructions to the government official: "Go back home. Your son is healed!" (John

4:50, TLB). He noted the date in the margin of his Bible. He was sure it applied to the spiritual healing of our son John, for whom we had been praying for years.

I met Ken at the Portland airport for a bit of vacation when he returned. Before long he was asking about John. I had to report that there was no news. "But there's good news about Peter. His heart has been healed!" We were not accustomed to hearing news like that in our church, so it was gracious of the Lord to confirm it to Ken on the other side of the world. The date he had written in his Bible matched the date of Peter's letter.

36

JANET

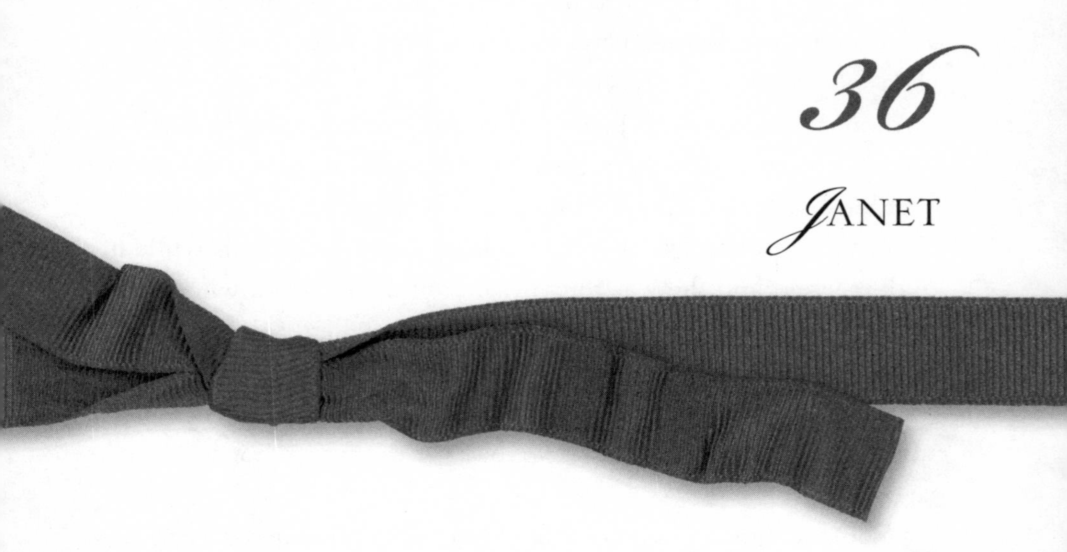

IN HER INFANCY we could soon see that baby Janet's eyes did not track together. When we moved to Wheaton, we had access to fine ophthalmologists. She was diagnosed as having amblyopia, "lazy eye." Janet got her first glasses at 22 months. It was a constant struggle to see that she kept them on and to find the glasses if she discarded them outdoors. Over the years, all of the standard treatments for "lazy eye," such as exercises and patching the good eye, were a trial that Janet had to bear to no avail. Eventually, at age 12, she had surgery to keep the weak eye straight.

Another problem we detected when Janet was very young was poor hearing. We found ourselves raising our voices to get her attention. An ear, nose, and throat specialist recommended that her adenoids be removed. There was marked improvement in her hearing as a result.

Janet didn't smile or laugh as an infant, and in that respect she was unlike our other babies. Perhaps the combination of poor eyesight and poor hearing explains her soberness.

Like Martha, Janet learned to read before going to kindergarten.

The way she remembers it is that words just fell into place one day, and she ran next door and announced to Mary Muir, "I can read!" Then she proceeded to teach Mary!

About that same time Janet started playing the piano by ear. We later learned that she is blessed with perfect pitch. With Becky, John, and Martha taking lessons, Janet heard plenty of simple pieces being practiced. We started Janet on piano lessons while in kindergarten, and she was the only one of the children who never asked to quit. She had lessons right through college. We were still living in the old house when her piano teacher urged us to get a grand piano for Janet's sake, and we were able to do that, paying as much for a good used piano as we had for the whole house 15 years earlier!

Janet made good grades in school but perhaps studied harder than some of her siblings to attain them. Like Becky, John, and Martha, she was active in the high school youth group at church and went on missions projects to needy areas in Kentucky.

She was sure that wearing glasses was the reason for her not having dates while in high school, though she was well liked. Getting contact lenses (finally) the summer following graduation boosted her morale tremendously. Surely she would have dates when she started at Wheaton College. And she did.

Janet had more reason to come home on weekends than Martha had; we had just moved into our new home (built in 1966), and she literally rolled like a dog on the shag carpeting in the family room to show her enjoyment.

In the summer of 1970, she and Ray Wells, a fellow Wheaton graduate, were married in France. None of the family attended. Later they had a family ceremony at a house in Cape Cod where we were vacationing. Without jobs they were free to go anywhere, and they decided on Oregon and settled in Salem. They taught and later had an experimental group home for troubled girls. But theirs was a troubled marriage, and it finally ended in divorce.

Janet was much helped by friends in a house church. And wanting to help others, she got a master's degree in counseling and became a family and marriage therapist. With that career, God has used her to bless many, many individuals and families.

All's Well That Ends Well

I WAKENED Ken in the middle of the night. Time to go to Geneva Hospital again, where Peter had been born. The roads were terribly icy, and we didn't relish the cold drive in our old Dodge, now three years older (and colder, if that could be) than when Ken had purchased it so he could drive from Chicago to Winona Lake for Janet's birth.

It had been a normal pregnancy, and fortunately, it was a normal delivery. I was given no anesthesia or pain killer, and only the night nurse was in attendance, as Dr. Mary didn't make it in time over the icy roads. Ken had to turn right around ("Drive carefully"), for we had left five sleeping children at home.

We named the baby Mark Douglas. Now we had three girls and three boys—the six children I had earlier thought would be the right-sized family. Lots of companionship—enough for game playing indoors or out (as if game playing were the most important thing in life, along with plenty of books, of course). That was what I relished about my childhood, and I wanted the same for our children. I could not foresee that TV would forever change childhood, plunging children into a commercial, adult world. Laughter would come from a pie in the face, not from watching an S-shaped row of dominoes tumble when the first one was pushed.

Mark was born on January 16, 1951, Janet's third birthday. That is not as uncommon in families as one might think. Mark himself now has five children, and two share a birthday.

Our three bedrooms were full, but we wouldn't always live in this house with the ugly coal stove smack dab in the middle of the kitchen, the oil stove in the living room, and no heat in the children's bedrooms. Or would we?

Ken went back to work as soon as I was home from the hospital. He was enjoying his work at Moody so much, directing two closely related departments—Moody Press and Moody Literature Mission. He dreamed not only of publishing more Christian books but also of opening more stores in Chicago to distribute them. His associate Bill Moore was already planning for the third annual Christian Booksellers Convention in August. Surely it would bring more like-minded Christian bookstore people to Chicago than the first two.

My father kept busy at his store, the Christian Supply Center, in downtown Portland, in addition to responsibilities at Central Bible Church, the Gideons, and the Union Gospel Mission. Both of our mothers were now in heaven, my mother having succumbed to lung cancer the previous September. She would never see this blond, blue-eyed baby so much like her own eight babies. And to walk down the driveway to our mailbox and never find a letter in her distinctive handwriting was hard. I was still trying to get used to it.

We did not know that my mother had a savings account in her own name that she had been adding to a little at a time through the years. According to her wishes it was divided between her seven surviving children. It amounted to around $800 for each family.

There were so many ways we could use that money, but when

the check actually arrived, all options but one were forgotten. It was just enough money to buy a new washer *and gas dryer* from Sears. None of my friends had a dryer yet, but they didn't need one as badly. They had basements in which to hang the laundry during winter.

Life was never the same again. The bath towels and diapers came out so soft and fluffy. I could damp-dry the shirts and dresses so they were just right for ironing. This was before perma-press fabrics. In fact, when clothes began to be made of wash-and-wear fabrics, I didn't know what people were talking about—you didn't even have to iron them, or very little. Since all of our clothes were coming from church and charity rummage sales, I had to wait two or three years before any started appearing on the sale racks! And then, because I was fussy, I still ironed them, but the ironing did go faster.

Parents are cautioned repeatedly to keep strong cleaning products, pesticides, and other dangerous substances out of the reach of young children, if not locked up. A fine theory, but mostly impractical. How high is "out of reach" when they are born climbers?

Mark discovered a hazard within easy reach—right on the floor—when he was a toddler. The tin can which caught the drip under the 50-gallon drum of fuel oil was an invitation to drink, and he drank some. We rushed him to Dr. Mary, thinking his stomach should be pumped. Instead, we were told to feed him as much bread as possible! Pumping was dangerous because some of the oil might get into his lungs. His breath was pretty potent for a couple of days.

We must have had to discipline Mark as a child, but if so I have forgotten. In contrast, his brother Peter got more spankings than the other nine put together, and neither he nor we have forgotten.

Because Mark's birthday was in January, he started school a year older than his brothers had been. It showed. He was definitely more mature. But his personality was different, too. He was a leader, not a reluctant follower. In kindergarten he was the room representative to the student council, a pattern that continued throughout his school years—being president of his high school class and president of the youth group two years in a row.

Our church had a fine high school choir in which our children were active. Mark also sang in school musicals. At Duke University he formed a Christian singing group that called itself the J. C. Power & Light Company, more or less under the sponsorship of a Presbyterian church near the campus. They sang at other churches and functioned as a discipleship group. The importance of that group to its members is attested by the fact that 30 years later the group continues at Duke, though it has now changed its name to Something Borrowed, Something Blue. Mark met his future wife, Carol Rogers, through that singing group.

When in high school Mark was an unusually kind brother to his four younger sisters. For one thing, he didn't take off with the family car and leave them to find their own way to school or youth-group activities. I was grateful. Perhaps the girls thought all big brothers were like Mark, but I knew better.

The summer he was 14 he worked as an "engineer" at Wheaton College's Honey Rock Camp in northern Wisconsin. Just before camp was over and he was going to join the family for a camping vacation in eastern Canada, he picked up a young skunk and was bitten. If a skunk can be picked up, chances are good that it has rabies (though why anyone would *want* to pick up a skunk is beyond me). Naturally, he had not counted on being bitten, as that would lead to a 14-day series of rabies shots.

Any reference to rabies shots is always prefaced with the word "painful," as they are given in the abdomen. Painful—and inconvenient when you are traveling. The serum had to be kept cold, which was not easy in a hot car, and the injections had to be administered by a doctor or skilled nurse. The rest of the family watched for hospital signs as we went through towns. Not Mark. Each emergency room encounter added to the dread of another.

These delays in the hospital parking lots, waiting for him to get his shot, did not make the rest of the family happy, either. It was never a quick in and out. There was an explanation each time of what we needed (yes, we have the serum with us), the inevitable insurance forms, plus waiting for a doctor to be free. Rabies was life threatening, but the shots removed the danger; only the pain and inconvenience had to be endured.

A few years later Mark found himself in another situation that could have been life threatening. He was lost in the woods in Alaska without a compass or map.

Instead of going back to Honey Rock Camp, he went to Fairbanks to assist an acquaintance in house building. Since we still expected the children to contribute to the cost of their college education, the higher pay in Alaska was the main drawing card.

We knew nothing of Mark's ill-fated adventure until we got a letter recounting the bare facts. Our imaginations filled in the rest.

The Tanana River runs through Fairbanks. What boy with access to a river hasn't dreamed of being Huck Finn? In Mark's case, he had access to the makings of a raft—empty 50-gallon oil drums and odd pieces of lumber. His plan was to drift 40 or 50 miles down to a small town, abandon the raft, hitch a ride back on the highway, and be back at work the next day, adventure fulfilled. Fortunately, he told his boss what he was doing.

How far down the Tanana River he got, I don't know, but he was at the mercy of the river current, his makeshift paddle of little use with the raft riding high on the water. Eventually the raft slammed into a log jam. Not a gentle bump. The raft broke apart, and barrels and boards were sucked under the log jam. Thankfully, Mark was able to clamber up onto the logs or he too might have been pulled under. Now he was a wet and shivering Robinson Crusoe, not Huck Finn. He would be dependent on a boat coming by, but when? and where?

He had been on a narrow channel of the river, and he was not within sight of the main channel or any passing boats.

The water was not much warmer than freezing, but he could see that he needed to cross over the channel to get to the main part of the river. Mark wrote that it took him an hour to get up his courage to enter the water. Holding his shirt, jeans, and boots over his head, he waded as far as he could, but then had to swim. He could no longer keep his arm up, and his clothes got soaked. He crawled up on land, numb but alive.

Eventually a man and his young sons who were on a fishing trip came by and made camp for the night, sharing their food and fire with Mark. But they were going in the wrong direction to help Mark get back to Fairbanks. Rescue was more likely if he could get to the highway. In the morning the friendly man pointed him in the right direction.

Mark walked and walked. But he had no compass, and there was no hint of the sun, so he had no idea if he was walking in a straight line—as straight as one could, clawing through brush and climbing over fallen trees. Or was he going in circles like he had read that people do when lost? And if so, do lost people go right or left? How could he compensate? He thought he heard trucks, and he plunged ahead. The road never materialized, nor did any sign of civilization. He was *really* lost. Not only could he not find his way, but no search party would ever find him, either. What would they think when they found the pieces of his broken raft? Mark shivered, though he was warm from the exertion of constantly pushing on.

With light of day waning, he climbed trees to try to get his bearing. Eventually a high tree brought success. He could see the river: "the most beautiful sight I have ever seen"—a temporal river of life.

When Mark reached the river, he gave thanks. Not for food, because he didn't have any, but for the river itself. The river that was his enemy the day before—wrecking his raft and ending his adventure—was now his friend. It spelled *hope*. He spent that second night alone but no longer as lost as he had been all day. The next afternoon a boat did come by, and he was given a ride back to Fairbanks. Meantime, his boss had rented a small plane to fly over the river, and he had spotted the wrecked raft but no Mark! He was just about to call us to tell us of the tragedy.

The following summer Mark returned to Alaska to build houses again. The next summer he worked at Tyndale House, participating in the launch of *The Living Bible* at the CBA Convention in Denver. After his junior year at Duke, he worked in Jordan, helping to construct a mission hospital for Dr. Eleanor Soltau, who had been a classmate of Ken's at Wheaton. Franklin Graham was a fellow worker.

Another event occurred in Mark's life—in all of our lives—that needs to be recorded. It was the night of the wedding rehearsal for Mark and Carol's wedding in Croton-on-Hudson, New York. The rehearsal and the rehearsal dinner were over. Our children mostly sat apart from Mark and Carol's college friends who would be taking part the next day. Ken and I were seated somewhat apart from our children. Then we saw Peter get up from his place to go talk to Janet, who started to cry. We had no idea what brought that on, and Ken and I slipped away to go to our motel room.

A couple of hours later the telephone rang. It was Mark: "Get up. We're all coming over." What was going on? We got up. What had happened? The message they brought—it was more of a "happening," a happy one—was that they loved us and wanted to express it with hugs and kisses. Nine of our children plus several spouses jammed into that motel room.

We learned that after we left the reception, one thing led to another between our children. They confessed old hurts and wrongs and forgave each other. Aware of family bonds in a way they never had been before, they wanted to express that closeness with us, and wanted to do it *right away*. Mark called Carol at her parents' home, where she was getting ready for bed, so that she too could share in this bonding experience.

We missed John, who had walked out of our lives five years before. Someone expressed the thought that surely something good must be happening in his life that night—wasn't he a part of this family?—even though we did not know where he was or what the "good" might be.

There have been many hugs and kisses exchanged in the years since, but we won't forget those significant ones in the early morning hours of May 28, 1973.

38

Rummage Sales

CHURCHES OTHER than College Church began to figure in our lives after I was introduced to their spring and fall rummage sales. Most of the mainline churches had them. Parishioners would clean out closets and garages, and the outgrown, outdated, and sometimes worn-out clothing and miscellaneous items were sold for pennies. This was before garage sales and yard sales became popular. Until the children were in high school and earning enough money to buy clothes on their own, almost everything they wore or played with came from rummage sales. Or boxes of clothes were given to us directly from kind neighbors and friends.

Since not everything I bought fit one child or another immediately (though most things did), I accumulated some extras. This was especially true with children's shoes. If they looked good and cost no more than 25¢, I bought them. Eventually I had a boxful. When a child outgrew or wore out one pair, we just pulled out the box from Ken's and my closet to look for the right size! Sometimes I was able to get shoes in my uncommon size at the Glen Ellyn Methodist Church rummage sale, but never anywhere else!

I learned to expect to buy the best clothes at the Episcopal Church sales (Wheaton and Glen Ellyn) and those of the Infant Welfare Society. Of course, other people were aware of that, too, and one had to grab fast!

I became an expert at mending. Apparently some women could not be bothered to fix a hem that was coming out or secure a sash that had pulled loose from a dress that was otherwise in good condition. I even bought girls' anklets with holes in them. I had more time for mending than money for buying new things. Socks with holes cost just two cents.

In the '50s local hospitals or charities began opening resale shops that were staffed by volunteers. Prices were a little higher than at rummage sales but still very reasonable. The resale shops were open five days a week all year long, so my shopping didn't have to be confined to a few days spring and fall. The children wore what I brought them, but they would never go in one of those stores with me. How embarrassing!

They got over that embarrassment when they married and had children of their own. Now, they all shop at resale stores on occasion, though not from necessity.

39

Number Seven

WE HAD a hard time naming our seventh child (fourth girl), who was born on Mother's Day, 1952. We had already exhausted the list of girls' names we could agree on! I suggested Gretchen again, as I did with every girl, but Ken vetoed it.

When the baby was three days old the hospital started putting some pressure on us. Finally I capitulated to Ken's latest idea: Cynthia. He had known a wonderful girl named Cynthia Ann in college. I became acquainted with her after we were married, but she had dropped Cynthia in favor of plain Ann.

I demurred at Ann for a middle name as we had already used Ann for Martha's middle name. My premise was that each child should have a distinctive name of his or her own. In this case, having decided on Cynthia, it would have to be a short middle name. We finally agreed on Ruth. Ken had a favorite aunt named Ruth, and I had a sister Ruth, not to mention Ruth in the Old Testament.

The whole family came to the hospital to bring Cynthia and me home after ten days. Dr. Mary was always insistent that I stay ten days. She knew I wouldn't have any outside help when I got home.

The diapers would pile up if nothing else. Mark was only 16 months old, so there would be two in diapers for a long time to come—again. Becky and Martha folded diapers, but other than that I tried not to burden them as junior mothers, lest they view playing with a fussy baby as a chore to be avoided. Fortunately, Cynthia was a good baby, and she charmed us all.

But even good babies required space. Our second crib had to be put up again. There was no room with her three sisters. The three boys more than filled the other bedroom. Putting the crib in Ken's and my bedroom was a less-than-ideal solution. Would we still have to share the space when she reached school age? That wasn't the American middle-class way, but for the time being it was the Taylor way.

One Sunday, when Cynthia was three or four, I was peeling potatoes after coming home from church. The children had scattered after trips to the bathroom. Out of sight, out of mind, they hoped, as the one in sight had to set the table or make the salad. Then a car pulled up behind the house, and ElsieBeth McDaniel came to the door with teary-eyed Cynthia.

How could that be? Had we actually come all the way home without anyone missing her? I was apologetic as I gathered Cynthia in my arms and thanked ElsieBeth for bringing her home. We had scooped up Gretchen and Mary Lee from the nursery, but then forgot Cynthia in children's church. She was too young to be released by the teacher to find her own way to the car, so ElsieBeth stayed until it became apparent that no one was coming for little Cynthia!

"It will never happen again, honey. We're so sorry. See if Martha will read your Sunday school paper to you." I put her down and picked up the potato peeler.

Of course, ElsieBeth would tell others about how we had left Cynthia at church. They might snicker about the hazards of growing up in a large family. But it was no joke. I tried to be a conscientious mother, and I was aware of my shortcomings, but to actually leave a child at church and not be aware of it while pulling out of the parking lot! Then to get home, pile out of the car, and nobody say, "Where's Cynthia? Did we forget Cynthia?"

"Never again" was a big promise. Too big, as it turned out. Just a few weeks later we left Cynthia at church again!

A year or so later I was stopped by my words again. Cynthia always played with Mark and the older neighborhood boys, and it was a blow when he and his friends started kindergarten. Since she could do everything they did, why couldn't she go to school, too?

"You will have to wait until you are five," became my theme song. Eventually Cynthia turned five, and she expected to start school that day. In May! It was not a small thing, but a major disappointment—like Christmas being postponed several months. I had said she could start school when she was five, and now she was five.

Eventually September came, and I drove the four grade-school children to register them and pick up lists of supplies to purchase. I went to the kindergarten room first. Wide-eyed Cynthia soon left my side to explore the housekeeping corner.

TAYLOR, CYNTHIA ________, I wrote on the first line of the registration card. But when it came to filling in her middle name, I drew a blank. I knew it wasn't Ann. Immediately my mind went back to the hospital, remembering our struggle to find a name. Well, if I went through all the girls' names it would naturally fall into place, whatever "it" was.

Rebecca Louise
Martha Ann
Janet Elizabeth
Cynthia ?
Gretchen Marie
Mary Lee
Alison Margaret

It didn't work. I filled out the rest of the cards (duplicate copies). Name of doctor: Dr. Mary Breme. Whom to call in case of an emergency: Virginia Muir. (I put her name down every time, just as she put my name for her five children.)

It was time to move on to first grade, fourth grade, and fifth grade. I should have left the middle name blank. Not all children have middle names. It wasn't an exam. I wouldn't get a lower grade. Or would I? A mother who doesn't know her own child's name! HELP!

Finally, I asked, "Cynthia, what's your middle name?" I tried to sound casual, like a stranger asking, "How old are you?"

"Ruth." Of course. I filled in the last blank, but *I* had failed kindergarten!

Did Cynthia grow up feeling unwanted, or did these incidents mark her for life? Was she emotionally crippled?

I don't know about small families, but big families spend hours reminiscing when they get together as adults. Having survived, they laugh not only about the really funny things that happened, but even the not-so-funny. Just the growing-up experiences that are remembered in common.

Since we didn't move again after November 1948, our children have memories of the same neighbors, same church, same schools, and some of the same teachers. Only their memories are not necessarily the same!

Cynthia is now married and a mother herself, in addition to being a family and marriage therapist. When she telephones from 800 miles away, sometimes her greeting is, "This is number seven." She is the only one of our children to use a number appellation. There is probably no significance, but seven is the biblical number for perfection.

40

TRANSPORTATION

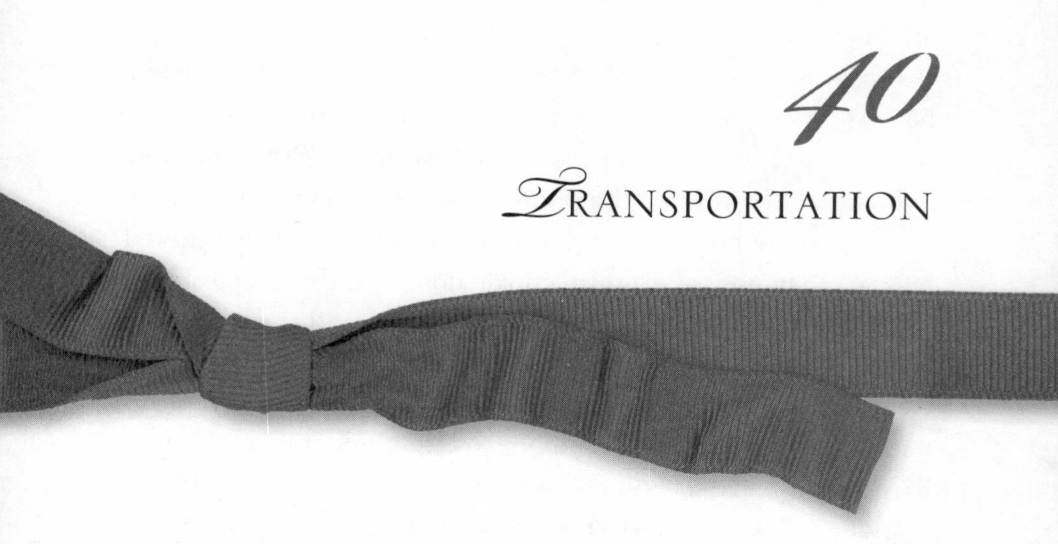

I WAS SURE we were referred to as "that big family in the old blue car—I wonder how old it is anyway? It's not a Ford, maybe a Dodge. One of these days it will break down for good. Wonder what they will do then?"

I was the mother of "that big family in the old blue car." It was already 20 years old when we bought it just before our fifth child was born. And now I could barely squeeze under the steering wheel toward the close of pregnancy number eight. My main concern was not that it would break down, leaving us without transportation. In the 1920s cars were made to last—and this was only 1954. No, my main concern was the fit of nine bodies (soon to be ten) in a five-passenger car. With three children sitting in the back seat, four others had to fit in as well!

That was okay for the mile and a half to church, but we could never go on a vacation trip like that. And vacation trips were important, especially since Ken—as a department head at Moody Bible Institute—got a month's vacation every year. This was almost unheard of for a man still in his thirties. Even if we went to a lakeside cottage in Wisconsin for two weeks, it still left two weeks to do fix-it jobs around the house and harvest garden products.

Car or not, there wouldn't be a vacation this year. We couldn't go before the baby was born in late June. And we didn't know of any owners who would rent their cottage to a family with eight children. What to do when you feel a poor-me syndrome coming on? Pray.

I looked out the kitchen window at the old blue Dodge parked behind the house as I dropped cookie dough on the baking sheet. "Dear Lord, you will have to do a miracle for us. I am embarrassed by that old car. Please forgive me for that. It doesn't seem to bother Ken. He isn't as worldly-minded as I am. I would like to replace it, but we don't even have the money to buy an old used car that would have a little more space, and I can't foresee us ever having that kind of money. O God, forgive me if I sound like I'm complaining. Ken is so happy with his work at Moody Press and Moody Literature Mission, and I know he could earn a lot more in the secular world, but he wouldn't be happy, so I can't even think about that.

"Faith is the substance of things hoped for, the evidence of things not seen. Dear Lord, I want that kind of faith. Amen."

There, that was final. I closed the oven door and closed my prayer. Now it was up to the Lord.

Not long after that I was mashing potatoes, knowing it was time for Ken to walk in from the train station. (Mashed potatoes are better than plain boiled potatoes even without meat and gravy.) I always had dinner timed so we could sit down as soon as Ken hung up his coat and washed his hands. Six o'clock. He was hungry, and the children were hungry. So catching up on the day's events came during dinner, not before.

Eight-year-old Peter exclaimed, "Daddy is getting out of a car, and nobody is with him." He ran out the back door to see why Daddy was driving somebody else's car. Then he was running back in, shouting, "Daddy says it's *our* car!"

Ken filled in with a few details. Leonard Unkefer (from Moody's personnel department) had told him that one of the Moody trustees had a car that he wanted to give to somebody who needed one. Leonard said he thought of our family right away. He lived in Wheaton, so our ancient blue chariot was a familiar sight to him. God had heard my cry.

The old Dodge did not have to go to the junkyard since it was old enough to be an antique. Ken sold it to a friend for one dollar!

Believe me, our almost-new car did not go unnoticed in the church parking lot. "Don't tell me the Taylors finally got a new car? Wonder how Ken managed that? He can't even buy a new suit for himself." I didn't have to hear anybody actually say that to know it was being said or thought. The new car was a 1952 Dodge. It was definitely roomier, though still not quite big enough for everyone to sit down.

But we would need more room if we were to go on a vacation with all the children. Twice we had left the youngest ones with friends.

After a few months of blending in with other cars in our suburban setting, Ken sold the '52 Dodge to another couple in Christian ministry for $1,200. In turn, he bought a 1942 black Cadillac limousine for $250. It was being sold by a nursery school in Chicago, but the original owner must have been a funeral home. Only funeral homes had limousines. It was 12 years old, but still quite elegant looking. So we were still noticed when we drove around town, since limousines were so uncommon. There was only one other in Wheaton, and it was chauffeur driven!

If I held the baby, there was now room for all the other children to sit down, not stand on the feet of those who were sitting. But because of the novelty, they all wanted to sit on the jump seats.

The bigger the car, the bigger the repair bill, and sooner or later the car would have to be replaced. We banked the remaining $950 and earmarked it "next car," for our regular budget could never include buying a car. We did eventually replace the limousine, and we were coming up in the world of cars. This time we bought a '48 Cadillac limousine for $450. This one had more lights and buttons, including an electric window between the driver's seat and the passenger seats. The window worked, and you can be sure the children worked it.

Shortly before that car gave out, Ken's car pendulum swung in a reactionary extreme, and he bought a little Renault. Five people, if they weren't too big, could squeeze in. Two trips to church, and two home again. The driver had to remember who was in the first load to know who to look for when going back. Of course I was always in the first load. The cook needed to check on Sunday dinner and fix last-minute dishes.

We didn't keep the Renault very long. After all, it was pretty inconvenient to be making two trips when one would do with a larger car. I remember driving it to Detroit with Becky and Mark for Margaret Baden's wedding. After the Renault we got a big Ford station wagon, just like other suburban families. Only ours was older.

We probably don't remember each car we have driven in the past 35 years, for to us cars are simply for reliable transportation. They are not a status symbol. I do know that all except one have been used cars.

Years later, Ken did buy a new car—a Mercedes! He was convinced that it was a very economical car. It would give good service for so long he probably wouldn't have to buy another car for the rest of his life. When he returned it to the dealer a few days later, the rumor spread that he was conscience stricken about driving such an expensive car. Wrong. He returned it because it didn't have enough pickup out on the highway. It was an expensive lesson about thoroughly test-driving a car before signing the contract.

41

Gretchen and Mary Lee

FINALLY I GOT a girl named Gretchen. On June 23, 1954, to be exact. Apparently I had worn down Ken's resistance to that name after so many previous attempts!

There was the usual problem of what to do with the other children and how to manage the housekeeping chores while I was in the hospital. Ken was on his hands and knees under the house installing a furnace. I don't recall which of us had the idea of bringing my niece Margaret Baden from Detroit. Would her parents think she could handle the responsibility? She wasn't quite 16. At home she was the oldest of four. At our house she would be the oldest of eight. She came and did very well. She could organize games and fun things, as well as cook a plain meal and do the laundry.

Fortunately, Gretchen was a good baby, and I had willing helpers in Becky and Martha during July and August. We did not take a family vacation that year as finances were tighter than ever. Gretchen complains wistfully that we have no baby pictures of her. Naturally, because film costs money. As a mother herself, she has never had to count the pennies that closely, so my saying "naturally" doesn't adequately explain the lack of pictures.

I am truly sorry we don't have pictures of that sweet, good-natured baby. And she stayed just as sweet when, at 14 months, she had to move over to make room for the next baby, and 14 months after that for still another baby.

These three girls—Gretchen, Mary Lee, and Alison—seemed almost like triplets (at least what I imagine triplets to be like) in their attachment to each other. They were their own best friends as preschoolers and all the way through grade school. They never took sides, two against the third. They never fought. It isn't that I have forgotten if they did, because I was aware—very aware—at the time how much they sought to please each other. And I thanked God for it, for such congeniality cannot be legislated. Nor inherited. Charlie and I made life miserable for little sister Ruth plenty of times when we deliberately tried to ditch her.

When Gretchen was in kindergarten, she brought home a sucker that another student had brought for a birthday treat. Gretchen had carried it home a mile without unwrapping it even to sample the flavor. She explained that she wanted me to break it into three pieces so she could share it with her little sisters, Mary Lee and Alison. I tried to hide my tears. Tears because the weekly food budget didn't include 39¢ for a bag of suckers, so we almost never had any hidden behind the canisters in the cupboard (the cans in which I had bought powdered skim milk). Tears at my own selfishness because I could not imagine wanting to share such a small treat with *anyone,* especially when there was ample opportunity to consume it while walking home from school. What a rebuke! What did I do to deserve such a sweet, unselfish five-year-old daughter? And how do you break a sucker into three pieces, especially when you have tears in your eyes?

About the time Gretchen was learning to sit up, I made an appointment with Dr. Mary. "Well, Margaret, what brings you in?"

I colored, as I had the year before, and said I was pregnant again. Of course she could guess that.

In Ken's book some of the later children just "came along." Nonsense. No woman would write like that of the longest nine months of her life. Mary Lee was one of those children who didn't just "come along."

During some of the earlier pregnancies, I had been bothered by varicose veins. I had injections to reduce the swelling, wore elastic hose, etc. While I was pregnant with Gretchen, my left leg was particularly affected, and I pretty much carried my weight, plus that of the baby, on my right leg. Except for meals and an afternoon nap, I was on my feet (or foot) all day long. Dr. Mary told me I should plan to have the problem taken care of as soon as possible after the baby's birth.

Now when does the mother of eight children, all of whom are under the age of 12, have time to go to the hospital and have a vein stripped under general anesthetic? With the pressure off, in more ways than one, the thought is pushed to a far corner of the mind.

"What about that leg of yours? Remember, we were going to take care of that."

Yes, I remembered. But Ken had been busy during the summer putting in the furnace. He couldn't be watching a slew of children while I went to the hospital.

"Well, since we didn't get it done before, let's get rid of that vein once and for all. I'll make arrangements at the hospital."

She said nothing about the arrangements I would have to make at 1515 E. Forest! But I was agreeable. Somehow we would manage, counting heavily on our neighbor Virginia Muir.

When we went for the surgery, Ken was asked to remain on hand at Geneva Community Hospital (rather than returning home to care for the preschoolers). If I needed a unit of blood, he would have to drive to St. Charles to pick it up at Delnor Hospital. I didn't need blood, but the surgery took four hours—longer than Dr. Mary had anticipated—and no one came out of the operating room to report to Ken. Since he tends to worry in the best of circumstances, it was an anxious time for him.

When I got home I had to keep off my feet so as not to pop open any of the five or six little incisions from my ankle to upper thigh.

Before I was fully recovered, the new issue of *Ladies Home Journal* arrived. Like millions of other readers, I turned first to the monthly feature, "Can This Marriage Be Saved?" After disposing of Joe and Judy Smith's probably reconcilable problems, none of which I related to, I was drawn to an article on the dangers of surgery that require anesthesia during pregnancy. Since there was a possibility of birth defects, any elective surgery should be postponed. I was stunned! My recent surgery had certainly been elective.

We had so much confidence in Dr. Mary. Surely she was aware of the dangers (though we had not been), so how could she have knowingly put our unborn baby at risk just to make me more comfortable for a few months? When we questioned her about it, she assured us, in her quiet way, that at this early stage of pregnancy it would be all right.

Ken and I buried the matter in the dark recesses of our minds, to be dug up periodically and reexamined in the middle of the night. "What if?" We couldn't *talk* about it, but each of us knew the other *thought* about it. How could we not? Still, the problem was so nebulous. We couldn't put a shape to it. We would have the answer in September.

The summer of 1955 was hot, hot, hot. Who in Illinois would choose to have a September baby and be in the last stages of pregnancy during June, July, and August? Who would even choose to have a ninth baby at all, especially so soon after number eight and with the space limitations of our house—not to mention limitations of income? What were our friends saying to each other?

It was still hot in early September. I was in the hammock under the apple tree, thinking about supper but not motivated enough to get moving, when my water broke. I got moving.

Since Ken wasn't home from work yet, and it would be reckless to drive myself 12 miles to the hospital in Geneva, I sent one of the children to ask Virginia Muir if she could take me. Almost immediately I was in pain. And not like anytime before, when first contractions had been several minutes apart. The trip was agonizing. Maybe we wouldn't even make it to the hospital. But we did. I didn't stop at the admitting desk but headed right for obstetrics. I knew where to go—it was my fifth time in that little hospital. And after a quick exam by a nurse I was taken right to the delivery room.

Soon the pain was over and a baby cried. "Another girl, Margaret, but it's a good thing it was a fast delivery. The cord was wrapped around her neck." Later Dr. Mary pronounced her healthy in every way that could be observed or measured. "Thank you, thank you, Lord. You protected our little one all the way."

Did we have names all picked out for our ninth child? No. Maybe we subconsciously put off that decision until we knew if the baby would be all right. Now we could forget about boys' names. As before, we went round and round with girls' names. Ken wanted Mary, but I didn't (with apologies to the Virgin). I had known a Mary when I was young who was overweight and slovenly, and that had spoiled the name for me. Still, Ken kept coming back to Mary, and I continued to object.

"If we put something else with it, like Mary Jane?"

"No."

"Mary Ann?"

"No. We already used Ann, remember?"

"Mary Martha?"

"There you go again. Can't you think of a name we haven't used?"

"Mary Lou."

"Louise is Becky's middle name!"

I don't know which one of us came up with Mary Lee. Both of us have Lee's in our family background. But I was adamant that we have no fancy spelling like Marilee. Mary Lee would be her name—her full name—with no middle name to make things difficult. Eventually even "Mary Lee" became cumbersome, and to her siblings and friends she became known as Maryl.

When Mary Lee was in second grade, she was relieved to learn that it wasn't a law of the Medes and Persians that everyone has to go to college. There was a lot of college talk with John and Marty in college and Becky in nurse's training. Mary Lee could relax a little—only ten more years of school instead of 14. But there was a breach in Mary Lee's wall of defense against college when she saw me take an 8" x 12" pan of sweet rolls to Marty at Wheaton College. A *whole pan* of sweet rolls for one person! Forget studies and pass the butter.

After taking just one semester of sewing in seventh grade, Mary Lee became an excellent seamstress and made all her own clothes. That way she didn't have to wear hand-me-downs from Cynthia and Gretchen.

In her senior year of high school, Mary Lee changed her mind about not going to college. For one thing, all her friends were going. Secondly, the alternative was working at Tyndale House, and she had already been doing that since she was seven! When Ken had a promotional mailing to send out, he put the little girls to work stuffing envelopes.

Tyndale House didn't have a separate phone line in the early days, when the "office" was still in our house, so the children answered business calls on occasion. Once, Mary Lee called to me, "Mommy, they want the order department. What's the order department?" Years later she confessed that once she tore up her notes about a telephone order because she was sure she had gotten it all wrong. Another time, she answered the phone and I heard a desperate, "Mommy, come quick, it's that lady we can't understand!" A German deaconess at a bookstore in New Jersey called frequently for one or two more copies of *Living Letters*. We all learned to recognize her voice.

Mary Lee finally chose to go to Westmont College in Santa Barbara, California. No other Christian college was as close to the beach!

42

Eggs and Cookies

CHILDREN NEED to learn how to handle money, and learning packs more of a wallop when the money has been earned rather than simply received in an allowance.

But suburbs come up notoriously short when it comes to ways for children to earn money—especially year-round ways. Energetic boys could mow a few lawns in the summer or shovel snow in the winter, though that often came under the "do good to others" clause, without remuneration in mind.

Our 1954 Christmas letter reported that "John (10) has had a paper route since last January and has been very faithful with it. He elected not to go to camp this year but bought an English racer bike out of his earnings. Peter (7) inherited [John's] old bike, and Peter's bike (a girl's model anyway) went to Janet (6). A familiar pattern in a large family!"

One day I read a story in *Christian Life* magazine about a family in Wheaton whose children earned money by delivering fresh eggs each week to their neighbors. I called Eleanor Carlsen, the mother, with questions. "Where do you get the eggs? How much do you charge?"

It turned out that the Carlsen children, somewhat older than ours, were no longer delivering eggs, but yes, she heartily recommended the "business."

Having learned that the egg farm was a few miles west of Wheaton in West Chicago, I called to find out if eggs would be available if our son Peter could find enough neighbors who would buy eggs regularly. The answer was affirmative, and the rest was up to eight-year-old Peter. He would mark the eggs up 10¢ a dozen over what he paid for them, so if he sold 30 dozen every week he could pocket three dollars. Three dollars! Every week! You could see the wheels turning. Why stop at 30 dozen?

The reality was that he would have to go farther than just up and down Forest Avenue to peddle even 30 dozen. Not everybody wanted eggs—even guaranteed fresh eggs—if they cost more than at the grocery store. But Peter did get enough orders to justify our getting started.

I say "our" because it also involved a commitment on my part. I would have to drive to the farm every Friday afternoon to pick up the eggs. I would pay for the eggs by check and Peter would repay me in dollar bills, quarters, dimes, and nickels. If several customers told him, "I don't have any money this week," then there wasn't any money left over for Peter. That was a hard lesson—but an essential lesson—in any business in accounts receivable. I explained that next week he would (hopefully) have twice as much money.

There were three sizes of eggs—extra large, large, and medium—with differing prices. Peter had to remove them from the crate that held 30 dozen and pack them in cartons that held a dozen. The customers returned empty cartons for reuse. Sometimes Mrs. Egg Lady gave me a couple dozen cracked eggs that she couldn't sell. Then we might have what I called a 10¢ supper. Not 10¢ each, but 10¢ for the whole family—French toast made with the stale bread we were getting at five cents a loaf. Another 10¢ supper toward the end of a month was split pea soup.

Eventually Peter tired of the egg route and found other ways to earn money. Janet gladly took over. The Taylor children with their beat-up coaster wagon and crate of eggs became a local institution in our neighborhood as the next five children after Janet inherited the business in turn. Their earnings paid for many weeks at summer camp.

It likely was my idea for the girls to bake cookies and peddle them in the neighborhood. I figured the cost of each recipe, and they paid me out of the money they collected. Of course, I did more of the baking than they did, making several kinds of bar or drop cookies in one day. It was shades of my Grandma West making cottage cheese on her kitchen stove and Papa peddling it.

These were some of the ways that our children learned responsibility—and learned to count out change!

43

On Taking Saucepans to Bed

IT IS NOT LIKE taking teddy bears or Raggedy Ann to bed. It is not like anything else. And the idea was not original. It came from my friend Emily Rodgers, except her children used coffee cans. But we drank instant coffee, so we didn't have coffee cans, which would have been preferable.

When does one send children to bed with saucepans (or coffee cans)? When Janet or any child is sent home from school. And it might be the beginning of a whole lot of things, but it probably is stomach flu, and that is as dread a disease as one could wish on any family.

Didn't we have bathrooms? Of course we did. The problem (and it was a problem only at night) was that the children and their bathrooms were too far apart. Most of the children were upstairs and the only bath was downstairs. So I sent the children to bed with saucepans "in case you get sick." I didn't say "vomit" because that was too descriptive.

I have heard mothers say, "Betty Sue erped last night." But I frown on that. It isn't even in the dictionary, and one ought to protect the English language (like the French do, only I wouldn't go that far).

And speaking of being protective, that is why you send the children to bed with saucepans. It is to protect the wide cracks in the bedroom floor, the grooved rubber stair treads, and the living room rug in case they get that far, and no farther, on the way to the bathroom. The rug was of no value, which is precisely why it needed to be protected. Carpeting with a luxurious pile is easier to clean (especially in the middle of the night) than one that is worn down to the warp and woof.

One should establish rules for being sick just as there are rules in case of fire: In bedroom A you open the window, climb out on the front porch roof, and jump. In bedroom B, open the window, climb out on the other porch roof, and jump. Or if you can see the apple tree well enough, you can climb into it, then down to the ground. In bedroom C, open the window, throw out the rope ladder that is under the bed, and climb down. Never go back into the house to get *anything*.

Rules when Sick at Night:

1. Stay in bed. Don't lean over the side, especially if you are in the top bunk. Try to get the pillow out of the way. (Remember how much laundry Mommy's going to have to do anyway, not including the pillow.)
2. Get on your hands and knees. Use the saucepan (or coffee can) if you have one.
3. Call Mommy.

Unfortunately, children do not follow these rules instinctively. Instinct says if you can't make it to the bathroom, lean over the edge of the bed. It's all part of training children.

I think you get the idea about the saucepans, and I've never seen this in "Heloise's Hints." Now if you send it in (the idea, that is) to somebody in a newspaper office, please give the credit to Emily. And hopefully the largest saucepan won't get used, because that's the one you use for cooking cereal in the morning.

44

We Learn about Prayer

KEN CLOSED the Bible storybook during our family devotions one night early in December of 1954. "Before we pray, there is something Mommy and I feel you should know. And it isn't easy for me to say it. We have some bigger bills than usual to pay this month, and we don't have enough money for Christmas presents." He paused for this to sink in, and the older children looked down, not wanting their eyes to betray them. No presents. Of course presents weren't the real reason for Christmas. But to come downstairs on Christmas morning and not find any packages under the tree. Tree? Even trees cost money.

"But we can pray about it," Ken continued. "If God wants to, he can send us a surprise. And if he doesn't, we can pray that we'll still be thankful for Christmas. Maybe we would appreciate God's gift more. What was God's gift, Peter?" He knew Peter was hoping for a bicycle, even if it was a secondhand one.

"Jesus." But there wasn't any enthusiasm in Peter's voice.

I swallowed hard and blinked back my own tears, realizing I was no better than the children in letting my thoughts stray, already thinking about what Christmas would be like without presents. The fall rummage sales were over, so that wasn't an option. Why hadn't I gone to the toy section instead of always heading for children's clothing?

"Janet, you can pray first tonight." There was a moment of shuffling as the row of blondes slid off the couch to kneel for prayer time.

There was a sameness to the childish petitions night after night. Very likely our house did not burn down because Becky prayed for years that it wouldn't—long before the awful night in January, 1964, when the Rodgers' house burned to the ground. Their children Cynthia and Bobby lost their lives, and little Joel was badly burned. And surely Uncle Doug and Aunt Betty in Africa were blessed because they were prayed for every night.

I found it hard to concentrate. Could I really turn this burden over to the Lord? Without scheming?

Maybe I had been dishonest last year not to tell the children that it was a generous check from my sister Ruth and her husband Bill that had put the gifts under the tree. We had always played down the Santa Claus myth, so there wasn't any confusion on that score. And for years I had used the annual $20 check that came from Ken's aunt Bertha ("to buy something for the children") to purchase the turkey and all the trimmings for a big Christmas dinner.

Later that week, the check from Aunt Bertha arrived. I didn't see that as an answer to our prayers, however, because we expected it. But at least Christmas dinner was taken care of.

The following Monday there was a piece of first class mail for Ken from *Reader's Digest*, but I wasn't even vaguely curious. Supper was ready when Ken came in the back door at six o'clock. The mail could wait. There wasn't any unusual news in the letter from his dad. I dished up the large pan of corned beef hash, the buttered green beans, and the plate of bran muffins. "Becky, please put the ketchup and blackberry jam on the table."

In winter it was easy to get the children to the table, because they would all be in the living room—reading, playing a game, or just tussling. I had vacuumed the carpet while supper was cooking, and the younger children had put away their toys and coloring books. We always tidied up just before Ken came home.

Dinner and the nightly devotions were over before Ken could look at the mail. Then he raised his voice in the old camp call, "Announcements, announcements, announcements," and he waved a piece of paper in his hand. "Look here—I got a check from *Reader's Digest* for $25. Or I should say *we* got a check. I think God is answering our prayers for money for Christmas presents. I sent an item to them way more than a year ago, and they decided to publish it but couldn't find who sent it in. Somebody was going through the files, and she found my name and address on the back. God knew about it all the time, and I guess he decided that now was the right time for them to find my name and address. Let's thank him right now."

In my heart I was having to say, "Forgive me, Lord, for doubting." At the same time I was thinking like the disciples, "What is this among so many?" (John 6:9), and had to pray for forgiveness for that, too. "Amen."

A few days later we received a somewhat rumpled letter from my sister Ruth. On the back of the envelope Bill had written, "I just found this in my jacket pocket." Inside was a check for $150 dated three weeks earlier!

We had a tree, a turkey dinner with all the trimmings, and *new* presents (not from rummage sales). And more importantly, that year we had more faith. God didn't stop giving gifts with the gift of his Son on that first Christmas day.

The following year the Denneys—Ruth, Bill, and their five children—flew from California to Detroit to pick up a new car. They planned the trip so they could stop on the way home to spend Christmas with us. Cousins Clifford, Billy, Harriet, Kathy, and Margy corresponded in age with our eldest five. Mary Lee was our baby that year. The children slept in sleeping bags on the floor.

45

What, Again?

I WOKE UP in the middle of the night having to go to the bathroom. I wondered what I had had to eat or drink that was responsible. The answer to that was nothing. It was so inconvenient, though I had done it hundreds and hundreds of times. Groping my way down the steep stairs, I clung to the handrail, watching my step where the stairs made a 90 degree turn near the bottom. The bathroom was just the other side of the wall, but to get there I had to go through the double living room, then reverse myself and go through the kitchen and back hall. There were no wall switches for the lights. I batted the air furiously for that elusive string.

The bathroom itself was *cold*. My memory is that it was cold even in summer, though that couldn't have been. We had a portable electric heater to lessen the chill when bathing in winter. Still, the big window that came right down to the edge of the bathtub breathed moving air—*cold* air.

The next night I was awake again. Now I suspected history was repeating itself. I only had to go to the bathroom during the night when I was pregnant! Getting back into bed, trying to find a warm spot for my feet, my mind was already turning pages of the calendar. The baby would come in November. Mary Lee had been born in September and was now a little over six months old.

And then there was a tear, followed by another, thinking of Mary Lee. We were so grateful for her safe arrival after learning that the umbilical cord was wrapped around her neck. But the pain. I hadn't forgotten the pain, the worst since our first baby. I didn't want to go through it again.

I had just had my 39th birthday. We were unaware (then) of the higher incidence of having a baby with Down's Syndrome at that age, so that was not a concern. I just didn't want to be pregnant *again,* to get big and heavy. Why, I wasn't back in shape from the last pregnancy, and Ken was starting to remind me about doing my exercises. I didn't want to wear maternity clothes again or face the stares of people at church. "Wonder if Margaret is pregnant *again*—the way she is walking?"

It was just the second night of suspecting this secret, and my mind was already running the whole gamut of being pregnant—right up to going to Community Hospital in Geneva and the nurses saying to each other, "Here she comes again."

Another tear soaked into the pillow. I was careful not to sob. Being pregnant wasn't the worst thing in the world by far. November would come and we would have another cuddly baby—*Another girl, please, Lord. I can't always handle the older boys.* But then the real problem would surface. I was already stretching the food money as far as it would go, and one more mouth was one too many. More milk after the baby was weaned, even one more potato in the soup or one more carrot. One more of everything week after week would add up.

My tired body needed sleep, so all these thoughts did not keep me awake. Soon enough Mary Lee was whimpering for an early morning bottle and I was going down the stairs again to warm it. During the day I was too busy with the present to worry about the future and its demands.

But during succeeding nights my mind tackled the space problem. Where would our new baby sleep? *Maybe we could get a third crib in the small bedroom where Gretchen and Mary Lee sleep in cribs. Eventually their cribs could be replaced with bunk beds.* How I hated bunk beds! The older four girls were already in two sets in the other bedroom—the bedroom you got to by going through a corner of the room with cribs. But this last baby, still a secret in a deep recess of my body, would have to sleep in a crib all its life! There simply wasn't enough room to replace that crib someday with a larger bed. Would we never get a bigger house? This was an occasional topic of discussion between Ken and me, but no matter which way we looked at the problem the answer always came up no.

That any children would eventually grow up and leave home, leaving empty spaces, was so remote as not to be a consideration. Except when it came to thinking about college, and then they were growing up by leaps and bounds, one right after another. Three in college at a time!

And that was why I put off telling Ken about this pregnancy. There was no telltale morning sickness, though I did munch soda crackers while I fixed his lunch and he was in the bathroom shaving. It would make his burden about college even heavier, and I instinctively wanted to protect him. Why, we were still paying his dad the $600 college debt we owed him. Well, it was probably paid in full by now, but we continued to send him $20 a month to supplement his meager income.

Weeks went by, and my secret was getting bigger. One day Becky guessed it when I gave her a big hug when she came in from school. "Mommy, are you going to have another baby?"

"Uh-huh." I nodded, and then said, "But don't tell the other children just yet." I didn't add that I needed to tell their father first!

But before I told Ken about being pregnant again, he had a question for me. "Would you like to go to Quebec with me and Peter Gunther during spring vacation?"

"What do you mean, 'Would I like to go?' Liking has nothing to do with reality. Would I like to go to South Africa with you? Would I like to go to the moon?"

To myself I thought, *Just go. You and Peter pack your bags and go, and don't bother me with hypothetical questions.* I might start feeling sorry for myself, which was always a dead-end street. *Turn around, go back, and get on Main Street again.* Main Street—between the sink, stove, and washing machine—with an occasional foray into the bathroom, just three steps away.

Quebec can wait, the moon can wait; I have to get at the ironing. Six white shirts a week for Ken, 12 minutes each. Iron a shirt, watch the cookies, nurse the baby, iron a shirt. . . .

And I don't want to hear about Susanna Wesley spending all that time with each child. She must have had help. I don't have anybody to help me. Poor me. Another dead-end street. Back up.

"I'm serious," Ken said. "You need to get away, and we could get a college girl to come stay with the children."

"No college girl is going to stay with nine children and think she has had a spring vacation. She would *need* a vacation."

"Well then, we'll get two girls."

"How much would it cost?" Always, always that question would tumble out. "How much?" It had been up to me for 15 years to make the money stretch to the end of the month. If the monthly commuter ticket went up, then the food budget went down by that amount.

"Call the college employment office before putting up any more excuses."

"All right," I said barely audibly. And the employment bureau located two girls, Margaret and Anna May. They liked children and thought it would be fun to be off campus and have a chance to cook and bake.

There were no catastrophes while we were gone ten days. What we heard from the children, not just for weeks but for years, was that

Anna May made incomparable sweet rolls. "They're even better than yours, Mom, and she cuts them with thread, not a knife." Apparently I was living in the Dark Ages, cutting sweet rolls with a *knife.* Such ragged edges. It seems Anna May had baked sweet rolls every day we were away. The aroma wafted clear over to the college, and some boys showed up to help eat them!

Many years after that spring trip to Quebec, I heard Dr. Wayne Detzler at church. He said he was married to Margaret Partridge of the class of '57. That name rang a bell. I spoke to him after the service and told him his wife had taken care of our nine children one spring vacation while in college. He gave me his card. They lived in Bristol, England. By then I had been to England once with Ken and the possibility of going again was no longer an impossible dream. I tucked the address away.

The evening of November 16, 1956, I called Virginia Muir (again) to ask if she could drive me to the hospital. Ken had stayed in Chicago after work for an evening meeting. Doug Muir went with us this time in case there was an emergency.

I wasn't in labor very long, and the pain was tolerable. It was another girl. (Thank you, Lord!) We named her Alison Margaret.

Baby Alison must have sensed that she was part of a large family and that she had better not make too many demands! And she didn't.

Edna Green loaned us a third crib, which we put in the little bedroom where Gretchen and Mary Lee slept.

When Alison was just a few weeks old, Ken left on a trip to the Far East that took him to many countries and eventually around the world. He had not been gone long when he received word from Moody that he was being given a raise. There would be enough money for baby food and eventually for that extra potato, extra carrot, extra everything! Again, thank you, Lord!

Between high school and college, Alison went to Nairobi, Kenya, where she lived with a missionary family and worked in the African office of Living Bibles International. Her friend Linnea Hansen was doing something in Mombasa, and occasionally they were able to get together. On her way home she spent the summer in France as an *au pair* for a family with four children. She expanded her high school French vocabulary, and she reported that she made lots of brownies!

46

Dad Taylor— or Grandpa

DAD TAYLOR visited us several times during the ten years after Mother died. He would be on his way to and from Connecticut, where he visited his sister, Bertha Dickinson. He had a clergy pass which enabled him to travel by train at a reduced rate.

Each time he came to see us we had another child, and it became less convenient to find a place for him to sleep. Still, we had a standing offer for him to come live with us when he tired of living alone and cooking for himself. But he had friends in the Portland area who invited him to stay for dinner when he dropped in for a late afternoon visit! We would get a description of the "eats" in his next weekly letter.

Finally a neighbor wrote us to say that Reverend Taylor shouldn't be driving anymore. His reaction time was slow, and there had been some near misses on the busy Canyon Road. In the spring of '57, on his way home from the Orient, Ken stopped in Portland to personally assess the situation. There was a new facet: Dad's car had given up the ghost and wasn't worth fixing. Bus service to Portland was convenient, but he could no longer visit friends in the Bethany area. Maybe it was time for him to accept our invitation.

Alison, our tenth child, had been born the previous November, and we were more cramped than ever. There was no option but to build an additional room. It sickened me to put any money—money we didn't have—into building on. It was like putting a patch of new cloth on an old garment. But Ken saw no other option, and we did not look for a larger house. He had our friend Otto Nystrom draw plans for a room to be built in the corner between the two enclosed porches (one on the front of the house and one on the side). The front porch had become bedroom space for the boys, so that common wall had to be well insulated for sound. The side porch had been our dining room for several years. The door to Grandpa's room would replace a window in the dining room.

Of course, the addition had to meet city codes, and that meant a concrete foundation. The rest of the house didn't have any foundation at all but simply rested on cement blocks at the corners. At least Grandpa's room wouldn't be as cold as the rest of the house in winter.

Ken dug the trench for the footings by hand in order to save money. A flat roof would be the cheapest, so we went that route, a decision we would regret in later years. I thought a picture window would be nice, but we did not place it on the front wall, overlooking our large front yard. I knew from observation that Dad got no pleasure from watching the children—ours and the neighbors'—at play.

In fact, he took little pleasure in the children at all and seemed not to know how to relate to the older ones, nor they to him. There were no warm expressions of affection. Grandpa was simply an old man who came to live with us at age 83—old enough to be their great-grandfather.

He arrived around Halloween with one suitcase and a large cardboard carton. He had precious few clothes, but he was proud of two sets of long woolen underwear. The carton contained the last few pieces of Mother's Haviland china and sterling silver wrapped in old linens, most of which I passed on to the Salvation Army. He brought no books except his worn Bible and some small scrapbooks containing samples of ads he had written 50 years earlier for patent medicines, windmills, and other products.

One scrapbook was a compilation of his gospel ads in newspapers. These five-inch ads were single columns under a headline of the "Man Bites Dog" variety. They were made to look like news items, but a line at the bottom said, "Adv. paid by Geo. N. Taylor." He had been producing these weekly columns for more than 40 years, and they were carried by several local papers in Oregon and Washington. He solicited funds from friends in a low-key way to pay for them. Sometimes the story was an incident from the Bible, other times from current events (like what his sons were doing at college). He was so proud of Doug and Ken's accomplishments. The ads were always evangelistic: "Believe on the Lord Jesus Christ and thou shalt be saved."

Dad continued writing his weekly column when he moved in with us. Composing the column took a great deal of time, as what he had to say was usually too long and had to be condensed. Then he had to type copies and get them in the mail. But being uprooted from his home of nearly 30 years took its toll in this area of his life. There was confusion and irregularity. Finally I intercepted his mail to those papers and wrote them that they should not expect any more columns from George N. Taylor.

Dad enjoyed taking walks through the neighborhood, venturing as far as Glen Ellyn. He talked to anybody and everybody he met, sometimes receiving brusque replies!

In the winter months it was too cold for him to take his walks. But with a gas heater he was able to keep his room as warm as he liked, which was around 80 degrees when the weather turned cold. He pretty much stayed in his room except for meals.

Ken found it more difficult than he had anticipated to have his father under the same roof—not for just three or four days but "forever and ever." Since he had no apparent health problems, he might live a long time.

I remembered in our high school days that Ken would unburden himself about his hang-ups regarding his father. These attitudes bothered him, and he would make it a matter of prayer. Having done that, he was confident that "tomorrow will be different."

But usually it wasn't. Just the way his father greeted him in the morning when he came downstairs might trigger the unwanted reactions. Why it was so he did not know.

Now at 40 he was the child again, and he could not overlook the peculiarities—or what he saw as peculiarities—of his godly father. I could see peculiarities, too, but he wasn't my father. (My father had his own peculiarities, but he wasn't living with us.) Ken didn't know how to exert his own fatherhood in front of his children and kindly ask his father not to do all the talking at dinnertime, for one thing. We heard the same stories over and over again.

Dad was used to getting up early and making oatmeal, so he continued doing it in our kitchen. When I came downstairs to fix breakfast for Ken, Dad already had the oatmeal cooked! I could hardly fix something else, so it was a steady diet of oatmeal. He didn't cook enough for the children, so they didn't have oatmeal every day, even though Gretchen thinks they did. ("When I grow up and get married, I am never, *ever* going to cook oatmeal." And she hasn't.)

Dad had sold his house to his neighbor, Olin Hamlin, for $7,500. This was much less than he had hoped for when he first started thinking of selling, but an appraisal came in at $7,000, so he had to be satisfied with the Hamlins' offer. They paid $3,000 in cash, and the balance was being paid in monthly installments of $100.

The $3,000 was put in our local savings bank, and Dad got great satisfaction in seeing that figure increase as he made monthly deposits of the Hamlins' checks. His little passbook was very precious. He frequently would take it out of the dresser drawer to look at it. What did he think about as he looked at the figures? Never in his life had he had so much money.

When he couldn't find his passbook, he was desperate. He had been robbed. It must be one of the children. When he was out of his room, I could usually find the missing passbook very quickly. There were only a few places for him to hide it—under the mattress or in a dresser drawer under some clothing. In order to spare the children from being falsely accused, we made Grandpa's room off-limits for them.

Dad enjoyed Wednesday night prayer meetings, and that meant Ken or I had to take him. We had not made it a practice to attend regularly, reasoning that to be home with the children was more important. Now we took turns because it was such a trial for Ken to hear his father's prayers, especially when he referred to himself as "a stranger within the gates." He never got over being "a stranger" at College Church. And Ken never got over his embarrassment as he relived childhood hang-ups, even though others spoke appreciatively of his father's pastoral prayers.

At this point, Ken had already completed his initial paraphrase of the New Testament epistles, but he was now in the process of reworking and revising the manuscript. He worked at it on the Chicago & Northwestern train to and from Chicago, and in the evenings he would check his work with other Bible versions and commentaries that covered his desk. They were always left open, so not a moment was lost in finding the right page.

Ken continued his practice of disappearing upstairs as soon as we were finished with family devotions. Dad would go back to his room disconsolate. There was no further opportunity to talk to his son about what was happening in Chicago, or on the political scene, or at that bastion of the faith, Moody Bible Institute.

Ken was not avoiding his father, though it might appear that way, for his pattern of going upstairs to his desk had begun at least two years earlier. A pattern, I might add, which still continues 35 years later. The secular world calls it being a workaholic; Ken says he has been "called."

We left Dad alone when we took our unforgettable vacation to

Colorado in 1958. The Muirs next door could keep an eye on him and take him to church.

On our return we found a little depression on the kitchen counter that Dad had covered over with red paint in an attempt to match the existing red. We never said anything to him about it, nor did he mention it to us. Apparently he had put down the iron and forgotten about it; then he had tried to repair the deeply scorched wood as best he could. We thanked God there was a house to come back to, with Grandpa alive.

The senior adults at Wheaton Bible Church had a monthly dinner meeting that Dad liked to attend. Invariably we would become hilarious on those nights, as if a cork had been removed from a shaken soda bottle. We needed those nights of spontaneous levity. But Dad needed the break, too, and he even tried to get a date with one of the younger women. He repeated that move once, when Ken took him to Moody for the day, and he asked Ken's secretary for a date. Poor Ken!

I stood up to Dad one time. It was so out of character for me that the older children have never forgotten. It wouldn't have happened if Ken had been home, but he was away. During evening prayers, as the 12 of us were kneeling in the living room, some of the younger children became restless, poking each other as Dad prayed on and on. He then invoked the wrath of a holy God on the miscreants, which was more than I could take.

I said firmly, "Dad, stop! You forget they're just children. They didn't mean to be disrespectful." There was an awkward silence as we got up off our knees. Dad went to his room muttering under his breath.

The children didn't know what to do, so I reminded them! Becky and Martha could do the dishes while I started "the littles"—Gretchen, Mary Lee, and Alison—on their bedtime routine of brushing teeth and going to the bathroom. The nightly routine was for me to carry all three upstairs at the same time. One on my back and the other two on each arm.

In late winter of '59 Dad seemed to lose interest in eating. Since that wasn't characteristic of him, we had a doctor come for a checkup. Was there something we should be doing for him? The doctor could find nothing wrong. Soon after that, when Ken was in the East, Dad didn't want to go to bed one night. I insisted and even helped him. He was obviously getting weaker. I prayed he wouldn't become bedfast, because I didn't know how I could handle that.

The next morning Dad was up as usual. The older children left for school, and I got the daily washing started. Mid-morning, I told Dad I would be out for a little while to solicit in the neighborhood for the Red Cross. Gretchen, Mary Lee, and Alison—ages four, three, and two—played so well together that I had no qualms at all about leaving them. Their harmonious play was truly a gift from God.

When I returned, Dad was slumped over the kitchen table, where he had been drinking his mid-morning cup of tea. "Grandpa's asleep," the children said, but I knew immediately that his spirit had taken flight. God's grace was evident in making Dad's Homegoing so peaceful.

For the first time in our lives we had to make arrangements for a funeral. Our pastor, Dr. L. P. McClenny, was of great help. Lyman came from Salt Lake City, but Doug could not come from Zululand. Lyman and Ken both paid tribute to the godly life of their father at the funeral service. We sang "Holy, Holy, Holy," which was Dad's favorite hymn. All that was missing was Dad's pastoral prayer. Now he was no longer "a stranger within the gates," but a son who had reached his Home.

Dad's death freed up his bedroom, and Becky and Janet immediately moved into it. Alison continued to sleep in a crib, but I was freed of the worry that she would have to sleep in it all her life!

47

Family Vacations

OUR FIRST FAMILY vacations were in lakeside cottages in Wisconsin—including Honey Rock Camp soon after Wheaton College acquired that property. We drove up in our old blue Dodge, which was an oddity both to young campers and college-aged counselors.

The summer of 1954, when Ken was putting in a crawl-space furnace under the house and I was having a baby, we didn't go on a trip but visited local sites of interest instead. We saw the Chicago stockyards, the roundhouse in West Chicago where steam locomotives were turned around, and the Falbo cheese factory on Geneva Road (all of which have long since disappeared). Ken also took the children to the Brookfield Zoo and the Museum of Science and Industry.

The following year we were ready for a *real* vacation again. My sister Harriet thought of a joint vacation with her family and the Schroeders (my sister Lois's family), who would be home from Hawaii for a few months. Harriet located a lakeside resort in northern Michigan where the three families could have cottages near each other and the 17 first cousins would have an unprecedented occasion for getting better acquainted.

That would be for one week, but how might we extend the trip on our slim budget? Ken had a full month's vacation. A fellow worker at Moody recommended tent camping as the way to go. That sounded good to Ken, especially when he learned that sites could be had for one or two dollars a night. And campgrounds were plentiful in upper Michigan and Wisconsin, where the weather would be cooler.

How much would it take to buy a tent and sleeping bags? Not much at an army surplus store. Twenty dollars for a huge canvas tent with a center pole, and wool mummy bags were a couple dollars each. Even two air mattresses for Ken and me and a Coleman stove for cooking didn't rob the investment fund too badly. And it really was an investment of sorts, because we could use the camping equipment year after year.

Before our real vacation began, we went to the Mississippi Palisades for a weekend trial run. It turned out to be a *real* trial. It was dark long before we arrived. Readers can't read in the dark, individual space shrinks, and arms sprout extra elbows, so we were at odds even before finding the campground. Furthermore, it was raining when we arrived. Our camping friend failed to tell us that it always rains sometime when you are camping. Sure as anything, some "local" will comment, "It's funny, but we've never had rain in these parts in July as long as we've lived here."

After finding the restroom, the younger children climbed back into the car, where I was holding baby Gretchen. By the light of the headlights, Ken and the older children were attempting to put up the tent. It was very heavy. Army tents, back then anyway, weren't made of light nylon. Seeing and hearing their struggle, a neighboring camper came to the rescue of the amateur tent-erecting team.

Pillows and sleeping bags were sorted out, and eventually ten bodies were stretched out on the ground, Ken and I with the luxury of air mattresses. I had reserved the spot closest to the tent flap, as I would have to get up during the night!

The rest of the weekend was a learning process. I learned that you can't bring water to a boil on the second burner of the Coleman stove, and it surely paid to have water heating while you ate in order to have hot water for washing dishes. We brought our unbreakable Melmac dishes from home on that weekend and every subsequent vacation as long as we camped.

The trial weekend wasn't a rousing success, but neither did it keep us from planning to camp for a week on our way to the cottage in northern Michigan.

A couple of weeks later our real vacation began. The first night we camped at Indiana Dunes State Park. It was so cold we were tempted to return home to get some blankets, but we didn't. We drove on into Michigan and camped in a county campground on Lake Michigan. Camping spaces and picnic tables were under trees on the back side of the dune, but Ken wanted to camp within sight of the lake. The manager agreed, but he must have thought Ken was crazy to want the tent on sand instead of pine needles. Ken hadn't thought about how far we would have to carry water for cooking and washing dishes or walk to use the rest rooms! And that big army tent didn't have a floor. The children's sleeping bags went down on the sand.

The first night we ate at a picnic table in the park. The table was on a cement slab. Our big jar of honey fell and broke on the cement, then baby Gretchen's bottle! It was her last bottle, so she was instantly weaned from a bottle, ready or not. It was not an auspicious beginning, and I was not very happy that night as I tried to get comfortable on the ground. I was seven months pregnant.

While the children romped the next day in the water and on the beach, I faced the reality of washing diapers by hand. We stayed a couple of days before moving on to another campground on the lake.

From our Christmas letter that year:

> You have our word for it that ten people can go camping without taking a trailer if they can put two luggage carriers on top of their car. This we can do on our old Cadillac limousine.

> Luggage included a stroller for Gretchen, who had just had her first birthday and wasn't walking yet. It served as her high chair and playpen.

We camped for eight days before joining Harriet and Lois and their families for a week in adjoining cottages. A happy surprise was to have my dad join us for the week as well. The children swam by the hour in the small lake. We all enjoyed the dark, sweet cherries for which the area is famous. And Ken played one of his first games of golf with my dad and my brother-in-law John Baden.

In August Ken took the four older children, ages thirteen to nine, to Washington, D.C., for the Christian Booksellers Convention, camping *en route*. They must have looked pretty disheveled when they arrived at their first-class hotel! They stopped at Mammoth Cave on their return trip.

Most of the children had an opportunity at one time or another to make a spring trip through southern states with Ken and his assistant, Peter Gunther. They visited schools, both "colored" and white, that used storybooks supplied by Moody Literature Mission. Staying in motels for the first time added to the children's enjoyment.

On his very first such trip in April of 1948, Ken wrote to me (back at the Garfield Hotel in Winona Lake):

> I was shaken this evening as we sat in the home of four sisters between 50 and 60 as they told story after story of lives transformed through reading the Colportage books, which they use in the local county jails. Seems incredible that *Rosa's Quest* could so soften and save. Mr. Hall [Ken's predecessor at Moody] told me of the WPA saddlebag libraries that carried books all through these hills, and the librarians complaining that the hill folks didn't seem to like the regular books supplied, but ate up D. L. Moody's sermons.

Our house in Wheaton was in the Glen Ellyn park district rather than Wheaton's, so we should have paid the large nonresident fee for a family swim pass at the Northside Park swimming pool. But Mr. Potteiger (husband of our children's sixth grade teacher year after year) was on the staff at the pool, and he made an exception for our family and sold us resident passes. The children could ride their bikes to the pool or even walk, if necessary. Occasionally we took advantage of the "families only" swimming hour from 5:00 to 6:00, so the preschoolers could have some water fun, too, followed by a picnic in the park.

We spent an unforgettable vacation in 1958 with our friends Ted and Mary Lou Benson and their 11 children in Colorado Springs. We drove our 1948 Cadillac limousine, but this time we pulled a trailer loaded with the tent, sleeping bags, and our luggage. The children didn't have suitcases, but used cardboard grocery cartons for their clothes. There was a separate carton for Sunday shirts and dresses. I held baby Alison on my lap, another child sat between Ken and me, four children were on the jump seats, and four were on the back seat. It made for pretty cramped traveling.

En route we spent a weekend on a farm in Iowa, our children's first exposure to farm life. Ken knew our hosts slightly. The children rode the tractor, rode a pony, watched cows being milked, fed the chickens, and played with the puppies.

I don't remember the morning church service in the rural Iowa church, but I haven't forgotten the afternoon baptismal service in the pasture pond. There was no Scripture, hymn singing, or even a prayer! Just the quick immersion of the candidates. A giddy girl was first, and when she came up out of the water, she exclaimed, "That was fun. Let's do it again!"

Our hostess was proud that all of the food she served us was homegrown except for one box of corn flakes. A cooking hint I learned from her was to prebake pie shells for cream pies and keep them in the freezer.

From that very brief exposure to farm life, 11-year-old Peter determined he would live on a farm when he grew up. And he did—for several years.

The Bensons lived in a three-story house that had been built by one of the city fathers. A fine home in its day, it had many fireplaces that were no longer used. The house had been moved from downtown to a lot near the edge of town. With some doubling up of girls with girls and boys with boys, there was room for all 25 of us. We stayed for a week, and we made the local paper with a picture of all the children on the staircase.

When we went on outings—such as to ghost towns in the mining area—Mary Lou insisted on staying home and keeping our babies as well as theirs. Even so, we filled up their station wagon and our limousine.

One day we drove the Gold Camp Road on the side of Pike's Peak to visit the Bob Rayburns and Franny Kramer in their summer cabins. The cabins could only be reached with four-wheel drive, so we left our vehicles on the road and hiked down. As we loaded up after our visit, Ted shouted back the long distance, "If we left anybody, send him to college!"

We went through many loaves of bread on that trip making cinnamon toast. Spread butter, honey, and cinnamon on pieces of bread, put them open-faced on a cookie sheet, and put them under the broiler for a minute or two.

Another memory is of a hailstorm in Colorado Springs. It was not unusual for the Bensons, but we had never seen anything like it.

On our return trip, when we were camped near the Platte River in Nebraska, a severe thunderstorm rolled through. We were sorry we had pitched the tent near a large oak tree, in case the storm toppled it. We prayed!

As much as we valued vacations, we could never manage to save money for them. We could afford to pay for gasoline and campground fees only because utility bills were lower in the summer, and Ken did not have to buy his commuter train tickets for a month. As for food, we ate pretty much the same as we did at home. In fact, I brought canned food from home as the basis for most dinners. We had no credit cards, so the money in Ken's wallet had to last for the entire trip.

Having to stop for inevitable car repairs was a big worry for Ken. Would he have enough money? Would we have to cut our vacation short? And the delays at repair shops did not make for a happy family, either. They would rather have been swimming or exploring a new campground.

Still, the good experiences outweighed the bad, and the vacation adventures made for several months of reminiscing before we began talking about where to go the next summer.

While in high school, Becky, John, and Marty went to Quebec with Ken for a week-long conference (all in French, except for Ken's part). They had to serve 20 hours of detention when they got back for missing a week of school, but they thought the trip was worth it.

During the summer of 1960, Ken and I made our first trip to the West Coast in 11 years. We left Becky in charge on the day after she graduated from high school! We flew to Oregon, which was a wonderful extravagance. After visiting family and friends in Oregon, the culmination was a four-day West family reunion at Lake Tahoe. My dad was there, as were all seven brothers and sisters, their spouses, and 25 of their children. Some of us were meeting for the first time, and others hadn't seen each other for varying periods of time—up to 20 years. How we wished our children could have shared that fun time! We decided that another reunion in five years was a must.

As it turned out, our next reunion was held four years later at a small oceanfront hotel in Seaside, Oregon. We took over the whole hotel. In the meantime, Tyndale House was up and running, and our circumstances had begun to improve. So we took the younger six, ages nine to 16, in our Ford station wagon, camping and sightseeing on the way there and back. Some of the great sights we saw on that trip were the Badlands in South Dakota, Yellowstone, Crater Lake, and Yosemite.

The biggest change in the ten years we had been camping was that we stopped for hamburgers every day for lunch instead of my making peanut butter and jelly sandwiches while we were driving, or eating at a picnic table in a small town's city park. That was a *big change*. Just ask the children.

Here is Cynthia's account of our next vacation from our 1965 Christmas letter:

> Our vacation last August was exciting and eventful. First we went to the C.B.A. convention at the Sheraton Hotel in Philadelphia. While Dad worked in the Tyndale House-Christian Reader booth, the rest of us went sightseeing. The 'rest of us' were Mom and six kids. Janet weakened at the last minute and came along. On the third day Mom drove us kids to Hillsdale, New Jersey, where we set up headquarters with our friends the Leon Headingtons to see the World's Fair and New York City. [Ed. note: Anyone who puts up our tribe for most of a week deserves to have his name in print!]
>
> Of course, we didn't see everything, and especially when we were driving we had to help Mom read the expressway signs. We didn't have any trouble except the first night we tried to drive back to Hillsdale from the World's Fair. We decided New Yorkers aren't very good at giving directions.
>
> After Dad joined us, we left to travel through New England to Prince Edward Island. It was farther than we thought, and it took us four days to get there. We camped at night. For one thing, we were slowed down because Mark had to get rabies shots (one per day) for two weeks because of a skunk bite. It meant going to the emergency room of a hospital every day and waiting for his turn.
>
> After visiting and sightseeing on P.E.I., it took us just as long to drive back again! Our destination was Hyattsville, Maryland.

> We got there the day before John's wedding. Becky flew from Chicago for the wedding, and she got to give Mark his last three shots. Finally home after three and a half weeks.

We vacationed twice at a lakeside cabin in Minnesota near the family of Bernie and Marge Palmer. It was there that our older children learned to water-ski, thanks to Bernie's patience. Later, the Palmers summered on Dore Lake in Saskatchewan, actually beginning a Christian community and reaching out to local residents—Indians and people who liked to live at the edge of civilization. We joined them three different times. Fishing rather than waterskiing was the big thing there. After a couple of hours we would come back to camp with 20 or more northern pike. Fish never tasted so good as when Marge cooked them over an open fire in the yard shortly after they were taken from the lake. Fishing was a new experience for the children, and also for Ken and me, as we had not grown up in families that fished.

And then there were the two summers that we rented the cabin of Art and Ruth Volle on Long Lake near Honey Rock Camp.

Years later, after the success of *The Living Bible,* we decided we would like to have our own summer place, something that would be available to the entire family. Several children were already married. While we liked the lakes in northern Wisconsin, the long drive was not appealing since it pretty much ruled out weekend use.

Peter and Sharon found a house in the Michigan dunes area near Sawyer in the fall of 1978. While not within sight of Lake Michigan, the deed granted access rights to a stretch of private beach within walking distance. The house was large, with six bedrooms, and of good construction, and there was an additional two-bedroom cottage. We bought it, and for 20 years now it has been the site for our ever-growing family to congregate for a joint vacation each summer. And traditions have grown up—the things we "have" to do that add to the collective enjoyment.

Since our children do not know most of their first cousins—and there are a lot of them—I'm especially glad that our 28 grandchildren know each other well because of time spent together at "the Michigan house," as well as at our house in Wheaton where they meet each Christmas. And now the married grandchildren are bringing their little ones to spend long hours at the beach.

48

EHAFF—1968

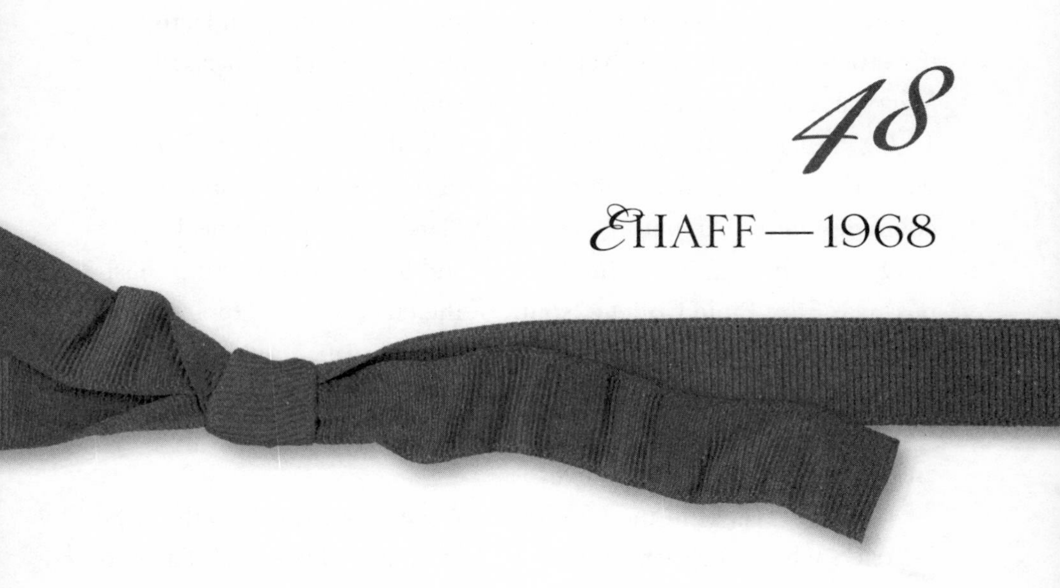

FORTY YEARS after my parents' memorable vacation in England, Scotland, and Switzerland, we made our own memories when we toured those same countries (and more) by car. Our Christmas letter of 1968 contained this brief summary of our six-week European vacation:

> We had been glibly telling friends that 1968 was an off year for the Taylors—meaning no weddings or graduations—when Ken announced that we were going to go to Europe as a family and, consequently, it became very much of an *on* year. Family meant seven now, with Ken, myself, and our younger five, ages 17 to 11. Except to allow for a couple of weeks for business in London, Ken had no preconceived notions of where we should go or what we should see. That being so, we were easy marks when Ken and Jean Hansen made the kind suggestion that we accompany them on their EHAFF (European Holiday and Family Fellowship) adventure. If you want suggestions on how two families can travel together for several weeks and still remain friends (despite dire predictions), see us.

In effect we signed up for a prearranged tour with Jean Hansen as the efficient coordinator. Maybe a couple can travel haphazardly (as Marty and her husband, Ken, did one summer in Europe, covering 10,000 miles in a Renault with pup tent and sleeping bags), but not when there are 16 to accommodate. All the reservations in eight countries were firm before we left O'Hare Airport on June 15.

Our family base for seeing London and for Ken to attend to business was Elim Bible College, south of the city, where "Uncle Jack" and "Aunt Elsie" Hywel-Davies kept their caravan (trailer). Jack and Elsie were our hosts. Jack was a superb tour guide who really knew his way around London. Other days we took the train into the city and did sightseeing on our own.

After two weeks in the London area, we drove north to the Lake District, where we met up with the Hansens in Grasmere. Their three youngest—Joyce, Jeannie, and Linnea—corresponded in age with Mark, Cynthia, and Alison. We celebrated the Fourth of July that week, and the chef at the Red Lion Hotel planned a special treat for their American guests—roast turkey. What a time we had shushing the girls. "Whoever heard of turkey on the Fourth of July! I think they got it mixed up with Thanksgiving." But we did appreciate that extra touch of hospitality. We all enjoyed hiking in the hills of that beautiful area. From Grasmere we went to Oban, Scotland.

At Ken Hansen's request the two families rode in their respective vehicles on days we traveled. And even though we often took different routes, we usually arrived at the next hotel within minutes of each other, whether it was in Germany, Holland, Belgium, France, Switzerland, or Austria. Usually the two families had evening devotions together.

The girls and Mark enjoyed the overnight ferry trip from England to Denmark, as being on a big boat was a new experience. A highlight for me was the gondola trip on Mont Blanc, surrounded by snow-covered peaks.

We spent some time with Janet in Belgium, where she was on a summer missions assignment at the Belgian Gospel Mission. And Becky found us in Zurich, Switzerland, on her way home from nursing service in Vietnam.

Our good friends John and Lorraine Winston and their son Jim showed us the major attractions in the Paris area. We stayed in student rooms at the French Evangelical Seminary in Vaux-sur-Seine, which the Winstons had founded. We enjoyed seeing the seminary both because of our friendship with the Winstons and because Tyndale House Foundation had made significant contributions to their work.

All in all, EHAFF was one super vacation.

49

Mistaken Identity

ANOTHER MEMORABLE vacation was in 1982, when Ken and I went to England with Janet and Cynthia. We rented a car, and Cynthia volunteered to drive the first day. She did so well driving on the left that we let her do all the driving. We had made no reservations, but I had made out a tentative tour based on the book *Turn Left at the Pub*. I had purchased a copy after first seeing it in the Wheaton Public Library. The book gives easy-to-follow directions for walking tours in certain English towns and in the countryside. We also had the indispensable book *Treasures of Great Britain,* plus *A Motorist's Atlas* and a volume called *Guest Houses and Farm Houses.* Friends who had recently been in England assured us it was easy to find accommodations day by day in B and Bs (bed-and-breakfasts). That sounded great to us—to be completely flexible about how long to stay in any one area before moving on.

Before we left home I found the business card I had collected several years earlier from Wayne Detzler, whose wife, Margaret, had stayed with our children when she was a college student. Perhaps we'd have a chance to visit Bristol and stop in to say hello.

Our first stop was Send the Light headquarters in Bromley, just south of London. Send the Light is the publishing and literature division of Operation Mobilisation, and we had close ties with them through Tyndale House Publishers and Tyndale House Foundation. The four of us had agreed that London itself was not on our itinerary. We had spent two weeks in London in 1968 with our friend Jack Hywel-Davies showing us the sights, including a visit to Parliament, Westminster Abbey, and the Tower of London. The British Museum would still be there another time. Out-of-the-way villages and moors were calling us.

On hearing that we had no place to stay that first night, except that we had marked a name in the guest house book, a new friend at Send the Light suggested an Anglican retreat center not too far away. It wasn't a guest house for casual travelers, but he knew they would be glad to take us if they had rooms available. He called, and there were rooms. Furthermore, he would drive us in our car to see that we got there without getting lost. It was a bit complicated, and we would want to have time to freshen up before dinner. He could catch a train back to Bromley. We objected, but not so much that our fairy chauffeur would disappear.

Our adventure in England had truly begun. In reminiscing about the trip we always include our playing Scrabble with a retired Bishop Taylor who lived at the retreat center. We have our own "Taylor rules" for Scrabble, but he played strictly by the book. We stayed a second night with encouragement from new friends—Anglican rectors vacationing with their families—and spent the next day visiting Leeds Castle and Canterbury Cathedral.

A walk around the town of Canterbury was the first tour in *Turn Left at the Pub,* but the reality of time meant we would have to confine ourselves to the cathedral itself after strolling through the Westgate Gardens. Almost as soon as we entered, a university student majoring in history offered her services as a guide. We were glad to be free of a guidebook as she turned back the pages of history at every nook and cranny.

We were impressed with the dedication of artisans who labored in the construction of great cathedrals but usually did not live to see the work completed. They and the cathedrals they erected stone by stone were truly relics of history. There was a faint shadow of that dedication here, for when we wanted to pay our guide for her time, she assured us there was no charge. She loved the cathedral and just wanted to share her knowledge and love with tourists as she had time.

A few days later we were prepared to "do" Bath, which rated two walking tours in *Turn Left*. It rained most of the day, and we did not have umbrellas, so we missed walking the numerous streets with architectural details that are pointed out by author Oakes. But we were delighted to explore the Roman baths that have been excavated after centuries of disuse, and after that, glad to get out of the rain, we located the Museum of Costume. We had learned by now to keep our eyes open for "Car Park" signs, as the narrow streets did not allow for parking.

Then what and where? Bath was as close to Bristol as we would get on my tentative outline of places to see. Bristol was where the Detzlers lived. Would they like unexpected visitors—four visitors? Ken was reluctant. My biggest problem was my unfamiliarity with the British telephones. Well, he would help me get the number, but I would have to do the talking. If no one had answered, he would have been relieved. He had never met Wayne Detzler, and our only connection with his wife had been in her student days, 25 years past.

"Hello, Mrs. Detzler? This is Margaret Taylor, Mrs. Ken Taylor from Wheaton, Illinois. My husband and I are vacationing in England with two of our daughters. If you are going to be home this evening, we would like to stop by for a visit."

Well, we must come for dinner, she said, and they would have room for us overnight—so I wrote down the directions. There was a midweek service at their church that night, and Wayne would surely want Ken to say a few words.

Margaret met us at the door, warm but not effusive, and showed us to our rooms upstairs while she went back to the kitchen to stretch the chicken-for-four to chicken-for-eight. Cynthia had something in her eye that was bothering her more and more, and one of the Detzler sons was appointed to accompany her to the local hospital. We were already at the dinner table when they returned.

Our attempts to get Margaret to share memories of caring for our children (including a seven-month-old baby) for more than a week drew only vague responses. She couldn't remember. Yes, she had done baby-sitting while at Wheaton College. So our only real connection with the Detzlers turned out to be a bad connection. Instead, we talked about mutual friends and acquaintances, Wheaton College, Wayne's writing, the rise and fall of *The Living Bible* in England, and the sad state of the church in England—a subject Ken always presses on British pastors. Why do so few people go to church? What were, or are, the causes? Is there hope? Any bright spots? Yes, the Detzlers' multiracial inner-city Baptist church was a bright spot. We could soon see for ourselves.

The bright spot was not evident in the drab building, but there was a midweek gathering—even young people who had their own meetings. The adults were not particularly impressed that Dr. Kenneth Taylor, "author of *The Living Bible,*" was there in person. They were more impressed that he had ten children, with Ken adding his usual quip, "and one wife." In his brief remarks Ken told our connection to their pastor, how Mrs. Detzler had many years ago cared for our (then) nine children during a spring vacation while at college.

Later at their home, while we were comfortably seated in the living room, the subject came up again—about that long-ago vacation, our old house, the boyfriends coming over to eat Anna May's sweet rolls. Wayne kept quiet. Apparently he hadn't been one of these college boys. Mrs. Detzler tried to cover her inability to remember any details. Finally Janet blurted out, "You *are* Margaret Prichard, aren't you?"

"No, I was Margaret *Partridge*. But I knew Margaret Prichard. We were in college at the same time."

Janet interrupted her, "Mom, you got the wrong lady!"

My face was red. My poor memory was the cause of our being there under false pretenses! Apologies and explanations flew back and forth, exploding in midair in laughter and more laughter until we were wiping away tears. Each fresh attempt to apologize simply brought more laughter.

Finally we were quiet enough to hear Margaret say, "But you are an answer to prayer. I have prayed, well maybe wished more than prayed, that you," and she looked at Ken, "would come here. But how could it be? We had never met. Why would you ever come to Bristol? But I wanted to tell you in person how much *The Living Bible* has meant to me, to us—our whole family." Our confusion about her identity had kept her from opening up earlier in the evening, but now she was free to share from her heart.

"And I know," Margaret continued, "that you must feel real kinship with William Tyndale, since you named your publishing company after him. Little Sodbury Manor is not very far away, and I would like nothing more than to take you there to see the manor house where he lived and tutored the lord's children. The house is open by appointment only, but I will be glad to call in the morning if you would like to go. Even if we can't get into the house, you can see the grounds."

What a bonus. We were becoming more and more sold on sightseeing in England without reservations. And to think that we were there in Bristol as an answer to prayer! Would that all my lapses in memory brought such happy conclusions.

Little Sodbury Manor is situated on the steep western slope of the Cotswolds and overlooks Chipping Sodbury, with distant views of the Welsh hills. It owes its unusual character to its great variety of architecture, with the medieval porch and Tudor oriel window, Jacobean mullions, and Queen Anne wing. But it was not the character of the architecture that interested us as much as the character of the man who occupied an attic room in the 1520s.

William Tyndale was born not too many miles away and studied at

Oxford and Cambridge. He was already something of a reformer when he met others of like mind at Cambridge—Frith, Barnes, and Latimer. When he came to Little Sodbury Manor as chaplain and tutor to Sir John Walsh's children, he was appalled at the ignorance of the local clergy. Gloucestershire had always been a stronghold of the church, and Tyndale's outspoken views soon incurred the displeasure of the Roman Catholic hierarchy.

Determined to translate the Bible into English, he probably did much of the preliminary work in his attic room after his young charges were dismissed for the day. Finally, though Sir John liked and admired Tyndale, he asked him to leave, fearing that he might bring ruin on them all.

Happily, Margaret Detzler was able to make an appointment with the owner of the manor. The lady of the house graciously showed us the public rooms. The Great Hall had been little altered since it was built around 1430. A gargoyle on the wall to the left of the fireplace chimney is a spy-hole, and the hall can be surveyed through it from an upper chamber. We could imagine Tyndale seated at a banquet table in the Great Hall, first conversing then debating with other clergy and friends of his host and employer. It was there in the Great Hall that he made his famous remark to a learned man of the cloth: "If God spare my life, ere many years I will cause a boy that driveth the plough to know more of the Scriptures than thou dost."

Then we climbed the steps to Tyndale's room at the top of the house. There would have been no telephone calls to interrupt his long evening hours of study, and when a candle burned low, it was replaced with another. We took pictures of Ken sitting in the window seat looking out over the fields where the plowboys formerly turned the soil.

Years before, Ken and I had seen the memorial erected in Tyndale's memory at Vilvorde, Belgium, on the site where he was strangled and then burned at the stake as a heretic. It was good to offset that with this glimpse of the pleasant surroundings he worked in when the fire that burned in his soul gave the English-speaking world its first printed New Testament.

We thanked Margaret Partridge Detzler for giving us the opportunity to let our heads and hearts be stirred by the memory of a man so devoted to God and his Word—so devoted that he gave his life to put the Scriptures in English for plowboys and for maidens at the spinning wheel.

And Margaret Prichard? We found out she lives nearby in Wisconsin, but we have never visited her!

50

I Can't Hear the Children

SOMETIME IN 1956 I made a decision that has affected my life ever since. Mornings were spent in a tight triangle between kitchen sink, stove, and washing machine. The doorway to the back hall was between the sink and the stove, and the washing machine was in the hallway just outside the doorway—with the drain hose snaking into the kitchen and hooked over the edge of the sink.

My mornings started with preparing Ken's breakfast (always something hot) and sack lunch, then breakfast for the children and five school lunches in the order in which they left the house—Becky in high school, John and Marty in junior high, Peter and Janet in grade school. Peter always had to be pushed. Finally they were all out of the house, after "Don't forget your violin," "Meet me in front of the school at 3:30 to go to Dr. Patrick's" (the orthodontist), or any one of the other last-minute instructions had been called out.

I would start washing dishes and turn on the portable radio that Ken had given me a year or two before. It was a luxury having WMBI at my fingertips. Our large console radio and record player was in the living room, too far from the kitchen for me to listen to. Now I could listen to prayer time, Bible exposition, or continued story reading while doing dishes, making cookies, loading and unloading the washer, and ironing. Improve my mind and spirit and let the outside world into my kitchen.

The potbellied coal stove had gone to the junkman a couple of years before, since we now had a gas furnace. (The large propane tank looked like a dirigible in the side yard.) The kitchen was now cleaner, and I no longer had to worry about the children falling against the stove and getting burned. Becky had a scar on her wrist from a burn she sustained while trying out roller skates in the kitchen when she was six.

However, there was a hitch to my escapism, an ever-present hitch—four young children. Mary Lee was in the playpen, but the other three romped noisily between kitchen and living room. I would raise my voice, "Children, please be more quiet. I can't hear what the man on the radio is saying."

One day, about to give the admonition again, I caught myself. Was this the kind of mother I had become, saying repeatedly, "Not so loud; please stop, NOW"? So, to the man on the radio I said, "*You* be quiet. I can't hear what the children are saying." And I deliberately turned it off. The tension was gone. I was a full-time mother again and not a mother who was saying (by her repeated admonitions to be more quiet), "I feel trapped. I want out." Babies, babies, messy diapers, runny noses, a bushel of ironing to do, socks to mend, bills to pay, bake something for lunches. I left the radio off.

Being the mother of this brood of children was God's choice for me. It meant full-time responsibility and attention. Listening—or trying to listen—to Christian radio programming in the background wasn't going to make me a better mother.

Now, so many years later, I can go for weeks without turning on the radio. I don't even have one in my car. When working alone, I am happy with my own thoughts, thinking of God's countless blessings on our family and the ministry of Tyndale House through *The Living Bible* and other publications.

51

FOOD TRIVIA

SOMETIMES IT SEEMS I am too preoccupied with food—having it on hand, its cost, using up leftovers, etc.

Food likes and dislikes are not usually covered in premarital counseling, but maybe they should be, especially when the husband and wife come from different ethnic backgrounds (though that was not true in our case). In some homes, for instance, garlic is a staple, but when we were first married, I didn't know what it was or what it tasted like.

I have often said that Ken is the easiest man in the world to cook for. He doesn't refuse to eat anything, demands nothing, and only rarely suggests, "Why don't we have such and such sometime?" On my next trip to the store I am sure to get the makings of whatever he expressed a wish for.

As mentioned earlier, however, married life did not begin with cooking for two. Ken had such an enormous appetite, it was like cooking for four to keep him satisfied. That would not have been a problem except that our monthly food budget in 1940 was only $20. That ruled out anything but the cheapest foods. For one thing, butter had to go. Being a dairyman's daughter, I was only vaguely aware that there was another spread. But now I bought margarine, added the color to make it look like butter, and we have been using margarine ever since.

Once, when walking toward a meeting at Wheaton College, I introduced myself to another woman. It was not characteristic of me to do that, but at least on occasion I do try to be more outgoing.

"I've heard of you," was her response.

"Oh?"

"Yes. I've heard you serve soup to guests." I didn't know how to respond, but by then we had reached the door of the meeting place and parted.

Was that good or bad to serve soup to guests? I rarely serve soup as one course of several. If we have soup, that *is* the meal. But were people talking about me behind my back for that? Did it mean I was cheap or unimaginative in meal preparation? Sometimes, after more than 50 years of cooking, I can be either or both. But would this woman have mentioned it if it were a negative criticism—my serving soup for a company meal? I'll never know for sure, but I chose to think she envied me. Serving soup was an indication that I could treat guests like family members, and that the consumption of food was not the most important reason for inviting friends—or strangers—to share a meal with us. For us soup is frequently the basis of a family supper.

Once, my husband was wakened early in the morning by a telephone call from a man several states away. "This is John Henry Doe. Do you remember me?" Ken didn't. John Henry went on to say that Ken had invited him to Sunday dinner at our home 25 years earlier after meeting him at church for the first time. Ken had given him a copy of *Living Letters,* the only portion of *The Living Bible* then in print.

He would not have been served soup, for I have maintained the Sunday dinner tradition with which I grew up: meat (pot roast 90 percent of the time), potatoes and gravy, a vegetable, salad, and dessert. If we have an unexpected guest, I cut the meat in the kitchen to make sure there is a piece for each person, and I add another potato to those I peeled before church. More likely than not, I would have been up early and baked two pies before the family was awake.

What John Henry remembered was "all those children" (see Psalm 128:3, TLB). He went on to say he had regularly prayed for our family ever since! Well, he wasn't an angel, but we have enjoyed heavenly blessings as a result of one meal shared with a stranger.

But going back to soup. . . . When Mother Taylor stayed with us for several weeks before Peter's birth, she taught me to make vegetable soup without a soup bone. (I can remember my mother telephoning an order to the butcher and ending with "and throw in a soup bone.") Without the luxury of a soup bone, an acceptable soup of three or four servings can be made with a bouillon cube, a potato, a carrot, an onion, a piece of celery, and a tomato—all vegetables that I had on hand. Any leftovers such as peas, beans, corn, or spaghetti can be added at the last minute. Mother Taylor didn't know about thyme, basil, or oregano in those days, and neither did I. Now I will add these herbs to vegetable soup in addition to salt and pepper.

For many years I shopped once a week for groceries, and that was always on Saturday. That way I would not have to take any children with me. Still, there might not be anything special for Saturday night, so it would be potato soup time and time again, until it came to be almost a tradition. Hot biscuits or muffins helped fill empty tummies.

I love the cartoon I once saw of a frazzled homemaker at the checkout counter of a grocery store. Two little ones were surrounded by groceries in the shopping cart, a third was fingering the candy bars within reach, and the fourth had just knocked over the display of cereal boxes. The manager, trying to be sympathetic, said, "Too bad you can't leave half of them at home." To which she replied, "I did!"

Occasionally Saturday supper would be homemade doughnuts—all you could eat. Our oldest daughter, Becky, was grown before she realized that having homemade doughnuts might have meant there wasn't any other food available for that night. I tried never to run out of sugar, flour, shortening, or eggs so that I could always bake cookies, brownies, coffee cake, or pastry—or, on occasion, those platefuls of doughnuts.

While I did not write out menus, I had a good sense of what would be needed for one week and how to make it stretch. For example, I couldn't decide on Thursday to run to the store to pick up something fresh, because I would have spent every available cent for the week the previous Saturday. Employees of Moody Bible Institute were paid only once a month, so if one "borrowed" on the week ahead, the last week of the month could be disastrous.

I kept fairly sharp at mental arithmetic because I always added up the price of the items as I put them in the shopping cart. This was a necessity, since I knew exactly how much I had to spend. If I made a mistake, then I had to ask the checker to put one or two items back. On such a tight budget, there was no room for impulse purchases—ever, for years and years. I regretted never being able to buy a child a box of animal crackers. They cost 10¢.

FHB. The three initials were not original with us, but on occasion we used them. They stand for "family hold back." If Ken came home with unexpected company, it was easy to set another place at the table, but not so easy to stretch the food that was ready to be dished up when they walked in the door. If he called before leaving the office, I could make biscuits or muffins to augment the spaghetti and carrots. We ate lots of carrots, the cheapest vegetable year-round. And men invariably like hot breads, especially with homemade jam or apple butter.

Number Seven (Cynthia) likes ice cream served in cereal or soup bowls, not little sauce dishes, because they don't hold enough. When she was young, ice cream was a rare treat. A single pint was sliced in ten or more slices. There were hardly enough bites to be sure of the flavor.

Once, when "Uncle" Doug Judson stopped in for a visit, he brought two half gallons (!) of ice cream. One would have to be eaten *immediately*. The freezer compartment in our old refrigerator would only hold one half gallon of ice cream, and then only if the two ice-cube trays were removed and the ice cream package was cut through the middle.

We did have dessert every night, usually something I had baked. I baked every day. Rarely bread, but sweet rolls, cookies, cake, or pie, and often more than one thing.

If we had a sheet cake or brownies for dessert, there couldn't be seconds because a half to a third needed to be saved for the next day's lunches. If the children traded desserts with a classmate—a square of homemade cake or peanut butter cookies for Oreo cookies—so be it. It was a case of win-win. A change from homemade oatmeal cookies or snicker doodles was day-old doughnuts, which were sometimes available for 13¢ a dozen from the National Tea Company.

Ken carried a lunch to work for 20 years—three sandwiches (six slices of bread), a homebaked sweet, and a piece of fruit. Sandwiches never included any cold meats. Too expensive.

When Becky started school, it meant another lunch to pack. Then there were three when John started first grade, and the following year four. Eventually we got up to eight. Consequently, it meant foresightedness to have all the supplies on hand. I always packed the lunches in the morning, trying to keep personal preferences in mind. Despite all my economies that saved a penny here, two cents there, I did not require the children to fold up their lunch bags and bring them home for reuse. I knew how humiliating such a small thing could be in front of other children.

I have always been very fond of candy, almost any kind. As a child, when my weekly allowance was 50¢, I could buy a 5¢ candy bar to eat after lunch if I wanted to walk to Dean's Drug Store in downtown Beaverton.

After we were married the nickels were harder to come by, and candy became a rare treat. If Walgreen's had a weekend special of six candy bars for 19¢ (limit six), I would try to take advantage of it. Six bars cut in half provided an instant dessert for the 12 of us.

Ten children do not consume huge quantities of food, for the simple reason that they are children and not adults. Once a couple without children wanted to entertain our family. An outdoor picnic seemed the best way to fulfill that desire. Mrs. H. would provide all the food. That would be a true picnic for me.

As she began to unpack the food and spread it out on the picnic table (on a proper picnic cloth), I couldn't believe the quantities. Mounds of fried chicken (fried chicken was an unknown commodity to the children), bowls of potato salad, pickles, potato chips, and on and on. I was embarrassed at how much food was left to take home—as if it were my fault that the children, especially the younger ones, ate child-size portions.

When we still had only seven children, Norris and Margaret Aldeen invited us for the weekend. Norris had been a college classmate of Ken's. On Saturday we went to the Aldeen family farm outside of Rockford for a genuine hayride. As expected, the children enjoyed the experience. I remember the quantities of Swedish bakery goodies for Sunday morning breakfast. Some of the children wanted theirs without nuts, but the selection was endless.

After church they took us to a Chinese restaurant. This was the first time most of our children had been in *any* kind of restaurant, so going to a *Chinese* restaurant with its quantities of food was a staggering experience. If we had rice at home, it was served like cereal, in a bowl with butter (read margarine), sugar, and milk. This was the way I had rice as a child. And very likely it was a carryover from my mother's childhood. It made a simple but satisfying supper. The children did not know what to do with all the platters of Chinese food that accompanied the rice. And the fortune cookies didn't even taste good!

Large families can testify that they do not often get invited out. Our children can count on one hand the names of the families who ever invited us all to dinner: Nystrom, Rodgers, Dresser, Fischer, Lundahl.

Now, a generation later, it is rare for families to entertain other families at all for a sit-down meal—other than a backyard barbecue—regardless of how many or how few children. But our children have expressed thanks for the example we set when it came to entertaining in our very modest old house on a food budget that didn't allow for frills.

From statistics published in newspapers, I knew I was feeding the family on less than families on welfare were expected to spend for food. Besides, my "food budget" always included soap and paper products such as waxed paper, lunch bags, toilet paper, and Kleenex. But *not* paper towels. I could do without them.

One reason I did not take the children to the grocery store with me was I did not want them to see all the things I was *not* buying, especially the fruits in the summer—apricots, cherries, plums, and melons—because of course they would want them. Eventually, I learned that it was I who wanted all those fruits we had in such abundance when I was a child. My children didn't want what they had never tasted. I bought bananas only when they were going soft and were marked down drastically. The good half of each banana was made into a salad the night of purchase, and the soft half became the basis for banana bread. I did buy peaches by the bushel for canning.

I also canned a lot of applesauce from windfalls, from either our own tree or others. When I had enough applesauce, I made apple butter. The blackberries that grew wild on vacant lots went into blackberry jam.

When ten-year-old Jill Dewey from across the street saw a row of jars containing applesauce, she mistook them for peanut butter. So much peanut butter! When I explained that it was homemade applesauce, she vowed that when she grew up she was going to be a homemade mother, though she was thinking more about sweet rolls and cookies than applesauce. Cynthia and Jill traded cookies at lunchtime. Oatmeal cookies for Oreos.

When our neighbor Lois Jack found that she could get day-old bread from a bakery at five cents a loaf, she shared the bounty with us—20 loaves for a dollar. The excess went into the deep chest freezer we had finally purchased. Our bread was never very fresh as long as that arrangement lasted, but neither was it very stale. It made wonderful toast and French toast, and the sandwiches were passable .

When Mark was in junior high, his standard after-school snack was six pieces of toast before heading out to the pink garage to pack orders of *Living Letters.*

Our children grew up on 2% milk. Not that it was marketed that way, but every day I made two quarts of powdered skim milk and mixed it with whole milk. I did this for economy, not health, but it quit being an economic issue years later when low fat became desirable, and the price of skim milk, both liquid and powdered, went up.

In the late '60s the success of Tyndale House allowed our food budget to become less stringent. The most noticeable change was Ken's demand for half-and-half for his oatmeal, or any cereal. It was his security blanket—we must never be out of it. And if perchance we were out of it, a special trip to the store was justified. If it meant going to his grave earlier from so much butterfat, so be it. He would die happy.

I have had a copy of Doris Greig's book, *We Didn't Know They Were Angels,* for years, and I have used some of her great recipes. But I had never read the editorial matter until recently. Well, I was surprised to find my name in the book! She said I would freeze biscuits and soup to be prepared for unexpected company. Not so.

For one thing, I can't imagine freezing biscuits. Biscuits should come out of the oven the moment you sit down to eat, or even later, after the blessing, in order to be *piping hot.* You can't have that if you are warming up frozen baked goods. I'm a crank about wanting my hot food really *hot,* not lukewarm. Naturally, I'm talking about making biscuits from scratch, with lumps of shortening the size of tiny peas. You roll out the dough and fold it over three or four times. You can't get the same flakiness from Bisquick or any other prepared mix. Is it too much trouble and too messy to make biscuits at the last minute? Well, biscuits can wait, so make them an hour or so ahead, then put them in the oven after your guests arrive.

I seem to have a reputation for serving soup to company, but soup is *not* our usual fare for guests. In addition to homemade soup, I do my share of keeping the Campbell's soup company in business, with no apologies. I may have a dozen cans on hand, but that is for a quick lunch for Ken and me, or for putting in casseroles or strata. Unlike some people, Ken is fond of casseroles. He wishes restaurants served them, including scalloped potatoes.

Peter's Science Project

IT WAS ONE of those gray winter days when the sky is so close to earth that one wonders what's holding the snow up there. It had to be snow. Whether he was "thinking snow" or not, Peter came home from school with a little more enthusiasm than usual.

"Mom, I know what I'm going to do for my science project."

What a relief! When I had promised years earlier "for better or for worse," I was ignorant of seventh-grade science projects and what a burden they placed on mothers. In our family, at least, Dad was more or less out of the picture when it came to school projects. Apparently his father had not helped him, so he felt the children should be self-motivated. For Peter's three older siblings that hands-off policy worked fairly well, but Peter needed all the help we could give him.

I sent for an educational booklet listing ideas for science projects. Too late. Most of them required weeks, if not months, of research and tabulating results. Obviously the list was made by a genuine card-carrying scientist, not a busy mother.

"What?" I tried not to sound skeptical.

"I found a dead cat on the way home, and I'm going to boil it and get its bones . . ."

Before he could continue, I was saying, "Not in my kitchen, you won't. I would be too squeamish."

"Well, where can I cook it?" Cooked cat! Something in a far corner of my brain said my problem was cultural. But cultural or not, I couldn't have a cat cooking in one pot while I was cooking supper in another.

"I could cook it on that kerosene heater Dad got."

"I don't think it would get hot enough," I said lamely.

"Well, I could try." When Peter got an idea, he would also get the last word. "I could do it in my bedroom."

Running out of sleeping space three years before, we had moved the three boys' beds to the enclosed front porch, dividing one-third with a partition so John could have his own space. The front door now opened into Peter and Mark's two-thirds of the porch, and the living room windows also looked out on their bedroom.

"If there's kerosene in it, I'm going to start now." It wasn't exactly a case of out of sight, out of mind.

I must say there is no particular cat odor to cooked cat meat, or else it was masked by the kerosene odor. That cat simmered for three days.

In the end (there had to be an end, for I needed the pot back in the kitchen), Peter abandoned the skeletal bones. They didn't stand up and hang together like skeletons in the Field Museum of Natural History! The bones went into a shoe box. Instead he made a descriptive diagram of "How a Telephone Works."

Two years later, on another gray November day, Janet got an idea for her science project. It came while she was practicing the piano. Those old cat bones could be mounted *flat,* even if they couldn't stand up.

She wrote a 25-page paper on cats to accompany the "Cat Skeleton" on poster board. The A she received was probably given for originality. After all, you had to start by skinning and cooking a dead cat. Thanks, Peter.

The score at this point was five seventh-grade science projects down, five to go. If you peek ahead, you can see a *papier-mâché* volcano spewing molten lava that looks like catsup (A & P brand, not the more expensive Heinz variety)!

None of our children became scientists. What did we do wrong?

53

Our Kids Wouldn't Let Us Have TV

JOHN ELECTED to attend Greenville College in southern Illinois rather than Wheaton College, where most of his friends from church were planning to go. He needed to attend a college in Illinois in order to qualify for an Illinois state scholarship of $600. In the end, however, he did not get the scholarship that year because he had $1,000 in the bank, saved from after-school and summer jobs. His friends who had had similar jobs squandered their earnings and received the state scholarships! That was a hard lesson for John. He had decided against Wheaton because of its compulsory ROTC program for underclassmen. He said he wasn't going to college to learn to carry a gun.

We had not allowed the boys to play with toy guns. Guns were meant to kill, and God had said, "Thou shalt not kill." Even Jerry and Roger Niles, who lived next door, learned to put down their play guns when they came over to play in our big front yard.

Greenville College prohibited televisions on campus during John's first year. Since a majority of the students were from Free Methodist homes that had no TVs, the restriction was no problem. The policy changed in 1962–1963, John's sophomore year, and the school put

TVs in the dorm lounges. John was dismayed at the lack of discernment and discipline on the part of some students who spent hours in front of the tube. John wrote that he was glad we were sticking by our policy of not having a TV.

Three years later Peter transferred to Greenville College from Southern Illinois University, where the lax moral code among students was more than he could tolerate. Once, when he came home for a vacation, he spotted a portable TV on the living room floor. It was not turned on, but even before removing his jacket he demanded, "Whose is that? Get it out of here." It was a command in a commanding voice. You would have thought it was one of our Puritan ancestors resurrected, with his arm extended and finger pointing at the Evil Monster, not a slim youth of 19 in the living room that had been his playroom since he was two. Peter made a special trip to Rogers TV on College Avenue to return the offensive tube that we had rented to view some special event.

We were out of step with most Americans when we did not watch the Vietnam War, battle by battle, as we ate dinner. That was the war that forever changed our culture because of the domestic protests it triggered. But our personal lives were more peaceful as we held fast to our decision not to let television get even a toehold in our household.

John was a conscientious objector and did not have to see active military service. Peter was classified 4-F when his number came up because of his heart problem. We did have some personal involvement in the war, though, as Becky served as a civilian nurse with the Agency for International Development in Vietnam.

A few years later, when Mark was home from Duke University during his sophomore year (1970–71), he apparently picked up the impression that his father might be weakening in his stance about owning a TV. We were on our way to O'Hare Airport when Mark suddenly said, "Dad, I am unalterably opposed to your getting a TV." In just a few minutes he would be flying back to North Carolina. If important words were to be said, they had to be said before the jet's roar obliterated them. (They are never easy to say—*the important words.* You squeeze them in between observations about urban sprawl, weather, coming exams, the lady driving that VW just ahead. Then come the important words.) These strong words—"unalterably opposed"—were not from father to son. He sounded like his father, as in, "I am unalterably opposed to your getting a car while you are still in school."

Mark continued, "Of course there are some good programs, but not as many as you think. And what are the chances that you would be home when they are on, or that you would have the inclination of watching, knowing your schedule? I can trust you and Mom, but I'm thinking of my sisters." *And you and Mom.* I supplied those words in my own mind. I suspect he wanted to shield us, as well as his teenage sisters, from the gaudiness, the materialistic lifestyle, the infidelity, and the hucksterism on channel after channel, hour after hour, day after day, year in and year out. He was afraid, without saying it, that the yelling, screaming, forced guffaws would overbalance the precept upon precept, line upon line that conscientious Christian parents slip in between those same observations about urban sprawl, weather, and coming exams.

I know how he felt, because I felt the same way in high school and college. One felt an obligation not to tell one's parents all that was going on in the world. Since they knew it was an evil world, waxing worse and worse, one need not fill in the details—the illicit liquor in certain boys' lockers, the girl who had to drop out of school because she was pregnant (there was only one while I was in high school as far as I knew), where the boys from Glenside were *really* going when they had that accident.

If we had a TV and Mark was 800 miles away at college, how could he protect us? He wouldn't know what his parents were watching. Would Dad get so enamored with pro football he would start watching on Sunday? And his sisters—what movies would they choose to watch? He had been an unusually kind and helpful big brother to them even when he was in high school. Cynthia was already at St. Olaf College, but Gretchen, Mary Lee, and Alison were still at home, all in high school. Now he was out in the world, and he knew what TV offered and how it was offered. He would have us miss the good TV specials rather than be exposed to the junk that calls itself entertainment, the blatant immorality, and the endless commercials urging viewers to buy, buy, buy. And that was a generation ago!

Mary Lee and her husband, Tim Bayly, were given a small TV set while they were still in college. It didn't remain in their apartment long. Tim threw it out the second story window!

All of our children became avid readers, and most made the high honor roll. They might rightfully fault us in other ways for our shortcomings as parents, but they have never said they felt deprived by not having TV in their growing-up years.

Peter, Mark, and Mary Lee in turn brought up their combined 13 children without TV. Janet had the same conviction. In the homes of our other children, TV viewing has been strictly regulated.

The Strawberry Worm

IN THE MID-SEVENTIES Peter, Sharon, and their young boys, who lived near Oconomowoc, Wisconsin, were taking a Sunday afternoon drive. Coming into a small town, Peter exclaimed, "There it is! I recognize it! That's the very place!"

Preston piped up, "I don't see anything." Peter had pulled over to get the full impact of his memories. What had happened here in his past?

"There, at that ice cream store—that's where Marty found the strawberry worm."

Sharon and Preston had never heard the story, if indeed it could be called a story. How could one re-create the feeling of 20 years earlier, of being part of this larger-than-average family on a three-week camping vacation, all 12 squeezed into an old Cadillac limousine? With so little elbow room, bare tempers were exposed along with arms, legs, and feet.

What was supposed to be an adventure in outdoor living became an endurance contest between campgrounds. Treats were so rare as to be thought nonexistent. Ken was always mentally counting his cash (we had no credit cards), dividing it by days and miles, camp admission charges, and allowing for a used tire in case the left rear gave out one more time.

None of our children travel now with the burden that their father had—wondering if the money will hold out. A telltale sign of his old worries still surfaces, as when a daughter and her family leave to return home after a visit. Ken will invariably ask, "Are you sure you have enough money—tolls and everything?" They always do. Enough for gas and a stop for hamburgers or ice cream. Even hamburgers *and* ice cream!

In the '50s we stopped for neither, except this once. Peter recognized the place, though it had probably changed hands several times in the intervening years.

"What about the strawberry worm, Dad?" Preston asked. Peter was mentally savoring how good the ice cream had tasted that hot, sticky July afternoon, when a treat really was a treat. None of the children ever begged for an ice-cream stop, for it was virtually an unknown occurrence.

Peter tried to sound matter-of-fact, a little embarrassed at his original show of emotion. It really wasn't such a big deal. "Once when our family was vacationing, we stopped here for ice-cream cones. Marty got strawberry ice cream, and she found a little green worm in one of the strawberries in her ice cream. Of course she didn't throw the rest of the cone away. She just put the worm on her finger while she finished her ice cream. John said she ought to show the ice-cream man what she had found. Not that he had grown or picked that strawberry, or even made the ice cream. Still, he should know. So Marty went in the roadside stand, finger aloft, and when she came out she had another strawberry cone, even bigger than the first."

Peter pulled back into the road. What he didn't add in the retelling was that from then on he always ordered strawberry ice cream rather than chocolate, his favorite. Maybe next time *he* would find the strawberry worm and get a second ice-cream cone.

LIVING LETTERS

THE STORY of *The Living Bible* is Ken's story, and he has written about it in his autobiography. It is *not* Ken's and my story. I have had the privilege of being his wife before, during, and since the unfolding of *The Living Bible* story—a divine unfolding, one new chapter after another—but I have been given undue credit. I'm afraid my position is like that of the Pharisees who gave their alms publicly in order to be esteemed more highly by others. Jesus said of them, "They have received all the reward they will ever get." Except in my case I have not sought any acclaim. It has come solely by virtue of being Ken's wife.

The rewards on this side of glory have been very great. On the other side, I hope we will rush to lay any crowns we have at Jesus' feet.

The story of *The Living Bible* has its roots in our parental homes, where family Bible reading was the norm. In both the West and Taylor homes, Bible reading took place in the morning right after breakfast.

With our children the devotional time was after supper, for Ken left the house in the morning to catch the commuter train before the children were even out of bed. As would be expected, the devotional time evolved as the children grew, from reading a short Bible story from a storybook, to reading from the Bible itself. And from singing choruses like "Jesus Loves Me," "Jesus Loves the Little Children," "Wide, Wide as the Ocean," and "The Wise Man Built His House upon the Rock," to hymns from the InterVarsity songbook. Later we obtained copies of the hymnal we used in our church. At first Becky played the piano while we sang, and later Janet.

In addition to reading and singing, we prayed all around—on our knees. Ken was in charge. To be honest, I have to say that as the children grew older (that is, as the first children grew older; we seemed always to have really young ones, too!), these devotions could be stilted, not happy and spontaneous. But we had them!

The story about how Ken began paraphrasing the New Testament epistles to make them more understandable for our children has been written and rewritten many times. He did the original draft on the train to and from work and "polished it" (his words) evenings and weekends, working at his big desk in the upstairs bedroom.

For six years he went over and over that manuscript. If he had been working on a secret invention, I could have said, "When are you going to stop tinkering? When will it be finished?" My unspoken thought was, *When are you going to join the family again—this big family you fathered?*

But what he was working on was no secret. It was all out in the open. It covered the whole desk. Bibles and commentaries, all open to the same chapter and verse. He never closed them, and I could never dust the desk. (Not that dusting was such a big thing in my life.)

I was so small-minded that I resented having to keep him supplied with 39¢ pads of yellow paper from my grocery money (39¢ equaled one can of tuna fish!). I have to confess I was not heart and soul behind this project that dominated his life outside of working hours. In my defense, however, I can say I was not railing at him, "You never spend time with the family." I may have thought it—hundreds of times—in the previous five or six years. But men hate nagging wives, and God does too, so I just kept quiet. I had more than enough work to keep me busy.

Except when he was away on annual trips, Ken was home every night, so I couldn't complain on that score. It wasn't as if he belonged to a couple of bowling leagues that ate up evenings. And he wasn't like my dad, who went to so many church-related or board meetings. No, Ken was home. He didn't even go to prayer meetings regularly. The problem was that he was *upstairs,* and the rest of the family was *downstairs*.

That manuscript, at whatever stage it was in—handwritten or typed—became Ken's most precious possession between the years of 1956 and 1961. When we went away on vacation, he did not dare to leave it in the house. The house might burn down. Billy Graham has been described as a worst-possible-scenario worrier, but Ken can't be far behind. But where could he put the manuscript for safekeeping? An old cupboard in the red shed was just the place. It was far enough from the house that it wouldn't burn, too!

The story about Ken's deciding to publish *Living Letters* himself after several publishers turned it down is also well known, so I'll skip over that. It was his own decision for Moody Press not to publish it, as he was aware that some conservative Christians who contributed to Moody Bible Institute might take exception to a paraphrase of the Scriptures.

The following paragraphs are from Ken's portion of our Christmas letter of 1962.

> MY WORK
>
> I am now spending all my time with Moody Literature Mission rather than only part-time as for the past 13 years. This has released me from the daily details of Moody Press, making possible extensive absences from Chicago. On March 1 I left for Europe, Africa, Malagasy, the Mideast, Hungary, and Yugoslavia, returning at the end of June.

> The trip appears to be bearing fruit with the development of several publishing centers. Apart from this serious purpose, the trip was also full of general interest as I visited 14 of the 28 new nations of Africa that have been formed during the last three or four years. Visits to Leopoldville, Johannesburg, Nairobi, and other much-reported trouble spots held special personal interest. Likewise an audience with His Imperial Majesty, Haile Selassie. My petition (for permission for the Bible to be translated and printed in diverse languages of Ethiopia) was denied, but it may turn out to be helpful to local Christians as they continue to press for this their longstanding request.

We were literally on our way to the airport for that four-month trip when Ken dropped a bombshell: "You will have to proofread *Living Letters* while I am gone."

"Me? I have never proofread anything in my life, much less a book. Remember I was a Home Ec major."

"You've got a good eye. You can spot misspellings or whatever."

"Can't somebody at Moody—" and then I broke off, remembering that this wasn't going to be a Moody Press book at all. This was going to be Ken's very own. "I don't know how to make the corrections."

"There's a page in any dictionary that shows you."

We had arrived at the airport, and he was unloading his Samsonite two-suiter (not that he had two suits). "Be sure to write. I left a list of addresses. And send me a second set of corrected galleys on thin paper. Good-bye. I love you."

I pulled away from the curb. Galleys? I thought that was something on boats.

A few days later, Norm Wolf, who worked at Lithocolor Press, dropped off the first galleys on his way home from work. They turned out to be long sheets of paper that contained the typeset text of the book. I draped them over the back of a dining room chair. It was nine o'clock that night before I could begin the proofreading.

Ken had been making changes in the manuscript right up until the time of his departure, so it was not a clean copy that went to the printers. If the typesetters couldn't decipher his cramped corrections, they threw in garbled type to fill in the estimated length. So I had to do the deciphering of these parts, all the while comparing the printed sheets with the hand-corrected typewritten pages to be sure no words or phrases were omitted. I began changing punctuation, too.

Ken had left some semicolons in, just like in the King James Version. I wasn't an English teacher, but I knew that semicolons were *passé*. Just as language had changed, so had punctuation. I tried putting in periods where he had semicolons. And exclamation points! There were too many of them. Since the old versions didn't use any exclamation points, they stood out and did their work. They said, "Wow! Did you ever think of that! And that!"

If Ken put them in, he wanted them. I wanted to take some out, but who was I? I couldn't talk it over with him, to explain my rationale. "Moderation in all things" applied to exclamation points in a paraphrase, too. But even worse, there were far too many commas. Commas are helpful, even necessary, but they can get in the way, too.

I was hired to look for typos, not rework the punctuation. When I say "hired," it didn't mean I was getting paid to stay up night after night going over every line of Romans, 1 Corinthians, 2 Corinthians, and all the way through Jude. This was my wifely duty. I did not have a long view at all. My only thought was that if this were going to be *in print* (and it already was in these galleys that kept coming), then I wanted it to be *right*. Of course that's what Ken wanted, too. Who decided what was right at this late hour?

But beyond quibbling over punctuation, I found myself (the first of thousands of readers) saying, "Is this what the *real* Bible says?" And I would look up verses in other versions. As if that were not what Ken had been doing for six years! (And that exclamation point belongs there.) So in that sense I was losing precious time and sleep.

In a letter to me from college, John wrote, "Sorry that the

proofreading is so tedious, but who knows how many people will be helped by this book?"

In addition to the proofreading, I was supposed to be following the commodities markets where Ken had invested some of his royalty money from the children's books he had written. Talk about fools rushing in. Ken wanted to make money faster than he might have in the stock market! You can guess what happened. He had given me a few rough guidelines. That explains some references in the next chapter, which contains excerpts from letters that the children and I wrote him during those four long months.

56

Life Without Father—1962

HERE ARE SOME EXCERPTS from letters we wrote to Ken while he was on his long trip through Africa.

MARCH 6 [TO LISBON, PORTUGAL]
When I think of the three women recently widowed in our church, I can hardly feel sorry for myself that you are to be gone four months. I think I am honest when I say that I don't. I feel that I am with you in the work, only you do the traveling, and my part is to stay here. Repeatedly the children have thanked the Lord that you have this privilege.

MARCH 8
Nothing much doing in the commodity market.

Martha can't afford to be complacent about being accepted at Wheaton, though she assumes that Dave Johnson and Bruce Cairns will get in. Among those who were turned down were Phyllis, Sharon, and Margie S. Remember Nancy S. was one of those admitted the week before school started last fall that caused a furor and the admissions committee resigned.

Gretchen wrote: "Mary Lee, Alison, and I got certificates for reading ten books. We all want to read 30 so we can pick a book of our own." *(They were seven, six, and five years old.)*

MARCH 11 [TO MONROVIA, LIBERIA]

There are still ways to save a few dollars. I noted that two of the eight Moody families I was to call about the potluck supper do not have telephones—Stockburgers and Hursts. Obviously they don't have teenagers!

Most of the letter was separate paragraphs from six of the children. Alison wrote: "I wish you could stay home with us. I said to myself that I didn't want any of my teeth to come out while you are away. We can't wait until you come home."

From Peter: "The car is generally OK. Two flats in one week. I can hardly wait till spring to get to work on the Cad. I went to the Father and Son banquet with Evon. It was pretty poor. Beans."

MARCH 19 [TO LAGOS, NIGERIA]

After much "blood, sweat, and *tears,*" Janet got the cat skeleton mounted, labeled, and delivered to school along with a 25-page report on cats. She is finding almost no time to practice the piano, and that disturbs me, but I don't know what to do about it.

APRIL 5 [TO SALISBURY, SOUTHERN RHODESIA]

We are out of the commodity market at present. I expect to finish the galley proofs of *Living Letters* this week. It is taking *much* longer than I anticipated. John says it would translate beautifully into Spanish!

Doug Judson stopped in this afternoon and sends his warmest greetings. You would have been proud of the children in the cordial way they greeted him.

APRIL 9 [TO DURBAN, SOUTH AFRICA]

Your royalty check has come ($653.69). I was just back from putting it in the bank when your letter came with instructions, which I shall follow.

I hope to work in a shopping trip as several of the children need shoes. Alison wanted to know if you can buy shoes at stores or only at rummage sales! This time she will get store shoes.

APRIL 12

From John at Greenville College: "Well, Dad, I suppose the biggest news is that two weeks ago I surrendered my whole heart and soul to the Lord, and now it is he who will have his way in my life. I feel so different now, so much better. . . . I gave my public testimony in church Sunday, and I've had plenty of chances to witness since then."

APRIL 22, EASTER SUNDAY [TO URUNDI]

Several of the children wrote:

Janet: "All of us have had a lot of fun playing ball and climbing trees and going on bike rides this past week during spring vacation."

Martha: "Only seven more weeks until graduation. I haven't decided where to go next year. Greenville seems like the most logical place. I have to let Wheaton know by May 1, so that doesn't leave much time to decide. Please pray about it.

"Last Saturday our [YFC] quiz team went to Dixon. We slaughtered two other teams with a final score of 190 to 50 to 30. There are quite a few more quizzes scheduled for the next few weeks. Then on May 18 and 19, the state finals will be held here in Wheaton. I need to do an awful lot of studying between now and then!"

Peter: "I have had several jobs this week, but all the money was to pay debts. I guess I'll never get ahead. Don't get shook about the Caddy because it won't run anyhow. It needs a complete ignition system replacement including the regulator, which rusted out during the winter."

May 5

This letter was carelessly addressed just to a P.O. box in Ethiopia (no city), but it reached Ken in Addis Ababa!

I reported that the lawn mower had blown up. Peter explained that because he had just worked on it the oil burned up real fast and Mark and Cynthia had not been cautioned that it would require more oil real soon or of the damage that would result. So no blame was laid on anyone but it was an expensive lesson to learn.

May 8 [to Khartoum, Sudan]

I reported we had sung "Happy Birthday" to him in absentia.

Alison wanted to send you a shirt, tie, socks, and a box of candy. She was in tears when I tried to explain it wasn't too practicable to try to send you a package when we didn't know how long it would take or just where to send it.

Last week I called Mr. Ziv [our broker] to place an order. It has not been executed. We missed by an eighth or quarter of a cent on July wheat—and now it is up three cents.

Yesterday I filled in the financial questionnaire required for John's application for a school loan. I had to put down an estimated figure on how much help we planned to give Becky and Martha this coming year. Even if Martha still gets the $600 scholarship now that she has decided to go to Wheaton, gets a job and saves her money this summer, and works through the school year, I figure she will still need $500 from us. This came as a kind of shock to me.

Then the boys want to know why we can't go to Seattle for our vacation (no camping please) to visit our West Coast relatives, etc. Romans 8:28.

June 4 [to Biel-Mett, Switzerland]
In your first letter about the copyright, I did not understand that you wanted your name omitted entirely, but simply that you wanted the copyright in the name of Tyndale House. However, from your next letter I gathered that you wanted your name left off, and this was confirmed in a talk I had with Pete G. And that's where you and I disagree (again!). You speak of a "spiritual constraint" to have it published, but there can't be any spiritual blessing if people don't buy it, and I think your name is its only selling point initially. Are there really lots of people looking for another paraphrase who will actually buy one without knowing who wrote it and if it's put out by a publisher that they never heard of before? I am dubious, to put it mildly. Or are you counting heavily on enthusiastic people in bookstores to bridge the gap of anonymity? And to every potential customer they will have to answer the question, "Well, if he wrote it, why didn't he put his name on it?"

John just said to me, "Say something to me to cheer me up" (He has not been able to find a job yet, and at one place he and Peter went to this afternoon, they learned they could have had jobs if they had been there this morning). I had to reply that I was so blue myself that I couldn't think of anything to say and of course immediately regretted having said it, but the tears were coming then, and I had to turn away. He and Peter were on their way out to go to Horsley's and replace the pants that had given such poor service. I took them in the other day, and he gave me full credit.

Well, the combination of my reaction to the copyright change (feeling that sales will be negligible if it can't be publicized as "another book by Ken Taylor") and the financial facts that stared me in the face after writing the first-of-the-month checks have taken all heart out of me for wanting to come to New York or wherever. Probably I would feel still worse if I knew how much the total bills for publishing are going to amount to. I can't go on a trip and feel happy about it (even with you) if it means leaving bills unpaid.

We are going to have to borrow (I suppose from the stock account) just to get through the month at home. Insurance premiums alone are $145. I haven't paid the car insurance yet, as it is not due until later in the month, and I am waiting to see if John is going to stay home or not, as that would make a difference in the insurance. After that premium is paid and we buy a family swim pass, pay for Peter's bed, and take care of a couple other obligations, there will be less than $50 in the bank for food and car expenses for the rest of the month. And I wanted the girls to have violin lessons. Cynthia wants to start. The children—Janet [14], Mark [11], and Cynthia [10]—are paying their own way to camp.

I am not blue for myself at the possibility of giving up the trip east (I fought that battle last month when I heard that Gladys had joined Dennis in Europe for the last month of his trip), but I am fearful of your reaction. Now Peter comes in to say we need new spark plugs and points!

There is the matter of a family vacation to be resolved, too. If it isn't practical to get the Cadillac running again, what then? As usual, the children have different ideas. Peter thinks that to go where we were last summer would be the worst yet, Martha says that if we go some place "real neat" she might even come along, etc.

Happy news: Cynthia went forward Friday night at the Billy Graham meeting. We went in with Fischers, and afterwards Debbie asked her, "Why did you have to go forward? You were already a Christian, weren't you?" I answered for her that if she were already a Christian, she would not remember having decided any time to be one and now she would know for sure. Fifty thousand out yesterday, so thousands had to leave. Prayers are being answered.

Yours always,
Margaret

P.S. The taxes are paid in full with income tax refund and your *Eternity* magazine check.

JUNE 10 [TO SWITZERLAND]

Mary Lee wrote: "I'm mad that school is out. I'm going to be in Mrs. F.'s room next year, and I don't like her! My tooth still hasn't grown in any! We got our report cards on Friday and we went over to Pappy and Bum-bum's [our neighbors], and since Sharon [Kawano] and Gretchen and Alison and Ruthie [Schoenthal] and I didn't get any N's she gave us a cookie and a sucker and a Tootsie Roll! Cynthia made some yummy chocolate chip cookies tonight. I never make anything anymore because you're not home!"

From Gretchen: "My birthday is coming up soon. It is June 23rd. Are you going to send a present to me? Martha was glad because you sent her a telegram. Mommy went downtown and got it so Martha would be surprised. She found it on her bed with her new watch when it was time to get dressed for graduation. Mommy and Becky and Janet and Cynthia went to Martha's graduation."

I wrote a postscript saying Mary Lee had had pneumonia but made a rapid recovery. Ken had sent directions for getting out a mailing regarding Living Letters. *Martha and Janet were going to do the addressing. I then added:*

I figure roughly that postage will come to $100. I shall call Mr. Ziv and ask him for $300 just to see us through the month—without coming to New York!

My reasons for not coming:

1. Children.
2. *Living Letters*—I doubt if I can get page proofs back to them

before a week from today, and then it will have to be checked once more. This time, changes are averaging three per galley.

3. Money.

Last week was a very difficult one, but things were looking up this morning. John kissed me good-bye. His first day as a supersalesman for *Collier's Encyclopedia.* He was in training last week.

57

CBA Convention—1962

KEN HAD been writing about his throat and husky voice that had been bothering him almost since the beginning of the trip. But when he got home, it was worse than I imagined. It was an effort for him to speak at all. A doctor could find no infection and said that giving his voice a rest was probably all that was needed.

Of course he was due back in his office at Moody right away. For some reason, dictating reports as he went from country to country had aggravated the voice, even more than the necessary talking at his daily appointments.

He didn't tell me about the concerned letter he had received in May from the vice president at Moody to whom he reported, but it couldn't help but cause inner tension. I quote in part:

> Ken, I understand that you are in the hole about $1,500 in advance royalties [i.e., money advanced by Moody against future royalties on his children's books] on the paraphrase. For many reasons I sincerely wish you could drop this project. But it may very well be that this indebtedness makes it impossible for you

> to drop it now. Certainly this indebtedness will make it practically impossible for you to clear anything on the work for a long, long time, if ever. Especially since the market is hardly crying for another such book. In case this is so, I think I should tell you now that I will approve a cancellation of this advance royalty account if you discontinue the project now. I don't want you to feel you've got a bear by the tail and can't let go.

The 13th Annual Christian Bookseller's Association Convention was looming, and there were final decisions to be worked out with Lithocolor Press. They had printed 2,000 copies of *Living Letters*, but Ken was disappointed to learn that the bindery was closed down for vacation. As a result, he wouldn't have a big stack of books to display. Lithocolor did, however, get 12 copies bound by hand.

As director of Moody Press, Ken had spent his time at previous CBA Conventions at or near the Moody Press booth, where he was available to talk to store buyers, authors, or representatives of other publishers. Since he was one of the founders of CBA, he was well known. Other years I had only attended the final banquet, if at all. Because of his balky voice, Ken asked me to help him in the booth all four days. The convention was in Chicago that year. If I wasn't a proofreader, I certainly wasn't a salesperson. But after his six years of working on it (and my proofreading), I was familiar with the product, and I did know the paraphrase better than anyone else!

Wouldn't every store want several copies of a book making the New Testament epistles easy to read and understand? No, they wouldn't. Unless the store buyer knew Ken personally, he or she passed by our little booth without a second glance. Our only sign was the small one provided by the convention for identification: Tyndale House Publishers, Wheaton, Ill. Nobody had ever heard of that before. We were only a few weeks old!

Very likely I had been ironing one day when Ken put the incorporation papers in front of me and said, "Sign here." That made me the 40% owner of a nebulous $1,000 company.

We had half of a 12-foot booth. The other half was manned by a couple from Alabama who also had only one product, molded plastic offering plates. Offering plates weren't a hot seller at Christian bookstores, so we couldn't snag their customers.

The booth was hardly large enough to invite prospective customers in. They would feel trapped. The little display table in front held all 12 books. How could arranging 12 identical books pose such a problem? But it did. Two symmetrical piles? Three? A planned carelessness?

This was bread—vital, life-giving bread to be cast upon the waters. One couldn't afford to be careless. But in what proportion was faith to be mixed with effort? If it was of God, wouldn't (or couldn't) he bless these loaves a thousand times over—or ten thousand times—despite our bumbling? Then reason would take over and say it all depended on sales. All was lost if we didn't get these first 2,000 copies into the stores where alert sales people would promptly recommend, nay, even *urge*, each customer not to let another day pass without becoming the proud possessor of this new Bible. Or we should get them into the hands of pastors who would hopefully recommend this new version of the epistles to all their parishioners.

"Hello, Ken, your booth looks great this year. Busy, too, every time I go by."

Well, Vern wasn't talking about this booth (in fact he hadn't noticed this booth yet). He meant the Moody Press booth, where the regular CBA conventioneers were accustomed to seeing my husband.

"Vern, take a minute to look at this new Bible. Look up your favorite passage in the epistles and see how it reads."

And that would start a succession of head and eye movements that was repeated over and over again, whether the listener was Vern, Bob, Bill, Chuck, or Mrs. Gray from Nippersink. This was surely Ken

Taylor they were talking to, but they looked at his yellow name badge just to be sure. Below his name was not Moody Press but Tyndale House Publishers. Then they would look up at the sign hanging at the back of the booth. It also read Tyndale House Publishers, Wheaton, Illinois. Ken Taylor of Moody Press they knew, but who was Ken Taylor of Tyndale House Publishers, and what was this little green book he was pushing into their ribs?

"Read a few verses. Here's an order card. Shall I put you down for ten, Vern?" Though Vern looked doubtful, Ken reassured him he couldn't lose—they could be returned if they didn't sell. Vern never did take the time to read any, but finally ordered five copies. After all he couldn't lose, and Ken's other books sold well. "Good luck, Ken," and Vern moved on. Was it a sale or not? Would anybody in Vern's store take the time to really read it and see the difference for himself, or would the volumes get lost on a shelf? Would they display the books in the Bible department, or would someone think it was just a devotional help and *Living Letters* would forever be lost to the residents of Kalamazoo?

A gentleman walking by recognized Ken. "Hello, Ken, good to see you again. Your new titles look great. I just left my order." (He was talking about Moody Press, naturally.) "Say, you've got a bad case of laryngitis for August. How long have you had it? Been to a doctor?"

"Yes, he says nothing is wrong with me."

"My wife's aunt had the same problem. She was an opera singer. Her doctor gave her the silent treatment. She couldn't talk or sing for three months. That did it. Her voice was all right after that. You better try it. Think he could keep from talking for three months, Mrs. Taylor? Maybe the children would like that. Well, I have an appointment with Bernie Zondervan right now. See you later."

And that man never saw *Living Letters* or the Tyndale House sign, and when would he have another chance? Did it all depend on one of us doing all the talking? And if it did, why did Ken's voice have to be so bad? It got worse each day. In the end Ken had nearly as many recommendations over what to do for his voice as we had sales, and a pocketful of evil-tasting lozenges.

"Meg, here comes Mr. What's-His-Name. Help me quick. Starts with a *Z*. Used to work at Moody Press."

"It doesn't start with a *Z*. It's Elmer Sawatzky."

Why could I remember Elmer's name and almost nobody else I had met at previous conventions? Ask any mother of ten children if she can't name every single family who ever had her whole tribe over for a dinner. Not only could I remember Mr. Sawatzky's name, I could tell you what we had for dinner. Piles of fried chicken with all the trimmings, topped off with chiffon pie.

If Ken could get people's attention long enough to explain that this was something he had written, had been working on for years, then he might get an order for two copies, five at the most.

"If you wrote it, then why didn't Moody Press publish it?" Good question. "Was somebody at Moody opposed to it?" Ken didn't want to get into the ramifications of that. His voice problem seemed (to me) to be partly psychosomatic, and it would be harder than ever to express himself if it involved defending his position.

If someone turned to the title page, he invariably would note that Ken's name wasn't there. Why not? Did he really do the work? What is a paraphrase anyway?

Ken was sure the book would sell itself if people took the time to look up a favorite passage. They would appreciate the clarity. Or would they? There were more "King James only" people in 1962 than there are now. For sure they didn't stock the Revised Standard Version in their stores, and they couldn't make a snap decision about this new rewrite of the epistles.

Just before the convention floor closed each day, Ken would urge anyone standing nearby to take a copy to his hotel room so he would have time to peruse it. "Just return it tomorrow. These are the only copies I have."

When the convention closed, Moody Press had done well, as usual.

And unknown Tyndale House could count on shipping 800 books when they arrived from Lithocolor's bindery.

Reorders were slow in coming and Ken agonized. Would his "baby" live or die? It did live—and around Thanksgiving he ordered a second printing of 2,000 copies.

Mark, 11, wrote in our Christmas letter that year:

> Daddy published his latest book this summer, *Living Letters.* The publishing house is called Tyndale House after the first translator of the Bible into English. *Living Letters* is a paraphrase of the New Testament epistles. In a way it is sort of a family project. Becky and Martha helped type the manuscript at various times. (It seems like Daddy has been working on this book for as long as I can remember.) Mother checked the proofs last spring when Daddy was in Africa, and now she helps him with the records. Cynthia and I help pack the books for mailing. Next week we will be busy, because that's when the second edition will be ready, and we have a stack of orders to fill.

Ken's Voice Problem

When Ken first returned from that long trip to Africa, it seemed that he had damaged his vocal chords by not giving his voice sufficient rest after a simple case of laryngitis. Since his itinerary was quite hectic and he was expected to speak wherever he went, he had pushed himself all through four months of travel. But if that were the case, his voice should have recovered when he returned home and was finally away from the pressure of daily speaking. But there was the internal pressure of getting *Living Letters* in print, presenting it to the booksellers at the CBA Convention, and then waiting for reactions. Would the response be good, bad, or just the indifference to which humans are so prone? He had poured so much of himself for several years into this little book, praying all the while because it wasn't *his* book at all but part of God's Book. The New Testament letters that spell out in detail what redemption is all about—the necessity of it and how Christ did the work of redeeming us from sin, death, and the grave. The books that tell us how we, as members of the church, Christ's body, should live in a corrupt world.

It was all in every Bible, but Ken's concern was that people weren't reading their Bibles. Certainly non-Christians weren't because of the general impression that it was "too hard to understand." And Catholics weren't reading it (at that time) because they were still discouraged from doing so.

It was the kind of pressure that gives some people ulcers. In Ken's case it seemed like his throat couldn't relax. Doctors could find no abnormality to treat. Was it all psychosomatic?

Certain sounds at the beginning of words seemed hard for him to pronounce. One could almost see the wheels in his brain turning to find a synonym for a word he was going to say in conversation but would stumble over. If it was in my presence, I struggled not to finish sentences for him when he came to a block.

During the next dozen years he consulted numerous voice specialists, psychiatrists who were known to help stutterers, and even a chiropractor in Wisconsin whose adjustments helped a famous preacher when his voice periodically gave out. The other specialists were as far apart as San Francisco and London. Some of them could help while he was in the office, but if it meant doing vocal exercises at home or singing "la-la-la" at a certain pitch, Ken always failed to follow through. He wanted an instant cure!

The adjustments by the chiropractor helped the first time. One could wonder about a psychosomatic correlation: The treatment helped because he fully expected it to help. But the relief didn't last long, and further treatments—which we coordinated with visits to Peter and Sharon on their farm—never produced the same positive results.

Since he could no longer speak with ease, Ken's personality changed. Anyone who didn't know Ken prior to 1962 would find it hard to believe that he was once a punster with the best of them or quick at repartee. Since his throat wouldn't respond fast enough to bat words back and forth, he quit trying. He always was of a serious bent, but now that he was more silent, it made him seem even more serious.

But there was a fairly obvious benefit to this "thorn in the flesh." With the increasing acclaim that came with the acceptance of *Living Letters* and the other "Living" books that followed, Ken was asked to speak at many functions across the country. Almost without exception he turned down the invitations because of his voice problem.

There were trips to England to start Coverdale House Publishers and to other parts of the world in the interests of Living Letters Overseas (later called Living Bibles International) to encourage, and even fund, the development of similar paraphrases in other languages. But most of the time he was in Wheaton, dividing his time between overseeing our growing publishing company and continuing to paraphrase other parts of the Bible. It was not until four volumes of the "Living" series were in print that Ken began to think about the possibility of completing the entire Bible, if God would be gracious in giving him continued good health. Up until then it had seemed too enormous a task to contemplate.

The long hours at his desk at home with numerous Bibles and commentaries open to the same passage had become a way of life. The desk had changed from the battered oak desk to an even larger mahogany desk (not new but still beautiful) installed in his first-floor study when we moved to our new home in 1966.

A few years later, when the end of the paraphrasing was in sight as he worked on the *Living History of Israel,* Ken began to hope that with the completion of the project God would do what the doctors couldn't and loosen his vocal chords so that he could speak normally. But his hopes were not realized. He finally finished his translation work, and *The Living Bible* was published as a single volume in 1971. Thousands upon thousands of *Living Bibles* (with the distinctive green padded cover) were loosed into an eager market, but Ken's voice did not improve.

Eventually he learned that his particular voice problem is called spasmodic dysphonia—the vocal chords are fighting each other instead of working in harmony. The only known cure was to sever the nerve leading to one set of vocal chords. Ken decided to have the surgery.

Since the surgery required general anesthesia, the surgeon wanted Ken's heart tested first. Ken failed the stress test and was soon in Presbyterian-St. Luke's Hospital in Chicago, where he had double-bypass surgery.

After recuperating from that open-heart surgery, the doctor was able to simulate the results of throat surgery by temporary paralysis of the nerve leading to one side of the vocal chords. The result was that Ken sounded like Donald Duck, so he decided against the surgery. His strained voice was better than one at such an abnormal pitch.

A few more years passed, and then a researcher at the National Institutes of Health asked if he would be willing to participate in a new experimental treatment of spasmodic dysphonia. The NIH was testing the effects of injecting botulin toxin into the vocal chords. He was happy to participate, and the treatment brought definite improvement in his ability to speak, though not total improvement in the quality of his voice. After some months the effect wore off, so another injection was called for. He made several trips to Bethesda, Maryland, at government expense. Each time it meant that he could stay with our daughter Marty and her family in D.C., which was a nice bonus.

The NIH was satisfied with the results of the experimental treatment, so otolaryngologists around the country were trained to give the botulin injections. Now Ken goes to nearby Loyola Hospital in Chicago when his voice needs another shot.

59

TEMPORAL REWARDS

FOLLOWING HIS WISHES, Ken's name did not appear in the first editions of *Living Letters,* an "omission" that was misunderstood by some. If he went to all that work, why not sign his name? It was not a case of modesty, real or false. Ken's answer is simple: "God is the author of the Bible, so why should I put my name on this edition?"

However, when Billy Graham decided to give away copies of *Living Letters* to listeners of his telecast in 1963, he insisted that Ken's name be on the title page, lest people misunderstand and think that he, Billy Graham, had done the writing. It was a very legitimate concern that Ken could not ignore.

The trickle of letters from enlightened readers, old and young, became a steady stream through the years, thanking Ken for making the Bible's epistles (then the Minor Prophets, and eventually the whole Bible) more understandable.

Readers of the Bible always have been and continue to be saved through any and all translations. But if a person is saved through reading a King James Bible, to whom can he write his heartfelt thanks? A publisher perhaps, and there are many different ones, but there is no person to whom the letter can be forwarded who had any part in the translation itself. The Gideons get their share of letters because of the millions of Bibles they have placed in hotels and other institutions—letters which encourage them to keep up their good work of distributing Bibles.

But Ken as an individual has been the recipient of countless letters of thanks. They have ranged from a few brief sentences to epistles of many pages. Perhaps no other person in the world has received such thanks as a human agent of translating God's Word.

In addition to the thousands of letters, Ken has received many awards, including honorary degrees from several colleges.

Rather than make my husband bigheaded, all this recognition humbles him to think that God chose him, an ordinary person, to do an extraordinary work in the 20th century. Not only through *Living Letters* and *The Living Bible,* but through the hundreds of Christian enterprises that have been helped by grants from Tyndale House Foundation.

I have traveled widely enough to know that we cannot be in a group of Christians anywhere in the world but that someone can give a personal testimony about how *The Living Bible* has blessed him or a member of his family.

Ken's office door is usually open to drop-in visitors. A recent one was a retired TEAM (The Evangelical Alliance Mission) missionary, who was prompted by something he had read in Scripture to come by the office to see if he should continue to pray for our family. It seems he was in our home *once* many years ago, and learning of the specific needs relative to some of our children, he had been praying for the Taylors ever since. Ken encouraged him to keep praying for our ever-growing family. Though the original problems have long since been solved by God's grace, there are always new ones. As our culture comes apart at the seams, we Christians, including our grandchildren, are exposed to issues and problems we could never have imagined in a bygone era.

But God still hears and answers prayers exceedingly, abundantly, above all we can ask or think.

The temporal rewards from the publication of *Living Letters* and the other "Living" books spilled over to our entire family, as Tyndale House became a profitable venture almost from the start. Part of that spillover included our ability to send the children to college.

While Ken would assent to the idea that a college education is not necessary for every young person, that was not the idea our children picked up from him. I think that Peter would have chosen not to go to college, or that he might have chosen a vocational school, but as he now puts it, "If your last name was Taylor, you had to go."

Not only did Ken want our children to go to college, he hoped they would finish without being in debt. That was a big hurdle, or series of hurdles, as our family grew in number. Our savings would never do it. Our savings plus their earnings would never do it. What an impasse! Ken's furrowed brow softened a little when his children's books began earning royalties, though his purpose in writing them had been pure and unadulterated—based solely on the need for devotional books and stories with an obvious moral for young children. If he invested the royalty money then maybe one or two hurdles would be cleared. In reality, however, that "maybe" became "forget it" as one scheme after another not only failed to *make* money but *swallowed* what he had invested!

The Scotch pine trees in our back lot that never shaped up to be Christmas trees are the remains of one such scheme. If our grandsons cut them down, at least we will have free firewood for a couple of years.

But God, who is rich in mercy and whose resources are never depleted, had a plan for financing our children's education—all ten of them. And throw in a couple of sons-in-law for good measure. But that plan was just a side benefit as thousands, and eventually millions, were being blessed spiritually through reading *Living Letters* and the six successive volumes that eventually comprised *The Living Bible*. While our children were growing and reaching college age, Tyndale House Publishers was growing, and Ken's salary—along with the children's earnings—paid all of their expenses. ALL. There were no loans. They could marry or begin careers without being plagued by debt. The blessings were heaped up, pressed down, and still ran over.

Ken was such a conscientious citizen that he wrote the Illinois State Scholarship Commission in January of 1964 that John and Martha would not need their scholarships for the second semester. The Commission had never received such a communication before and didn't know how to handle it! After that Ken never let any of the children apply for scholarships. We could handle the payments ourselves.

In the end, our children attended nine different colleges, not counting semesters at other colleges or semesters abroad.

60

Our New House

AFTER 18 YEARS of living in the old farmhouse, we were finally able to follow my sister Harriet's advice to tear it down.

But it was not an easy decision, at least for Ken, even though we could finally afford to move. When a larger home on West Street or Wheaton Avenue was for sale, I would pull Ken away from his desk to go inspect it. But we never actually got inside one of those homes because invariably he would say, "No yard. . . ." They *did* have yards—normal yards for a city lot—but only a fraction of our 250-foot front yard. If a house had "no yard," he didn't care how many bedrooms it had, whether the kitchen had been modernized, or what was the condition of the hardwood floors.

For sure I could never get him to tour model homes in the new subdivisions like Arrowhead where the houses were big, but the yards were even smaller than around the old homes on Wheaton's north side. And they lacked the mature trees that had so much appeal.

Then why not keep *our yard* and big trees and sacrifice our old *house?* I was the one who came up with the idea. We could build a new one in our spacious front yard. The economics of such a move made sense to me. Even with the mortgage interest added to the original purchase price, we had probably paid out no more than $10,000 over 17 years! That came to pretty cheap housing when you considered the good education our children had received in Wheaton schools, the influence of College Church with its fine youth groups and Pioneer Girls, and the friends we all had made.

An architect would be fine but not necessary. We could probably find a stock plan that suited our needs. Otto Nystrom, the same friend who had built Grandpa's room a few years earlier, agreed to be the builder and general contractor. He had learned the trade in his home country of Sweden.

Marianne Miller, who was typing Ken's manuscripts at her home, saw magazine pictures of a house in Houston that she thought would appeal to us. It did. There were four bedrooms on the second floor, one on the first floor, and a study, in addition to a living room, dining room, family room, and kitchen with a large eating area. There was also a laundry room next to the kitchen. From the pictures, Ken especially liked the family room with its large fireplace and beamed ceiling.

For five dollars we got a copy of the plans. Then I worked with a draftsman whom Otto recommended to tailor them to fit our ideas and draw up blueprints. It would have brick siding on the first floor with aluminum siding above. The draftsman suggested an overhang of a few inches to give more interest to the exterior. I wanted more windows than the original house—three instead of two in the living room, two instead of one in the dining room and all the bedrooms. I was going to have light and views after the years of having neither in our old living room. I reversed the placement of stairs and fireplace in the family room to make for a better traffic pattern. Now some of my dormant home ec training in art and architecture was being put to use. There would be closets galore and a full basement whether or not there was anything to store in it.

I made all the decorating decisions. The living room and dining room, which were divided by folding partitions and could open into one larger room, would be blue and white. Blue carpeting and draperies, white walls. The bedrooms would have painted walls, not wallpaper. I was tired of wallpaper. I bought all of the bathroom cabinets from a "truckload sale." We kept the old dining room table that Herman Fischer had given us years earlier, but we bought new dining room chairs. Living room furniture came from Toms-Price when they had a seasonal sale. I got seven chests of drawers through John Thorne from a damaged-goods sale, though they looked fine to me. Economizing continued to be a way of life!

Our good friend Ken Hansen did not want to see us economize on carpeting, so he steered us to a company in the Merchandise Mart. There would be ceramic tile floors in the front hall and baths, tile-patterned linoleum in the kitchen, but wall-to-wall carpeting everywhere else. No more cold floors!

In our Christmas letter of 1965, I reported that "being on the spot to watch progress on our house is ideal, but we remind ourselves that essentially it is a tent for us pilgrims, and we look for a permanent Home whose builder and maker is God. By late spring we will have room to put up more pilgrims, and everybody goes through Chicago. Right?"

The next year 12-year-old Gretchen described the new house and added, "We all like it *very much.* A bulldozer knocked down the old house. We children only got to watch the beginning as we had to go to school. Mom thought she would be sure to be away that day, but as it turned out she was so happy in the new house that she stayed home and watched and didn't cry a bit."

We were able to pay Otto as the house was being built. So another of God's blessings was that we never had to take out a mortgage on our new house. And we still had those big yards, front and back, which made Ken happy.

The Rest of the Story

THERE WERE SEVERAL printings of *Living Letters* in 1963 as the book gained in popularity. Since Ken was still working at Moody, I was the one who typed the invoices, recorded them on four-by-six-inch index cards for our simple accounting system, and took the packages to the post office. Mark packed the books when he came home from junior high.

Ken had always dreamed of publishing a magazine modeled after *Reader's Digest*—a magazine that would present condensations of the best articles from dozens of Christian magazines. With the initial success of *Living Letters,* he asked our friend Ted Miller to help Tyndale House publish just such a magazine. Ted began working part-time as editor, and the first edition of *The Christian Reader* was launched in December 1963.

Bob Hawkins, a retailer from Oregon, was very successful in selling bulk quantities of *The Christian Reader* through churches, so Ken asked him to join our fledgling company. His first job was to beef up the magazine's circulation, but he soon became sales manager for the books as well.

Now that we had our first full-time employee, it didn't seem practical to continue operating from our dining-room table. Something had to give, so we rented office space in the windowless basement of a building on Washington Street, next to the railroad tracks. The entrance was in the rear of the building, and to get to it, one had to go past the garbage cans used by the people occupying apartments on the second floor. It was not a very auspicious beginning for the Tyndale House office; we never took pictures to memorialize the place. There was a flurry of buying used office furniture. Both Ken and I juggled time between home and office. I tried hard to be home when the children came home from school. We stayed in that location only until 1967, when Tyndale House moved to its own office and warehouse building on Gundersen Drive in Carol Stream.

Tyndale House's second CBA convention was in Washington, D.C. We drove with Ted Miller, one of the Rodgers girls who was going to visit her grandparents in Pennsylvania, and a big roll of butcher paper that we tried not to squash. That paper, when unrolled, would hang at the back of our half of the 10-foot booth, which we shared again with the offering-plate couple from Alabama. In bright poster paint it said, "STOCK UP NOW. Billy Graham is going to give away copies of *Living Letters* on his telecast this fall."

We hoped the promise of increased publicity due to Billy Graham's involvement would bolster sales, but the plan backfired. If Billy Graham was going to give away copies, how could store owners hope to *sell* many copies? Most played it safe and placed minimum orders.

But that fall stores did begin ordering more copies. The hundreds of thousands of free paperbacks that the Billy Graham Association mailed out made for powerful advertising. People who hadn't seen the telecast went to Christian bookstores to get the little book their friends were recommending.

But the rapid growth of Tyndale House deserves to be the subject of another book, and Ken has written many more details in his autobiography, *My Life: A Guided Tour.* Another interesting book would be about the impact of *The Living Bible* on the rest of the world of modern translations.

Tyndale House Foundation was set up to receive royalty money from the sale of *Living Letters* and the other "Living" books that followed. Among other ministries, the Foundation supported Living Bibles International, a separate organization that Ken had founded to encourage modern translations of the Bible in major languages of the world. Often the predominant translation in use was even more difficult to read than the King James Version was in English. We heard firsthand stories from Europeans who were reading their Bibles with fresh understanding as they read *Living Letters,* even though English was their third language! In the '70s and '80s, I traveled extensively with Ken, promoting the interests of Living Bibles International both in this country and around the world. That work also deserves to be written up in another book!

I also did considerable speaking to women's groups at churches within driving distance and occasionally out of state. Usually I spoke about the development of *The Living Bible,* with family stories thrown in. I told the story of Ken's dream of making the Scriptures more understandable, which had begun with our own children and was now blessing hundreds of thousands, if not millions, of lives all over the world.

In 1981, at age 64, I retired from Tyndale House after having worked for 18 years. Other people could handle the payroll and accounts payable. The company had grown from ground zero to being one of the larger Christian publishing companies

The social upheaval of the late '60s and '70s did not bypass our family. There were a few divorces among our children's marriages. The odds had been against a few of the marriages from the start, but as parents we had been unable to prevent them.

A heavy burden at that time was for our son John, who, for reasons he has not shared with us, suddenly disappeared. For many years we did not know of his whereabouts or even if he was still alive. Then one day we learned from a high school classmate of his that he was in California—teaching English at the College of Marin! Peter and Sharon were able to visit him for a weekend. But after that, John again put up the No Trespassing sign. More years went by. The family grew through weddings and the births of many grandchildren, but still there was that vacant place, and our hearts ached.

On June 9, 1990 (a date we won't forget!), John showed up without any announcement at Peter and Sharon's house in Wheaton, having driven almost nonstop from San Francisco. Meeting family in the area was gradual over several days. He needed time and space to recover both from the long drive and from the great leap to cross the gap of 23 years.

For several years I had worried that I might not recognize John if and when he showed up on our doorstep. Would he look much different? What if he had a big beard (as our other two sons had had at different times) and I couldn't see his face? But my concerns were for naught. He was not hiding behind a big beard but had only a small mustache. Of course I recognized our lanky blond son!

In a letter to my West brothers and sisters soon afterward, I quoted from Psalm 26: "When Jehovah brought back his exiles to Jerusalem, it was like a dream! How we laughed and sang for joy. And the other nations said, 'What amazing things the Lord has done for them.' Yes, glorious things! What wonder! What joy! . . . Those who sow tears shall reap joy" (Psalm 126:1-3, TLB).

Since that first visit John has joined the family for special occasions and celebrations numerous times.

Beginning in 1984, the seven West brothers and sisters and their spouses have met together every year for a several-day reunion. "Otherwise," we said, "we will only see each other at our funerals!" (Harriet's husband, John, was already deceased.) Ken and I have not missed any of those happy occasions, which are usually in Oregon or California, where the majority of my siblings live. And there have been funerals—Harriet's and Bill's—where we celebrated the memory of their lives and God's grace in bringing us into his family with the assurance of eternal life. Harriet was tragically murdered at age 75. Bill died of liver cancer. He was the much-loved pastor of the Bible Church in Carson, Washington.

I have taken several trips with some of my brothers and sisters but without Ken (his choice). I have enjoyed vacations in Alaska, Hawaii, and the national parks of the southwest. But my most memorable vacation was not with my family but with Beatrice Sutherland and her extended family.

Beatrice was a missionary in western China with China Inland Mission from 1938 until she was forced to leave during World War II. Later she served the Lord in Hong Kong. With China opened to Westerners, Beatrice wanted to show her family where she had worked. Since it involved several days and nights of train travel, she wanted a party of 12 in order to fill three first-class compartments and avoid the possibility of sharing space with eleven smoking Chinese travelers! Beatrice's sister Dorothy had been a classmate of Ken's at Wheaton. Dorothy's husband, DeWitt Jayne, taught art at Wheaton College for a number of years, and I had known their daughters Nancy and Wendy years earlier. Wendy and I roomed together on the trip.

Beatrice had chosen to travel by train rather than by airplane so that we could stay on schedule. She was in touch with Christians in several locations, and she was taking Chinese Bibles and commentaries to leave surreptitiously at prearranged sites. Beatrice distributed the books among us in Hong Kong. Our bags were crammed. After a relaxing three-day boat trip up the coast, we went through customs in Shanghai—none of our bags were opened!

At that time Janet was in Taiuan (a city in mainland China) for a year, teaching English in a technical college. I was not allowed by the police to break away from our tour group to visit her, but she and a couple of friends were able to meet us in Beijing. They luxuriated in hot showers at our first-class hotel and immediately broke into the goodies I had brought.

The whole three-week trip was an experience of a lifetime—with new sights, smells, and foods every day. To top it off, it turned out that the young guide assigned to travel with us was a Christian!

From China I went to Taipei, Taiwan, for a wonderful visit with Clayton and Esther Barker at Morrison Academy. From there I flew to Paris to meet Ken, and we had two days of concentrated sightseeing with our missionary host. Sweden was our next stop, for a Living Bibles International conference with coworkers from Asia, Africa, and Europe—always a joyful experience. Our travels ended with a couple of days in England with Jack Hywel-Davies and his second wife, Joan. We love England and our friends there.

We had a very different vacation in England in 1995 when we traveled on a narrow boat for a week with Becky, John, and Janet. We didn't travel very far in the Midlands at four miles per hour! Narrow boats are only 7-1/2 feet wide, and ours was 50 feet long. These pleasure boats operate in the network of canals that were constructed in the pre-railroad days of the nineteenth century. That week would have been more pleasurable if it hadn't been one of the hottest weeks on record. John and Janet did most of the navigating, and she and Becky usually jumped off to open and close the many locks—an energetic experience.

When the week was over, we rented a car and drove to Stratford-on-Avon, where we had reserved rooms at a B-and-B. We bought tickets for *Romeo and Juliet* at the Royal Shakespeare Theater. No disappointment there!

Our purchase of the large summer home in the sand dunes area of Sawyer, Michigan, turned out to be a brilliant success. With access to a stretch of private beach on Lake Michigan, our summers at the Michigan House are times of wonderful fun and family togetherness that have surpassed our fondest dreams. The impact of that house was summed up by our granddaughter Heather Bayly when she was a college sophomore:

> Thanks for the Michigan house. I don't know if you realize how much it means to us, especially the cousins. Some of my best friends are my cousins, and I never would have gotten to know them if it hadn't been for spending that time with them every summer. When my boyfriend asked what my happiest memory was from growing up, I told him it was a combination of everything at the Michigan house. I told him about collecting cans, swimming in Lake Michigan, sleeping under the stars, skit night, etc. I love it! The proof of how much we love it is the fact that we all come back every year. It's amazing that all of us teenagers will hang out with our family for fun as a vacation during the summer. Thank you for making it possible!

We have rejoiced with our children and grandchildren at countless births (several of them at home), birthdays, recitals, musicals, graduations, baptisms, showers, and weddings, not to mention all the family feasts at Easter, Mother's Day, Thanksgiving, and Christmas. We simply cannot count the blessings our wonderful family has brought, and still brings, to us. God be praised!

Recently the family celebrated Ken's and my 60th wedding anniversary at a Sunday brunch with appropriate decorations and loving tributes. Old age is made easier because our children have forgiven us our many mistakes and shortcomings. They love us as we are!

But even more important than the love of husband, children, grandchildren, and great-grandchildren is the love of God. "God showed his great love for us by sending Christ to die for us while we were still sinners. And since we have been made right in God's sight by the blood of Christ, he will certainly save us from God's judgment. For since we were restored to friendship with God by the death of his Son while we were still his enemies, we will certainly be delivered from eternal punishment by his life. So now we can rejoice in our wonderful new relationship with God—all because of what our Lord Jesus Christ has done for us in making us friends of God" (Romans 5:8-11, NLT).